ABCTE

Elementary Education/Multiple Subject Practice Questions

I0894325

Mometrix
TEST PREPARATION

Dear Future Exam Success Story

First of all, **THANK YOU** for purchasing Mometrix study materials!

Second, congratulations! You are one of the few determined test-takers who are committed to doing whatever it takes to excel on your exam. **You have come to the right place.** We developed these practice tests with one goal in mind: to deliver you the best possible approximation of the questions you will see on test day.

Standardized testing is one of the biggest obstacles on your road to success, which only increases the importance of doing well in the high-pressure, high-stakes environment of test day. Your results on this test could have a significant impact on your future, and these practice tests will give you the repetitions you need to build your familiarity and confidence with the test content and format to help you achieve your full potential on test day.

Your success is our success

We would love to hear from you! If you would like to share the story of your exam success or if you have any questions or comments in regard to our products, please contact us at **800-673-8175** or **support@mometrix.com**.

Thanks again for your business and we wish you continued success!

Sincerely,
The Mometrix Test Preparation Team

Printed in the United States of America

TABLE OF CONTENTS

Practice Test #1

Reading and English Language Arts

1. Young children's skills in phonological awareness are focused on:

a. Morphologies
b. Speech sounds
c. Word meanings
d. Word sequence

2. A student encounters a multisyllabic word. She's not sure if she's seen it before. What should she do first? What should she do next?

a. Locate familiar word parts, then locate the consonants
b. Locate the consonants, then locate the vowels
c. Locate the vowels, then locate familiar word parts
d. Look it up in the dictionary, then write down the meaning

Refer to the following for question 3:

A fourth-grade student struggles to decode several words in her science textbook, including *organism*, *conclusion*, and *prediction*.

3. Which strategy would best help the student decode these and other similar words?

a. Using context clues to select words that make sense in the sentences
b. Slowly stretching out the letter sounds
c. Blending the phonemes
d. Looking for known word parts, such as prefixes and suffixes

4. While reading a book about animals, a student struggles to decode the word *giraffe*. He then points to the picture and says, "Those are giraffes. I saw them at the zoo." Which cueing system is the student using to figure out the unknown word?

a. Semantic
b. Syntactic
c. Graphophonic
d. Pragmatic

5. When should students learn how to decode?

a. Decoding is the most basic and essential strategy to becoming a successful reader. It should be introduced to kindergartners during the first two weeks of school.
b. Decoding is not a teachable skill. It is an unconscious act and is natural to all learners.
c. Decoding should be taught only after children have mastered every letter–sound relationship as well as every consonant digraph and consonant blend. They should also be able to recognize and say the 40 phonemes common to English words and be able to recognize at least a dozen of the most common sight words.
d. Decoding depends on an understanding of letter–sound relationships. As soon as a child understands enough letters and their correspondent sounds to read a few words, decoding should be introduced.

6. A second-grade teacher is designing a word sort to help her students identify inflectional endings. Which pair of words should she use in this activity?

a. Jumped and eating
b. *Blew* and *boo*
c. Crunch and trash
d. *Day* and *weigh*

7. A kindergarten teacher says the words *tap* and *top* aloud. She asks students to identify whether the sound that is different is found in the beginning, middle, or ending of the words. Which skill does this activity practice?

a. Phoneme substitution
b. Phoneme discrimination
c. Phoneme deletion
d. Phoneme insertion

8. Regarding the relationship of phonemic awareness to reading and writing, which is NOT true?

a. Phonemic awareness is a listening and speaking skill, not a reading and writing skill.
b. Including print letters and words in teaching phonemic awareness is more effective.
c. Using print letters and words alone in teaching phonemic awareness is sufficient.
d. Pointing to printed letters while saying them aloud to draw attention to sound-letter connections is helpful.

9. Which choice represents a likely progression of phonological awareness skills?

a. Onset and rime manipulation, rhyming, phoneme deletion, syllabification
b. Phoneme deletion, syllabification, onset and rime manipulation, rhyming
c. Rhyming, syllabification, onset and rime manipulation, phoneme deletion
d. Syllabification, phoneme deletion, rhyming, onset and rime manipulation

10. Among some of the critical components of good phonics lessons, which one is taught for the purpose of helping students to decode unfamiliar words?

a. Introducing sound-spellings
b. Blending phonemes into words
c. Discriminating phonemes in words
d. Reviewing to overlearn sound-spellings

11. The primary purpose of guided reading is to:

a. Help students develop a deeper understanding of literature
b. Help students develop their oral reading skills
c. Help students improve their phonological awareness
d. Expand students' reading power to increasingly difficult texts

12. A first-grade student that is struggling to decode high-frequency CVC words likely needs intensive and explicit remediation in which of the following areas related to phonics instruction?

a. Differentiating open and closed vowel sounds
b. Phoneme substitution and deletion
c. Identifying beginning, medial, and ending phonemes
d. Letter-sound correspondence and blending

13. Which text(s) are likely to foster the greatest enthusiasm for reading and literature among students?

a. Free choice of reading texts, provided that students complete class assignments, projects, and discussions
b. An all-in-one textbook that includes all reading material for the year, study guides, and sample test questions
c. A variety of texts, including books, magazines, newspapers, stories from oral traditions, poetry, music, and films
d. A small selection of current best-selling books for children, some of which the children may already have read and liked

14. Which of the following statements is true regarding the relationship of reading fluency to reading comprehension?

a. Reading fluency and reading comprehension should be considered separate, equally valuable skills that can be taught independently of one another.
b. Reading comprehension is an important component of achieving a level of overall reading fluency.
c. Reading fluency refers to a set of skills that should be continually improved upon, so that students can consistently comprehend that which they read.
d. Reading comprehension and reading fluency are so intertwined that a child struggling in one area is often incapable of making progress in the other.

15. Which choice is the most accurate and appropriate for quickly assessing students' reading fluency and comprehension skills at any given point?

a. The teacher listens to each student read a short passage aloud and asks questions at the end to determine whether or not the student comprehends.
b. Use a reading scheme or set that includes readers (short books), worksheets, comprehension activities, and applications at the end of each month.
c. Assign worksheets that include both phonics work (to monitor fluency skills) and reading comprehension passages, followed by basic comprehension questions.
d. Lead a group or class discussion on the major concepts in any given unit of study, allowing students to vocalize what they feel confident with and address areas where extra instruction may be needed.

16. Prekindergarten students tell their teacher, Mr. Clark, that they want to write about their field trip to the zoo. Mr. Clark writes down the students' sentences on chart paper, and then reads them back to the class, pointing to each word and modeling appropriate fluency. After reading the story multiple times, Mr. Clark invites the students to read with him. Which type of interaction is Mr. Clark demonstrating?

a. Language experience approach
b. Writing workshop
c. Trait-based writing
d. Modeled writing

17. As one approach to gathering student input, what is correct about a K.I.M. chart for learning vocabulary?

a. The K in K.I.M. stands for Know, the I for Identify, and the M for Meaning.
b. Under the K in a K.I.M. chart, the student enters the definitions of the word.
c. Under the K in a K.I.M. chart, the student enters the new vocabulary words.
d. When students make K.I.M. charts, they never include drawings or pictures.

18. Among effective reading strategies, which one involves recalling relevant past experience and existing knowledge to construct meaning from the new information in text that one reads?

a. Inferring
b. Activating
c. Questioning
d. Summarizing

19. Which of these correctly represents findings about research-based vocabulary instruction?

a. Children need word repetition consisting of drills for vocabulary development.
b. Children need only be exposed to new words once or twice to remember them.
c. Children learn the vocabulary in texts best indirectly through simply reading them.
d. Children require direct instruction and word exposure in various contexts.

20. Which statement accurately reflects a principle regarding self-questioning techniques for increasing student reading comprehension?

a. Asking only what kinds of "expert questions" fit the text's subject matter
b. Asking only those questions that the text raises for the individual student
c. Asking how each text portion relates to chapter main ideas is unnecessary
d. Asking how the text information fits with what the student already knows

21. When adults use narration to develop young children's language, which of these most places vocabulary into natural contexts for more authentic comprehension and better retention?

a. Communicating locations and directionality to children
b. Describing the intensity and manner of actions/speech
c. Narrating child actions to initiate positive reinforcement
d. Labeling present objects/current actions with new words

22. A student in a fourth-grade class struggles with reading comprehension and writing. This student reads at a much slower pace than classmates, and when writing, often misspells high-frequency words and writes several letters backwards. This student has been receiving Response to Intervention (RTI) services to improve literacy skills, but the teacher has noticed minimal progress. Based upon this information, the teacher has the professional responsibility to do which of the following?

a. Refer the student for an initial evaluation with the school special education department.
b. Contact the students' parents to address concerns.
c. Consult grade-level colleagues for instructional strategies that may benefit the student.
d. Offer this student extra tutoring sessions before and after school hours.

23. A third-grade teacher is preparing to introduce an informational text to students. As a prereading strategy, the teacher reads a portion of the text aloud to the class and pauses at unfamiliar vocabulary. The teacher then asks students to identify surrounding words that may indicate examples, synonyms, antonyms, or definitions of the new words. This strategy is likely intended to develop which of the following skills?

a. Contextual analysis
b. Structural analysis
c. Phonological processing
d. Decoding and encoding

24. A second-grade teacher would like to promote students' ability to read independently and retell stories by recalling major details, such as the characters, plot, setting, and central message. Which of the following instructional resources would be most beneficial in achieving this?

a. Story maps that students can complete as they read
b. Comprehension questions that correspond with each story
c. Anticipation guides for students to complete prior to engaging in reading
d. Pretests to activate students' prior knowledge

25. A second-grade teacher is working with a student individually on reading aloud. While reading from a short passage, the teacher tells the student to follow along with the text using his index finger. This strategy is likely intended to develop which of the following skills?

a. Prosodic reading
b. Accuracy and rate
c. Blending and segmenting
d. Word recognition

26. A first-grade teacher has included some non-decodable words on students' weekly vocabulary list. Each day, the teacher reviews these words using flashcards as a whole-class activity. During class circle time, the teacher reads aloud a story that incorporates these vocabulary words. Students also practice tracing and writing the new words, as well as using them in sentences. These strategies are likely intended to promote the development of which of the following skills?

a. Recognizing consonant-vowel-consonant (CVC) words as individual units
b. Morpheme division in multisyllabic words
c. Irregular sight word recognition
d. Distinguishing between digraphs and blends

27. A fluent reader does NOT:

a. Consistently read at a sufficient rate of speed
b. Pause frequently to sound out difficult words
c. Adjust pitch to reflect punctuation
d. Recognize words rapidly and automatically

28. Which of the following MOST accurately summarizes the relationship between reading fluency and reading comprehension?

a. As students develop greater reading comprehension, their reading fluency also improves.
b. When students develop greater reading fluency, their reading comprehension improves.
c. The relationship between reading fluency and reading comprehension is a reciprocal one.
d. Reading fluency and reading comprehension are two separate, mainly unrelated skill sets.

29. Which of these statements about guided reading is NOT true?

a. Guided reading promotes fluency.
b. Guided reading fosters social interaction.
c. Flexible grouping allows students to progress at their own rates.
d. Guided reading is generally a whole-class activity.

30. Which of the following activities is widely used in building students' reading fluency?

a. Sole focus on phonetic instruction.
b. Repeated oral readings combined with feedback.
c. Participation in vocabulary-building activities.
d. Utilizing speed-reading techniques often used in adult literacy courses.

31. Which of the following choices is not a component of reading fluency?

a. Speed
b. Comprehension
c. Accuracy
d. Voice Modulation

32. A struggling reader has difficulty comprehending vocabulary words when they are encountered in unfamiliar texts. She frequently uses a dictionary to look up the unknown words. While this helps her figure out the meanings of the words, it interrupts her fluency and affects comprehension. Her teacher, Mr. Palmer, would like to teach her other strategies she can use instead that will minimize the disruptions to her fluency and increase her comprehension. Which strategy would likely be most effective?

a. Quickly asking a classmate for the meanings of the words
b. Creating a list of the unknown words and looking them up later
c. Trying to determine the meanings of the words from context clues
d. Skipping over the words she does not know as long as the sentences make sense

33. Which strategy can be used to build readers' confidence and increase both comprehension and fluency when introducing an unknown text?

a. Introducing new vocabulary before reading
b. Reading the first few pages aloud before asking students to finish it independently
c. Listing what students want to learn about the topic
d. Asking students to predict what the text will be about based on the title and cover

34. Which of the following statements is correct about recognition of letter combinations that occur across many words?

a. This ability interferes with automaticity of word recognition.
b. This ability undermines accurate word recognition in reading.
c. This ability decreases the demand on the reader's memory.
d. This ability is a separate development from reading fluency.

35. Corey is a second-grade student who receives special education services due to a specific learning disability in the area of reading fluency. Which of the following is the best strategy for ensuring success for Corey if he is severely impacted by his reading fluency deficiencies?

a. Providing additional support in the classroom
b. Pulling Corey for small-group reading fluency intervention
c. Modifying the material that Corey is to complete
d. Pulling Corey for one-to-one reading fluency intervention

36. A third-grade teacher has noticed that a student often skips words or guesses them incorrectly when reading aloud. When writing, the student often uses inventive spelling, particularly for complex words. The student would likely benefit from intervention to develop which of the following skills?

a. Listening responsively to spoken language
b. Initiating and responding appropriately in conversations
c. Irregular sight word recognition
d. Decoding and encoding

37. Which of the following is NOT true regarding grammar instruction?

a. Grammar is primarily important in writing; therefore, it must be taught predominantly within the context of writing instruction.
b. Teachers must not only teach grammatical concepts in abstract but also show students how to contextualize that knowledge and apply it to reading, writing, and speaking.
c. Knowledge of grammar can be both declarative and procedural in nature.
d. Many students find grammar to be boring, necessitating engaging teaching methods and discussions about why grammatical knowledge is important.

38. Of the following statements, which one is accurate regarding teacher promotion and management of active listening and participation by students in collaborative discussions?

a. For students inexperienced in group discussions, teachers should use topics below their age levels.
b. To challenge students, teachers should assign group discussion topics above their age levels.
c. If teachers explain appropriate discussion behaviors first, modeling them becomes unnecessary.
d. Teachers should model and explain active listening behaviors for students before discussions.

39. Which of the following methods would give students the most *objective* feedback to enable them to monitor their own performance and progress in speaking and enacting through giving oral reports and presentations?

a. Having classmates offer peer reviews
b. Having a teacher evaluate their work
c. Comparing their work to classmates' work
d. Viewing videos of their performance

40. Which of the following approaches to writing instruction is characterized by setting clear writing goals, observing concrete data, and applying learning to written composition?

a. Prewriting strategies
b. Modeling strategies
c. Inquiry strategies
d. Process writing

41. What advice to teachers does research indicate about writing instruction strategies?

a. Explicitly instruct sentence combining to develop sophisticated sentences.
b. Computer word-processing is a crutch that defeats student independence.
c. A process writing approach is incompatible with research-based strategies.
d. Help students analyze writing models, but do not let them imitate models.

42. Which of the following choices describes the best introduction to a unit on oral traditions from around the world?

a. Introducing games that practice new sight words, encoding words based on phonics rules, and answering short comprehension questions.
b. Setting up video-conferencing with a school in Asia so that students can communicate with children from other countries.
c. Inviting a guest speaker from a nearby Native American group to demonstrate oral storytelling to the class.
d. Creating a slide show presentation about various types of oral cultures and traditions and characteristics of each.

43. In three pieces of informational writing, Sample 1's author provides evidence tangential to his argument. Sample 2's author cites anecdotal evidence which is inaccurate. Sample 3's author cites accurate, directly related evidence, but it is an isolated example uncorroborated by any other sources. Which choice correctly matches each sample to the evidence criterion it fails to meet?

a. Sample 1's evidence is not sufficient, Sample 2's is not relevant, and Sample 3's is not factual.
b. Sample 1's evidence is not factual, Sample 2's is not sufficient, and Sample 3's is not relevant.
c. Sample 1's evidence is not relevant, Sample 2's is not factual, and Sample 3's is not sufficient.
d. Samples 1 and 3's evidence is insufficient, and Sample 2's is factual but irrelevant

44. Which of the following is true of a coherent body paragraph in an essay?

a. Explanations support details, which support the topic sentence.
b. Supporting details are in order from greatest to least importance.
c. A closing sentence that echoes keywords the topic sentence contains is needed.
d. The topic sentence includes references to each supporting detail.

45. Which of the following should adults include in their conversations with young children to help them build strong oral language skills?

a. Simple vocabulary and simple sentence structures
b. Primarily telling things rather than asking questions
c. Doing the majority of the talking to model for them
d. Questions requiring them to express abstract ideas

46. Which choice completes the text with the most logical and precise word or phrase?

Given the intricate relationships in the coral reef ecosystem, it's not surprising that the impact of climate change has lacked __________ explanation. Marine biologists have conducted extensive research, and Dr. Olivia Chang's recent findings offer hope for the preservation of these fragile ecosystems.

a. an intricate
b. an elusive
c. a conclusive
d. a clear

47. Which choice completes the text with the most logical and precise word or phrase?

In George Orwell's *1984*, a bleak future is dominated by totalitarianism, and the protagonist, Winston Smith, symbolizes resistance against the oppressive Party. Amidst the struggle for truth and freedom, Winston encounters ______ Party loyalists who feign moral superiority while perpetuating the regime's cruelty. Orwell's powerful prose and vivid portrayal of this nightmarish world continue to captivate readers, offering a chilling commentary on unchecked authority.

a. solicitous
b. serendipitous
c. sanctimonious
d. surreptitious

48. Which of the following best develops student oral vocabulary, spoken narrative skills, and connections between spoken and printed language?

a. Correctly spelling, pronouncing, and using new words in telling stories to the class
b. Learning new vocabulary words and spelling them correctly in written narratives
c. Learning new vocabulary words in listening, speaking, and storytelling activities
d. Correctly identifying new vocabulary words in listening and reading exercises

History and Social Science

49. When the prices farmers receive for their crops decline in a developing country, this typically results in which of the following?

a. Increased urbanization
b. Increased college enrollment
c. Declining literacy rates
d. Higher prices for those crops in developed countries

50. Inflation has what effects?

a. Harms all members of an economy
b. Helps all members of an economy
c. Harms no members of an economy
d. Harms some members of an economy, helps others

51. Which of the following represents a discretionary expense?

a. Textbook
b. Rent
c. DVD
d. Groceries

52. According to Karl Marx, which two groups are in continual conflict?

a. Farmers and landowners
b. Workers and owners
c. Kings and nobles
d. Politicians and voters

53. Which of the following is most likely to benefit from inflation?

a. A bond investor who owns fixed-rate bonds
b. A retired widow with no income other than fixed Social Security payments
c. A person who has taken out a fixed-rate loan
d. A local bank who has loaned money out at fixed rate

54. Which geographic features were most conducive to the development of early civilizations?

a. Rivers
b. Deserts
c. Forests
d. Mountains

55. The Erie Canal is 363 miles long and connects which body of water to Lake Erie?

a. The Mississippi River
b. The Hudson River
c. The Susquehanna River
d. The Lehigh River

56. Land is typically more expensive in urban areas than in rural areas. Which geography concept does this reflect?

a. Location
b. Distance
c. Pattern
d. Interaction

57. The Andes Mountain Range is located on which continent?

a. North America
b. South America
c. Australia
d. Asia

58. If you know the longitude of a city in the United States, what can you determine?

a. The state in which it is located
b. The time zone in which it is located
c. Exactly how far it is from the equator
d. Approximate average winter temperature

59. The concept of checks and balances is evident in which of the following?

a. Federal judiciary appeals
b. Presidential veto
c. States' rights
d. The House and the Senate

60. What does the 10th Amendment establish?

a. Any power not given to the federal government belongs to the states or the people.
b. The president is responsible for executing and enforcing laws created by Congress.
c. Congress has the authority to declare war.
d. The Supreme Court has the authority to interpret the Constitution.

61. Criminal cases are tried under:

I. State law
II. Federal law
III. Civil court

a. I and III
b. II only
c. I only
d. I and II

62. The vice president succeeds the president in case of death, illness or impeachment. What is the order of succession for the next three successors, according to the Presidential Succession Act of 1947?

a. President pro tempore of the Senate, secretary of state, and secretary of defense
b. Speaker of the House, president pro tempore of the Senate, and secretary of state
c. President pro tempore of the Senate, Speaker of the House, and secretary of state
d. Secretary of state, secretary of defense, and Speaker of the House

63. One reason the Articles of Confederation created a weak government was because it limited Congress's ability to do what?

a. Declare war
b. Conduct a census
c. Vote
d. Tax

64. How was the vice president chosen before the 12th Amendment was ratified?

a. The president chose the vice president
b. Congress chose the vice president
c. The vice president came in second in the Electoral College
d. There was no vice president

65. A researcher is collecting data for her study on parenting. She hypothesized that countries where mothers carry their infants on their person have children who have more secure attachments as toddlers. Which method would be the most helpful in collecting data for this study?

a. Interviewing parents in the United States about their methods of carrying babies.
b. Determining methods of carrying babies and studying the toddlers in several countries.
c. Researching popular methods of carrying infants on the internet.
d. Collecting data on the number of strollers sold in several countries.

66. A historian is writing a book about George W. Bush's years as governor of Texas. All of the information she uses is derived from original public records, Bush's personal letters, and interviews she conducted with various government officials who served during his administration. Which of the following is the historian's book based?

a. Only on primary sources
b. Only on secondary sources
c. Mostly on secondary sources
d. Equally on primary and secondary sources

67. The social scientists who are concerned primarily with the ways in which societies use resources and distribute goods are:

a. Anthropologists
b. Economists
c. Historians
d. Psychologists

68. Before the Civil War, to which of the following did Southern states object?

a. An increase in Southern tobacco production
b. An increase in tariffs on Northern manufactured goods
c. An increase in western mining for gold
d. An increase in the voting rights of slaves

69. What did the Mason-Dixon Line divide?

a. The East from the West before the western states were incorporated
b. The East from the West along the Mississippi River
c. The North from the South before the Civil War
d. The Senate from the House of Representatives

70. Which list of events is in the correct chronological order?

a. The French and Indian War (Seven Years' War)
The American Revolution
The French Revolution
The War of 1812

b. The American Revolution
The French Revolution
The War of 1812
The French and Indian War (Seven Years' War)

c. The French and Indian War (Seven Years' War)
The French Revolution
The War of 1812
The American Revolution

d. The French and Indian War (Seven Years' War)
The French Revolution
The American Revolution
The War of 1812

71. What was the purpose of Lyndon Johnson's Great Society?

a. To eliminate poverty and racial injustice in America
b. To erase the last vestiges of the Great Depression from the American economic landscape
c. To encourage economic prosperity through trickledown economics
d. To increase educational standards in the United States

72. Which of the following was NOT a tax levied on the American colonies by the British government in the 1760s and '70s?

a. The Sugar Act of 1764
b. The Stamp Act of 1765
c. The Lead Act of 1772
d. The Tea Act of 1773

73. Of the following statements, which is true about the March on Versailles during the French Revolution?

a. The March on Versailles was an action undertaken by equal numbers of both men and women.
b. The March on Versailles was an action undertaken primarily by women.
c. The March on Versailles happened prior to the storming of the Bastille.
d. The March on Versailles was not effective in accomplishing its purpose.

74. Which of the following played the most influential role in the Spanish defeat of the Incas in the 16th century?

a. The scarcity of roads in the Incan Empire prevented the Incas from easily defending their cities.
b. Francisco Pizarro's forces outnumbered the Incan warriors.
c. The centralized power structure of the Incan Empire left the Incas vulnerable after Atahualpa was captured.
d. New diseases introduced by the Spanish decimated the Incan army.

75. How did Plato's Theory of Forms most influence Christianity?

a. It held that what is most real and most good is outside the physical realm.
b. The theory described a cosmic conflict between ideal forms of good and evil.
c. It held that the form of the good formed a trinity with ideal forms of knowledge and reason.
d. The theory described Socratic reasoning as a means of redemption from sin.

76. In about 1428, the Mesoamerican city-states Tenochtitlan, Texcoco, and Tlacopan formed a Triple Alliance. How did this influence Aztec history?

a. Texcoco and Tlacopan secretly conspired against Tenochtitlan, using the Alliance as a front.
b. Disagreements about strategy between the city-states weakened Aztec resistance to Spanish invaders.
c. The alliance agreed that each city-state would offer a specific number of human sacrifices each year.
d. The allied city-states joined forces to conquer other city-states, incorporating them into an Aztec Empire.

77. During the 15th century, Johann Gutenberg invented a printing press with moveable type. How did his invention influence science?

a. It did not influence science; the printing of Gutenberg Bibles directed public attention away from science and toward reforming the Catholic Church.
b. It led to scientific advances throughout Europe by spreading scientific knowledge.
c. It influenced scientific advancement in Germany only, where Gutenberg's press was based.
d. It did not influence science; though texts with scientific knowledge were printed, distribution of these texts was limited.

78. Which of the following is NOT true about the Crusades?

a. Their purpose was for European rulers to retake the Holy Land (Jerusalem and surrounding areas) from Muslims.
b. The Crusades succeeded at European kings' goal of reclaiming the "holy land."
c. The Crusades accelerated the already incipient decline of the Byzantine Empire.
d. Egypt saw a return as a major Middle Eastern power as a result of the Crusades.

Mathematics

79. Which type of function is represented by the table of values below?

x	y
−2	8
−1	2
0	0
1	2
2	8

a. Linear
b. Quadratic
c. Cubic
d. Exponential

80. Given that x is a prime number and the greatest common factor of x and y is greater than 1, compare the two quantities.

Quantity A	Quantity B
y	the least common multiple of x and y

a. Quantity A is greater.
b. Quantity B is greater.
c. The two quantities are the same.
d. The relationship cannot be determined from the given information.

81. A car is accelerating. Which of the following accurately describes the appearance of the position-time graph?

a. It is a line with a positive slope.
b. It is a line with a negative slope.
c. It is a curve with an increasing slope.
d. It is a curve with a decreasing slope.

82. Which of the following graphs represents the solution to $y \geq 3x - 6$?

a. 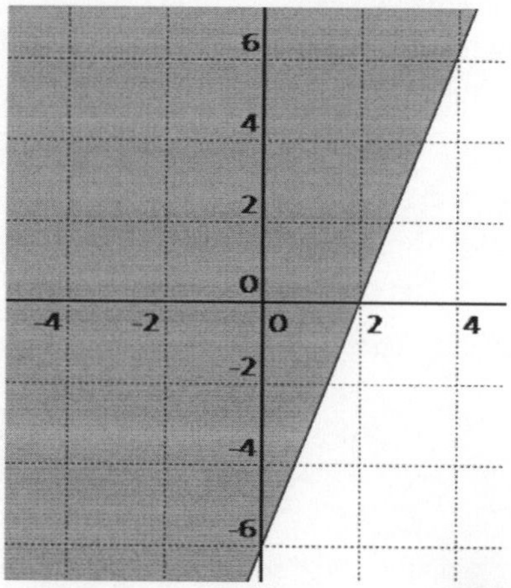

b. 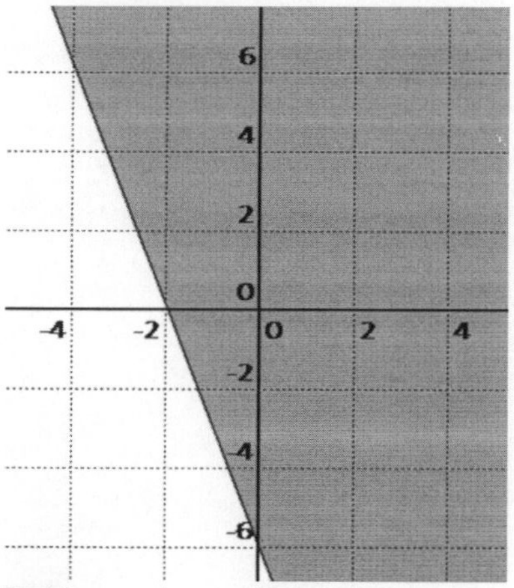

c. 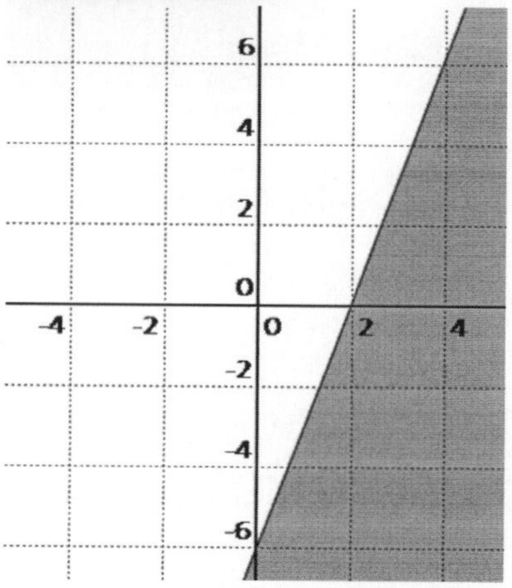

d. 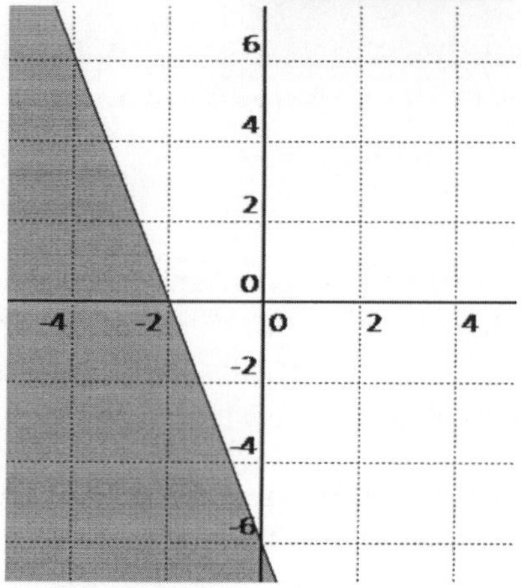

83. What linear equation includes the data in the table below?

x	y
-3	1
1	-11
3	-17
5	-23
9	-35

a. $y = -3x - 11$
b. $y = -6x - 8$
c. $y = -3x - 8$
d. $y = -12x - 11$

84. What linear equation includes the data in the table below?

x	y
−6	1
−2	3
4	6
8	8
10	9

a. $y = -2x + 2$
b. $y = -\frac{1}{2}x + 2$
c. $y = \frac{1}{2}x + 4$
d. $y = 2x - 2$

85. Myles has a \$60 budget to purchase a team lunch. He plans to buy sandwiches and salads. He needs to purchase a minimum of 15 items to make sure everyone has food. Each sandwich costs \$3 and each salad costs \$5. Which of the following graphs correctly shows the possible combinations of sandwiches and salads that he may buy, assuming that the x-axis represents sandwiches and the y-axis represents salads?

a.

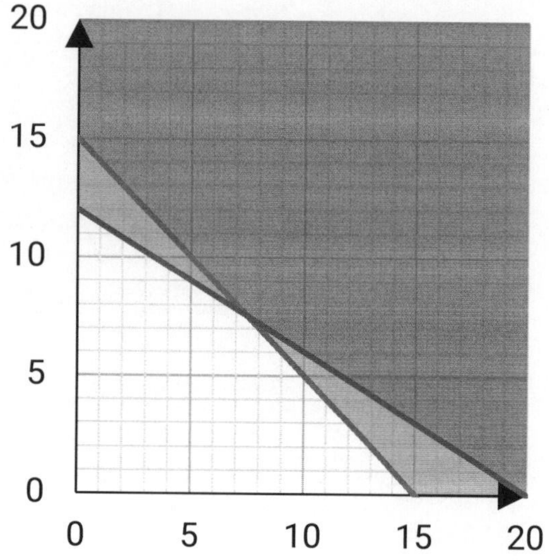

b.

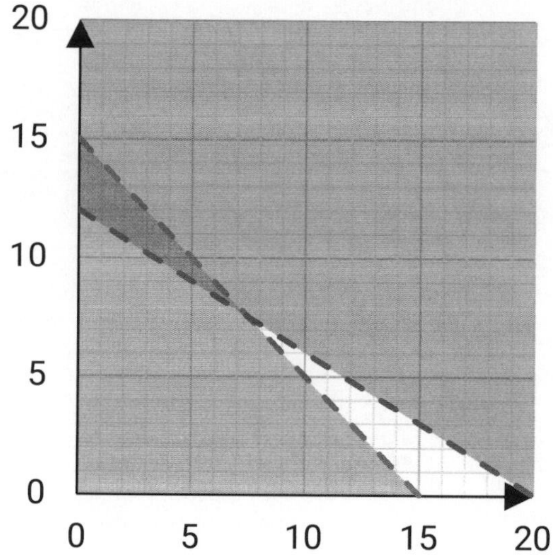

c.

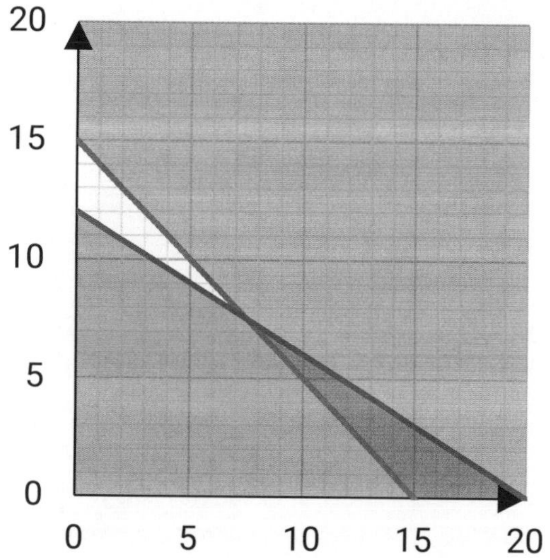

d.

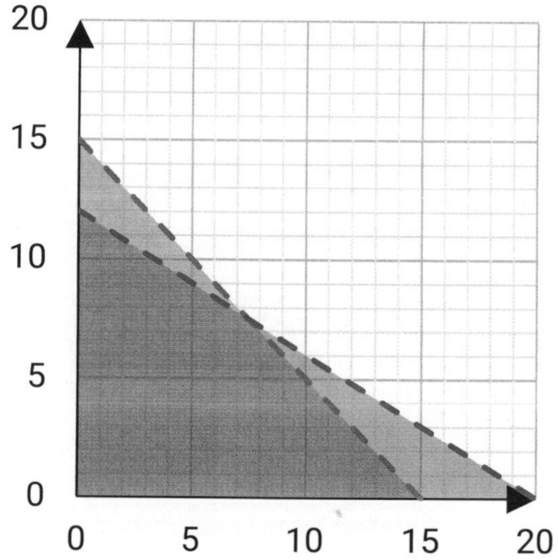

86. Tom needs to buy ink cartridges and printer paper. Each ink cartridge costs \$30. Each ream of paper costs \$5. He has \$100 to spend. Which of the following inequalities may be used to find the combinations of ink cartridges and printer paper that he may purchase?

a. $30c + 5p \leq 100$
b. $30c + 5p < 100$
c. $30c + 5p > 100$
d. $30c + 5p \geq 100$

87. Solve $\frac{x-2}{x-1} = \frac{x-1}{x+1} + \frac{2}{x-1}$.

a. $x = 2$
b. $x = -5$
c. $x = 1$
d. No solution

88. What is the perimeter of the trapezoid graphed below?

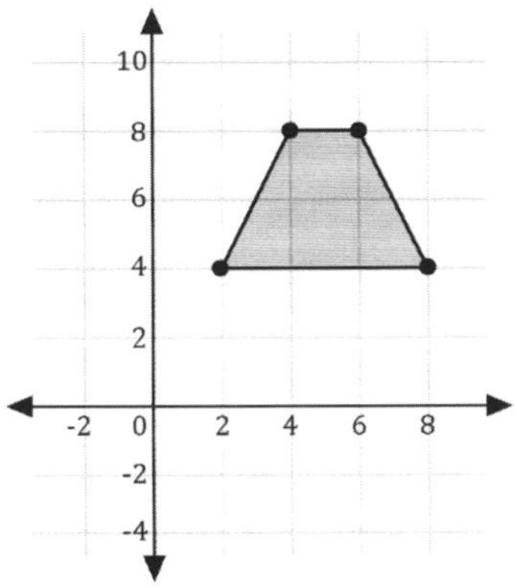

a. $4 + \sqrt{10}$
b. $8 + 4\sqrt{5}$
c. $4 + 2\sqrt{5}$
d. $8 + 2\sqrt{22}$

89. Which of the following represents the net of a triangular prism?

a. 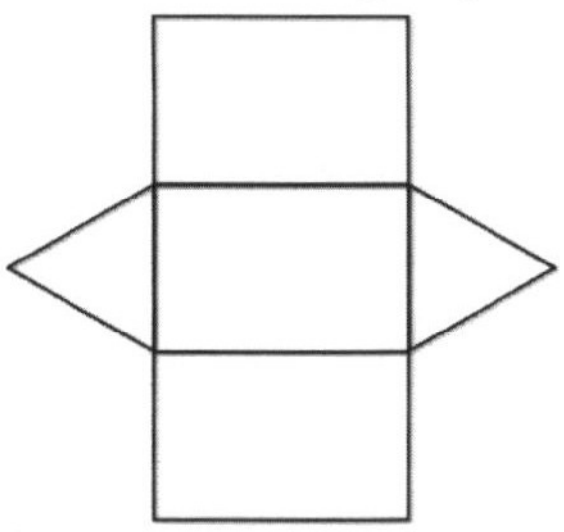

b. 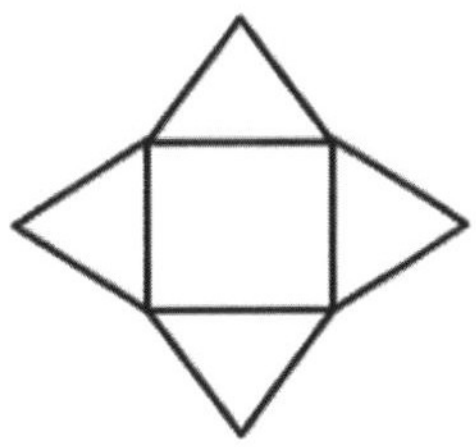

c. 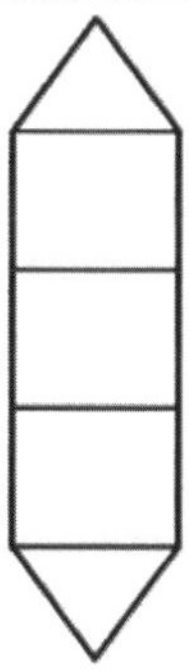

d. 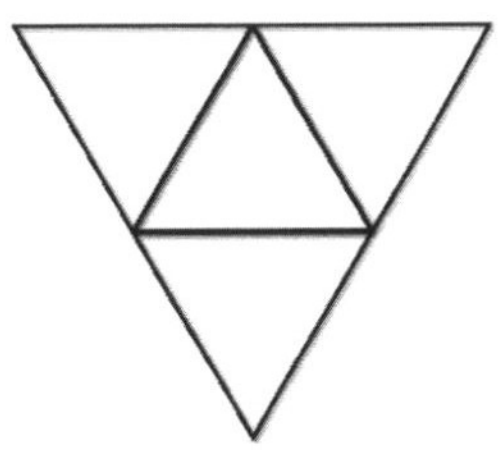

90. A gift box has a length of 14 inches, a height of 8 inches, and a width of 6 inches. How many square inches of wrapping paper are needed to wrap the box?

a. 56
b. 244
c. 488
d. 672

91. A lotion bottle is in the shape of a square pyramid. If the base has a side length of 3.5 inches and the height of the container is 6 inches, how many cubic inches of lotion can the bottle hold?

a. 18.6 cubic inches
b. 24.5 cubic inches
c. 28.9 cubic inches
d. 32.5 cubic inches

92. Which of the following choices best describes a three-dimensional figure comprised of only one square base and four triangular sides?

a. Square prism
b. Triangular prism
c. Triangular pyramid
d. Square pyramid

93. During a unit on geometry, Ms. Nifong instructs her students to sketch two congruent polygons. Which of the following sketches completes this task correctly?

a. Two rectangles with the same perimeter
b. Two polygons with the same shape
c. Two polygons with the same side lengths
d. Two squares with the same area

94. Which of the following measurements is the best approximation of 2,012 square inches?

a. 11.85 ft^2
b. 12.28 ft^2
c. 13.97 ft^2
d. 15.29 ft^2

95. What is the approximate area of the shaded region between the circle and the square in the figure shown below? Use 3.14 for π.

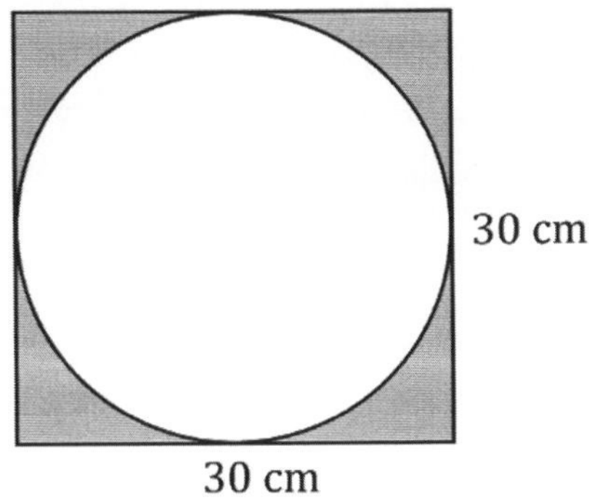

a. $177\ \text{cm}^2$
b. $181\ \text{cm}^2$
c. $187\ \text{cm}^2$
d. $193\ \text{cm}^2$

96. What is the slope of the leg marked x in the triangle graphed below?

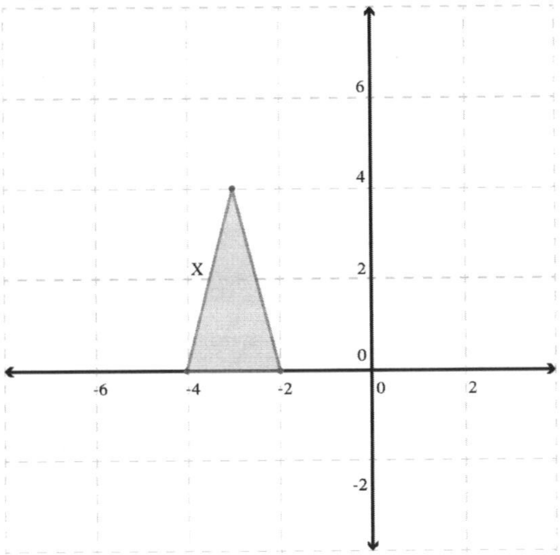

a. 2
b. 3.5
c. 4
d. 4.5

97. Given that premises "all *a* are *c*," "all *c* are *b*," and "no *d* are *c*" are true and that premise "all *d* are *b*" is false, determine the validity and soundness of the following arguments:

Argument I: All *a* are *c*. All *c* are *b*. Therefore, all *b* are *a*.
Argument II: All *a* are *c*. No *d* are *c*. Therefore, no *d* are *a*.
Argument III: All *c* are *b*. All *d* are *b*. Therefore, all *c* are *d*.

a.

	Invalid	Valid	Sound
Argument I		X	X
Argument II	X		
Argument III		X	

b.

	Invalid	Valid	Sound
Argument I	X		
Argument II		X	X
Argument III	X		

c.

	Invalid	Valid	Sound
Argument I		X	
Argument II		X	X
Argument III	X		

d.

	Invalid	Valid	Sound
Argument I		X	X
Argument II		X	X
Argument III	X		

98. Which of these statements is (are) true for inductive reasoning?

I. A general conclusion is drawn from specific instances.
II. If the premises are true and proper reasoning is applied, the conclusion must be true.

a. I
b. II
c. I and II
d. Neither statement

99. Sofia is learning to match equivalent fractions. Her homework question asks: "Circle the fraction(s) equivalent to $\frac{1}{2}$." The options given are: $\frac{2}{3}$, $\frac{2}{4}$, $\frac{3}{4}$, and $\frac{3}{6}$. Sofia circles $\frac{2}{3}$ and $\frac{3}{4}$. When her teacher asks her to explain her reasoning, what might Sofia say?

a. "I multiplied the top and the bottom of the fraction by the same numbers."
b. "I added the same numbers to the top and the bottom of the fraction."
c. "I drew a pie and split the $\frac{1}{2}$ into two pieces and into two more pieces."
d. "I drew three pies and split one into thirds, one into fourths, and one into sixths. Then I colored in the pies to match the fractions and circled the ones where I had colored in one half of the pie."

100. Marielle says the best descriptor of the data set $\{67, 2, 67, 73, 85, 60, 68\}$ is the range. Choose the option that best describes Marielle's error.

a. Marielle is incorrect because the range should never be used to describe a data set.
b. Marielle is incorrect because this data set has an outlier.
c. Marielle is incorrect because the mean is always the best choice for describing a data set.
d. Marielle is incorrect because the range for this data set is too small.

Refer to the following for questions 101–102:

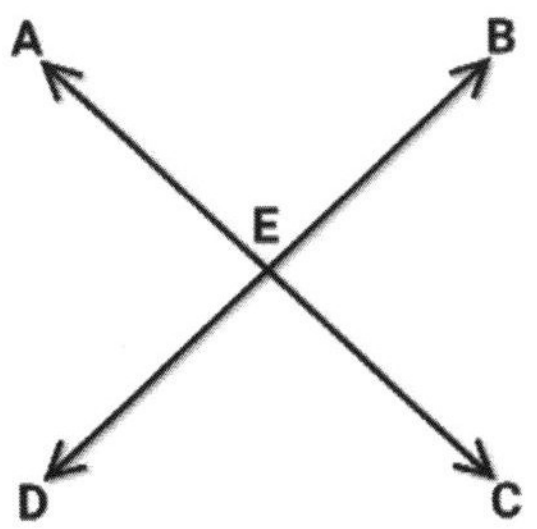

Statement	Reason
1. $\angle BEA \cong \angle DEA$	Given
2. $\angle BEA + \angle DEA = 180°$	Linear pair angles add up to 180°
3. ________	Substitution
4. $2 \times \angle BEA = 180°$	Combine like terms
5. $\angle BEA = 90°$	Division property of equality
6. $\angle BEA$ is a right angle	Definition of right angle
7. $\overleftrightarrow{BD} \perp \overleftrightarrow{AC}$	________

■

Given: $\angle BEA \cong \angle DEA$
Prove: $\overleftrightarrow{BD} \perp \overleftrightarrow{AC}$

101. Step 3 in the proof should contain which of the following statements?

a. $\angle BEA - \angle DEA = 0°$
b. $\angle BEA + \angle DEA = 2(90°)$
c. $\angle BEA + \angle BEA = 180°$
d. $\angle BEA = 180° - 90°$

102. Which of the following justifies step 7 in the proof?

a. ASA
b. Corresponding parts of congruent triangles are congruent
c. Definition of supplementary angles
d. Definition of perpendicular lines

103. Which of the following correctly describes a characteristic of students with effective problem-solving skills?

a. Students develop hypotheses via repeated trial-and-error tests.
b. Students have demonstrated skills for self-regulation.
c. Students are cautious in solving problems and avoid taking a risk.
d. Students quickly switch to another problem if their solution fails.

104. Chef K is dividing flour into plastic bins to use in his bakery. The weight of each flour bin is listed below.

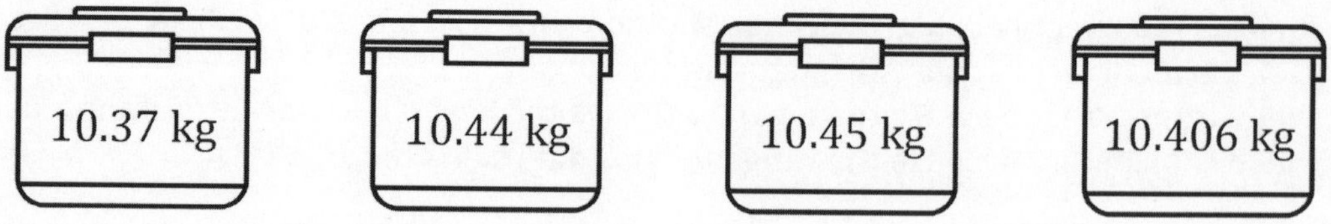

Chef K claims that all the bags can be labeled 10.4 kg because all of the bags round to 10.4 kg when rounded to the nearest tenth.

Describe the error in Chef K's statement.

a. Chef K's error is that all the bags of flour round to 10.5 kg not 10.4 kg.
b. Chef K's error is stating that all the bags of flour round to 10.4 kg when rounded to the nearest tenth. It is true that three of the bags of flour round to 10.4 kg. However, one bag does not round to 10.4 kg.
c. Chef K's error is stating that all the bags of flour round to 10.4 kg when rounded to the nearest tenth. It is true that two of the bags of four round to 10.4 kg. However, two bags do not round to 10.4 kg.
d. Chef K's error is stating that the bags of flour round to 10.4 kg when rounded to the nearest tenth. Chef K should have said that the bags of flour are rounded to the nearest hundredth.

105. Which number is not a factor of 648?

a. 3
b. 2
c. 7
d. 8

106. A taxi service charges \$5.50 for the first $\frac{1}{5}$ of a mile, \$1.50 for each additional $\frac{1}{5}$ of a mile, and 20¢ per minute of waiting time. Joan took a cab from her place to a flower shop 8 miles away, where she bought a bouquet, then another 3.6 miles to her mother's place. The driver had to wait 9 minutes while she bought the bouquet. What was the fare?

a. \$20
b. \$91
c. \$92.80
d. \$120.20

107. Ben's current monthly rent is \$750. He is moving to another apartment complex, where the monthly rent will be \$900. What is the percent increase in his monthly rent amount?

a. 15%
b. 17.5%
c. 19.25%
d. 20%

108. The table below shows the average amount of rainfall Houston receives during the summer and autumn months.

Month	Rainfall (in inches)
June	5.35
July	3.18
August	3.83
September	4.33
October	4.5
November	4.19

What percentage of rainfall in this timeframe occurs during October?

a. 13.5%
b. 15.1%
c. 16.9%
d. 17.7%

109. Which of the following correctly compares the sets of rational and irrational numbers?

a. The set of rational numbers is a subset of the set of irrational numbers.
b. The set of irrational numbers is a subset of the set of rational numbers.
c. The sets of irrational and rational numbers are disjoint.
d. The sets of irrational and rational numbers are equal.

110. Which of the following is true about the sum of two prime numbers?

a. It is always odd.
b. It is always a prime number.
c. It is always even.
d. None of the above are true.

111. If 1 inch on a map represents 60 feet and one yard is equal to 3 feet, how many yards apart are two points if the distance between the points on the map is 10 inches?

a. 1,800
b. 600
c. 200
d. 2

112. Consider the number set $\{-1, 19, -5, 0, 15.3, 15.05, -3\}$. Which of the following choices shows the number set in order from least to greatest?

a. −1, −3, −5, 0, 15.05, 15.3, 19
b. −5, −3, −1, 0, 15.3, 15.05, 19
c. −5, −3, −1, 0, 15.05, 15.3, 19
d. 0, −5, −3, −1, 15.05, 15.3, 19

Refer to the following for question 113:

The box-and-whisker plot displays a district's standardized test scores by subject.

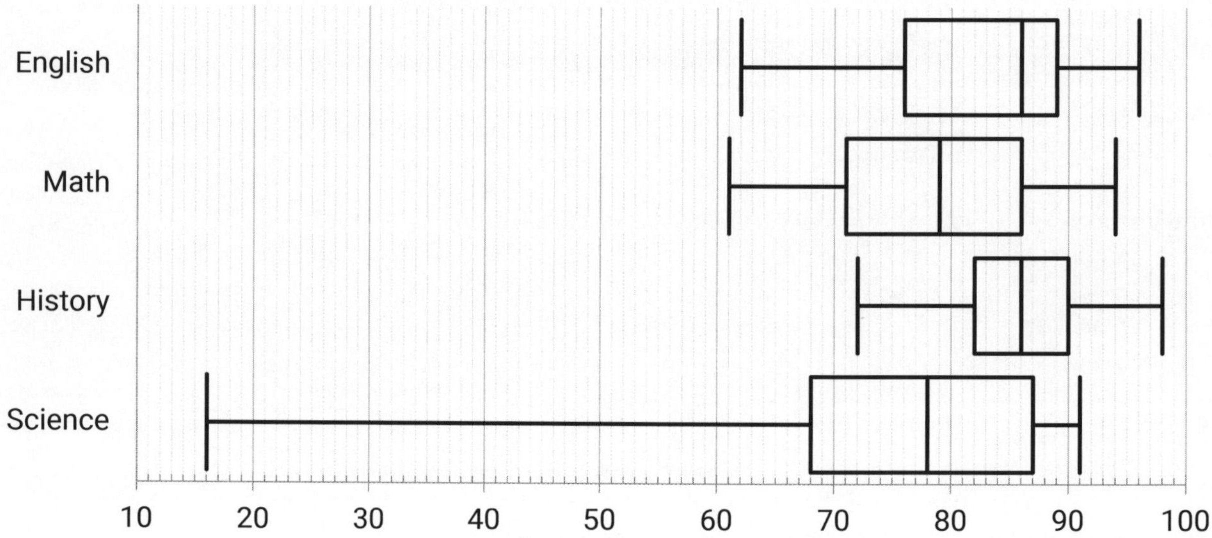

113. Which of the following statements is NOT true of the data?

a. The median better reflects student performance in Science than the mean.
b. The mean test score for English and history is the same.
c. The median of the History scores is the same as the 3rd quartile score for Math.
d. The median test score is above the mean for English.

114. Andrew rolls a die. What is the probability he gets a 4 or an even number?

a. $\frac{1}{4}$
b. $\frac{1}{2}$
c. $\frac{2}{3}$
d. $\frac{3}{4}$

115. In order to analyze the real estate market for two different zip codes within the city, a realtor examined the most recent 100 home sales in each zip code. She considered a house which sold within the first month of its listing to have a market time of one month; likewise, she considered a house to have a market time of two months if it sold after having been on the market for more than one month but before the end of the second month. Using this definition of market time, she determined the frequency of sales by the number of months on the market. The results are displayed below. Which of the following is a true statement for these data?

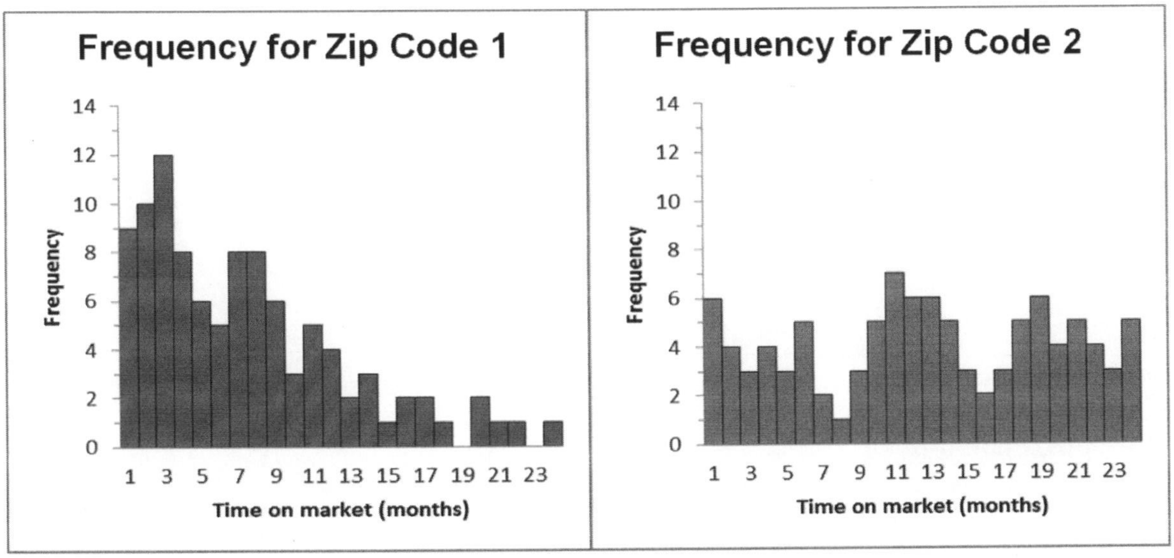

a. The median time a house spent on the market in Zip Code 1 is five months less than Zip Code 2.
b. On average, a house spent seven months longer on the market in Zip Code 2 than in Zip Code 1.
c. The mode time on the market is higher for Zip Code 1 than for Zip Code 2.
d. The median time on the market is less than the mean time on the market for Zip Code 1.

116. Kayla rolls a die and tosses a coin. What is the probability she gets an even number and heads?

a. $\frac{1}{6}$
b. $\frac{1}{4}$
c. $\frac{1}{3}$
d. 1

117. Adam rolls a standard six-sided die. What is the probability he rolls a number greater than or equal to 5?

a. $\frac{1}{6}$
b. $\frac{1}{5}$
c. $\frac{1}{4}$
d. $\frac{1}{3}$

118. Addison tosses a six-sided die twelve times and records the results in the table below.

Toss	1	2	3	4	5	6	7	8	9	10	11	12
Results	2	5	1	2	3	6	6	2	4	5	4	3

Which of the following statements is true?

a. The experimental probability of tossing a 6 is greater than the theoretical probability.
b. The experimental probability of tossing a 3 is greater than the theoretical probability.
c. The experimental probability of tossing a 1 is greater than the theoretical probability.
d. The experimental probability of tossing a 2 is greater than the theoretical probability.

119. Which of these tables properly displays the measures of central tendency that can be used for nominal, interval, and ordinal data?

a.

	Mean	Median	Mode
Nominal			x
Interval	x	x	x
Ordinal		x	x

b.

	Mean	Median	Mode
Nominal			x
Interval	x	x	x
Ordinal	x	x	x

c.

	Mean	Median	Mode
Nominal	x	x	x
Interval	x	x	x
Ordinal	x	x	x

d.

	Mean	Median	Mode
Nominal			x
Interval	x	x	
Ordinal	x	x	x

120. Erika must choose her outfit from 4 pairs of jeans, 6 tops, and 5 pairs of shoes. How many possible outfits may she create with one item from each category?

a. 12
b. 24
c. 60
d. 120

Science

121. Which of the following is false regarding solar energy?

a. Solar energy is environmentally friendly
b. Solar energy has the greatest conversion efficiency
c. Solar energy is low maintenance
d. Solar energy is silent

122. Which of the following statements about the Moon is NOT true?

a. Only one side of the Moon is seen from Earth.
b. The Moon only rotates once in one orbit around the Earth.
c. The Moon is slowly moving closer to the Earth.
d. The gravitational acceleration on the surface of the Moon is approximately one-sixth of the gravitational acceleration on the surface of the Earth.

123. World weather patterns are most influenced by which of the following?

a. Wind belts
b. The Earth's orbit
c. Ocean currents
d. Atmospheric conditions

124. Which of the following is NOT one of the five major physical properties of minerals?

a. Chemical composition
b. Hardness
c. Luster
d. Streak

Refer to the following for question 125:

After a laboratory experiment that involved using various chemical solutions, you and your lab partner are asked to clean up your workspace. The teacher states that any chemicals that have been poured into a new container should be disposed of, but the chemicals still in their original bottles can be placed into storage.

125. Which of the following is NOT a recommended storage practice for laboratory chemicals?

a. Chemicals should be stored at the appropriate temperature and humidity.
b. Chemicals should be dated when received and when opened.
c. Chemicals may be routinely stored on bench tops.
d. Chemicals should be stored on shelves with raised outer edges.

126. Which of the following is considered a non-renewable resource?

a. Glass
b. Wood
c. Cattle
d. Soil

127. James Hutton is best known for:

a. Establishing the first observable evidence for the Big Bang Theory
b. Suggesting the Third Law of Thermodynamics
c. Proposing the theory of uniformitarianism
d. Introducing the Law of Superposition

128. This organelle contains digestive enzymes that break down food and unneeded substances. They are also thought to be linked to the aging process. What part of a cell does this describe?

a. Lysosomes
b. Chromatin
c. Plastids
d. Golgi apparatus

129. The following is the anticodon sequence formed during translation. What is the mRNA codon sequence?

A C G U A C G C U

a. T G C A T G C G A
b. U G C T U G C G T
c. U G C A U G C G A
d. U C G A U C G C A

130. Which of the following habitats would provide an opportunity for secondary succession?

a. A retreating glacier
b. Burned cropland
c. A newly formed volcanic island
d. A 500-year-old forest

131. Which of the following animal structures is NOT paired to its correct function?

a. Muscle System – controls movement through three types of muscle tissue
b. Nervous System – controls sensory responses by carrying impulses away from and toward the cell body
c. Digestive System – breaks down food for absorption into the blood stream where it is delivered to cells for respiration
d. Circulatory System – exchanges gases with the environment by delivering oxygen to the bloodstream and releasing carbon dioxide

132. Cardiac output is the product of what two factors?

a. Heart rate and stroke volume
b. Stroke volume and blood pressure
c. Heart rate and pulse
d. Stroke volume and oxygen consumption

133. Which of the following plant structures allows for gas exchange?

a. Xylem
b. Phloem
c. Cuticle
d. Stomata

134. Plants begin to break down the products of photosynthesis through respiration. What is the result of respiration?

a. Water
b. Oxygen and glucose
c. Carbon dioxide and sugar
d. Carbon dioxide and water

135. The main function of _______ is to reduce the number of chromosomes to half the number of parent cells.

a. mitosis
b. telophase
c. meiosis I
d. meiosis II

136. How many electrons are in an uncharged atom of $^{45}_{20}Ca$?

a. 20
b. 45
c. 65
d. 25

137. Most organic molecules have all of the following properties EXCEPT:

a. High solubility in water
b. A low melting point
c. Covalent bonds
d. High flammability

138. Chemical compounds are formed when:

a. Valence electrons from atoms of two different elements are shared or transferred.
b. Valence electrons from multiple atoms of a single element are shared or transferred.
c. The nuclei of two atoms are joined together.
d. The nucleus of an atom is split.

139. Which of the following is the best prediction for solubility at 150 degrees Celsius?

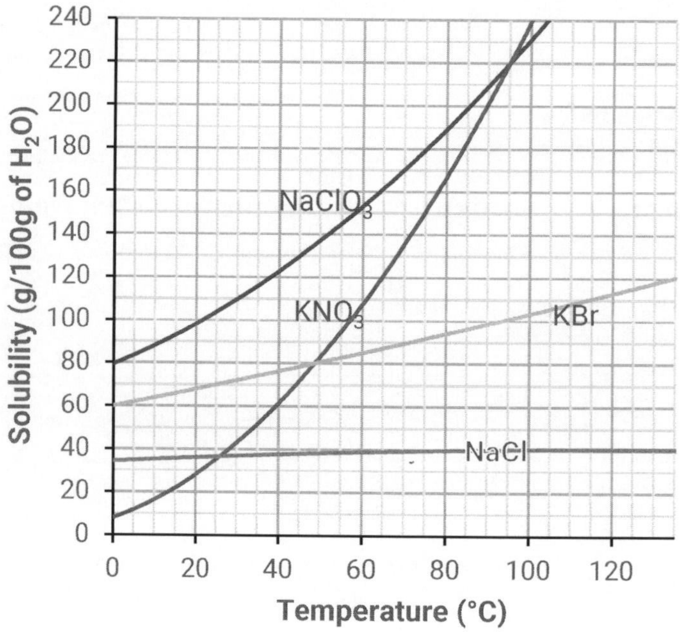

a. 260 g $NaClO_3$ per 100 g H_2O
b. 250 g KNO_3 per 100 g H_2O
c. 130 g KBr per 100 g H_2O
d. 80 g NaCl per 100 g H_2O

140. Which of the following is true about how light interacts with matter?

a. The sky is blue because molecules in the atmosphere scatter short-wavelength (blue) light more than other colors.
b. The sky is blue because the atmosphere absorbs only blue wavelengths.
c. Glass is transparent to all of the frequencies of light within the spectrum.
d. Wood, metal, and other opaque materials reflect all wavelengths of light.

141. Which of the following statements is NOT true about the period of a simple pendulum?

a. As the mass of a pendulum increases, the period increases.
b. For small amplitudes, the period of a pendulum is approximately independent of amplitude.
c. A pendulum swings more slowly at higher elevation.
d. To double the period of a pendulum, the length must be quadrupled.

142. A worker applies a force of 500.0 N to a pulley for a distance of 1.5 m to move a crate that weighs 1,000.0 N a distance of 0.5 m. What is the ideal mechanical advantage of this pulley?

a. 4
b. 2
c. 3
d. 5

143. How does adding a solute to a liquid solvent affect the vapor pressure of the liquid?

a. The vapor pressure increases by an amount proportional to the amount of solute.
b. The vapor pressure increases by an amount proportional to the amount of solvent.
c. The vapor pressure decreases by an amount proportional to the amount of solute.
d. The amount of solute present in a liquid solvent does not have any effect on vapor pressure.

144. Which of the following best describes the relationship of this set of data?

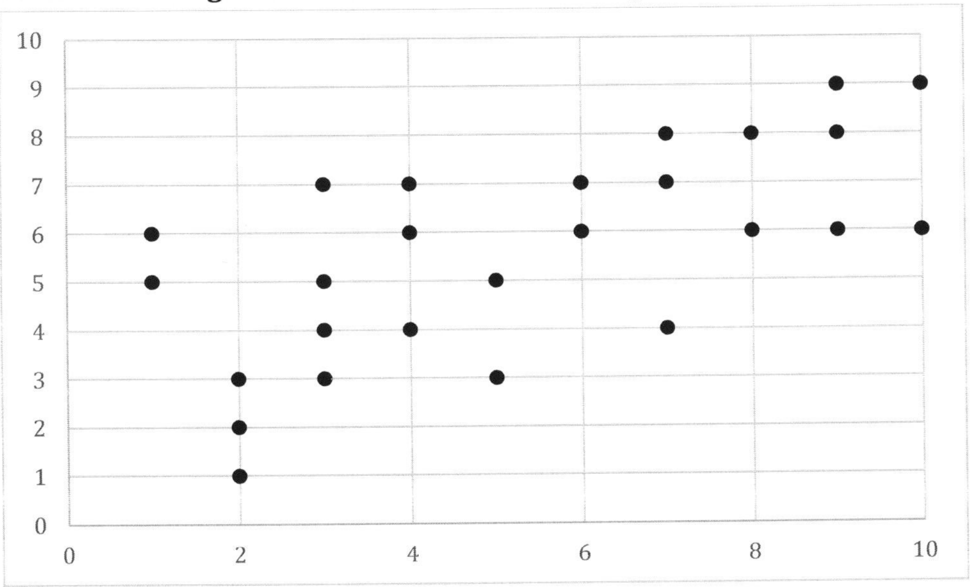

a. High positive correlation
b. Low positive correlation
c. Low negative correlation
d. No correlation

145. Which of the following subskills best fits the process skill of observing?

a. Using the five senses to collect evidence and write descriptions
b. Grouping objects based on similarities, differences, and interrelationships
c. Explaining or interpreting collected evidence
d. Reporting to others what has been found by experimentation

146. Once a hypothesis has been verified and accepted, it becomes which of the following?

a. A fact
b. A law
c. A conclusion
d. A theory

147. Scientists often form hypotheses based on particular observations. Which of the following is NOT true of a good hypothesis?

a. A good hypothesis is complex.
b. A good hypothesis is testable.
c. A good hypothesis is logical.
d. A good hypothesis predicts future events.

148. For what reason is repetition important to scientific inquiry?

a. It is the only way to prove that an experiment is reliable.
b. It adds to the number of statistics supporting the concept.
c. It assists the scientist in determining which data to consider.
d. It requires many groups of investigators working on a project.

149. Of the following actions, which best represents the science process skill of Inference?

a. Formulating new hypotheses based on experimental results
b. Finding patterns and meaning in the results of experiments
c. Identifying properties of things/situations using the senses
d. Reporting experimental results and conclusions to others

150. Which of the following is NOT provided as a result of the valid research and observations recorded by scientists?

a. A better understanding of the physical world
b. The ability to predict possible outcomes affected by actions
c. The ability to prevent earthquakes and other natural disasters
d. The creation of various substances and technologies that enhance our world

Answer Key and Explanations for Test #1

Reading and English Language Arts

1. B: Speech sounds or phonemes are the focus of phonological awareness skills, as well as the relationships of speech sounds to written language symbols. Morphologies (A) are the structural aspects of letters, syllables, and words that reflect grammatical changes. Word meanings (C) are called semantics, not morphology or phonology. Word sequences (D) or sentence structures are called syntax.

2. C: She should locate the vowels, then locate familiar word parts. Syllables are organized around vowels. In order to determine the syllables, this student should begin by locating the vowels. It's possible to have a syllable that is a single vowel (*a/gain)*. It isn't possible to have a syllable that is a single consonant. Once the word has been broken into its component syllables the reader is able to study the syllables to find ones that are familiar and might give her a clue as to the word's meaning, such as certain prefixes or suffixes.

3. D: Multisyllabic words often contain smaller parts that students recognize, such as prefixes, roots, and suffixes. Identifying these known parts can help students figure out the words. Context clues can help students guess words that make sense, but students should be able to apply word analysis skills to cross check their guesses and ensure they are selecting the correct words. Stretching out the sounds and blending the phonemes are helpful strategies for decoding shorter words with predictable spelling patterns. However, these strategies are less reliable for decoding multisyllabic words with more complex spelling patterns.

4. A: The student is using both the picture in the book and his prior knowledge to make sense of the text, which demonstrates use of the semantic cueing system. When using the syntactic cueing system, readers select words that sound right using knowledge of grammar and sentence structure. When readers use the graphophonic cueing system, they use knowledge of letter/sound relationships to decode words. When using pragmatic cues, readers consider their purposes for reading in given situations.

5. D: Decoding depends on an understanding of letter–sound relationships. As soon as a child understands enough letters and their correspondent sounds to read a few words, decoding should be introduced. The act of decoding involves first recognizing the sounds individual letters and letter groups in a word make and then blending the sounds to read the word.

6. A: An inflectional ending is a letter or group of letters added to the end of a root word. It is sometimes used to change the tense of the root word, as in the case of adding *ed* to *jump* to indicate past tense. Both *-ed* and *-ing* are inflectional endings. The words in choice B end in diphthongs, which are formed when two vowel sounds are combined within a syllable. The words in choice C end in consonant digraphs, or two or more consonants that are combined to form a new sound. The words in choice D rhyme, and they use different spelling patterns to make the same sound.

7. B: In this activity, students are identifying the discriminating phoneme in two words. In the example of *tap* and *top*, it is the middle phoneme that is different. To practice phoneme substitution, the teacher would give students a word and then instruct them to change one of the phonemes and identify the newly formed word. In phoneme deletion, the teacher would give students a word and instruct them to remove a phoneme and identify the newly formed word. In phoneme insertion, the teacher would give students a word and instruct them to add a phoneme and identify the newly formed word.

8. C: While it is true that phonemic awareness is a listening and speaking skill rather than a reading and writing skill (A), it is equally true that children develop phonemic awareness better when instruction combines print with speech sounds (B). This helps children realize how speech sounds and printed letters connect and apply this insight. However, just including print is not sufficient (C). Teachers should also point to printed letters while saying them aloud to draw children's attention to sound-letter connections (D).

9. C: Phonological awareness skills typically progress in a similar manner. The ability to rhyme often develops first, as it is considered the simplest skill. Later, children develop the ability to break words into syllables, which is usually followed by the ability to manipulate onsets and rimes. Phoneme isolation and other phonemic awareness skills typically develop last, as they are the most complex.

10. B: Introducing sound-spellings (A) is for teaching students which written letters correspond to which spoken sounds, which they must know *before* learning to decode words. Discriminating individual phonemes within words (C) is for teaching students phonological awareness, which they also must have *before* decoding new words. Reviewing sound-spellings to overlearn them (D) is for phonics maintenance rather than word decoding. Blending phonemes into words (B) is for helping students learn a strategy to apply their sound-spelling learning to decoding unfamiliar words.

11. D: By choosing texts for students and leading them in discussion, teachers are able to introduce young readers to increasingly complex reading material. The primary focus of guided reading is not specifically on literature study, fluency, or phonological awareness.

12. D: CVC words are those that follow the consonant-vowel-consonant pattern, such as "hat," "put," and "big." These words are often the first to be introduced to emergent readers because they are typically familiar, spelled phonetically, and easy to pronounce. In order to begin recognizing and decoding CVC words, young children must first develop a sense of letter-sound correspondence and the ability to blend letter sounds for correct pronunciation. Students with weak phonics knowledge in this area will require intensive and explicit instruction to improve their skills to a developmentally appropriate level, as decoding CVC words is a foundational step for increasingly complex word recognition, and ultimately, reading fluency.

13. C: Students can easily become bored or disinterested in reading if they are not exposed to a variety of reading texts. Also, reading can be overwhelming or frustrating for students who are still learning to read fluently or to comprehend what they read. By incorporating media, oral stories, and various types of print, students of all ability levels can build both fluency and comprehension skills. This approach also enables the teacher and students to discuss the relationship between all aspects of literacy—including speaking, listening, thinking, viewing, and reading.

14. C: Reading fluency is defined as a set of skills including speed, accuracy and inflection when reading words on a page. Reading comprehension generally refers to the ability to understand what is being read. Both sets of skills are important, and reading fluency is vital to comprehension, which is the ultimate goal of the practice of reading. It is possible, even common, to isolate skills for the purpose of skill-building or to compensate for areas in which a student is struggling; however, all skills are inter-related. Children can make progress in some aspects of reading while still working on more difficult areas. Based on these ideas, choices A and D can be ruled out as possible answers. Comprehension is typically not classified as being part of fluency skills, which eliminates choice B.

Reading fluency should be considered a vital part of overall reading skills: fluency must be improved so that, ultimately, the student can comprehend what is being read more fully.

15. A: This choice provides the most direct route for assessing a student's reading fluency and comprehension. Having the student read aloud is the best way to monitor all aspects of fluency, including speed, accuracy, and vocal expression. In asking questions at the end, the teacher will not be relegated to correct or incorrect answers written upon a page. He or she will be able to hear the student's vocalization, which may reveal degrees of understanding not found in a worksheet.

16. A: In the language experience approach, students decide on a story they want to tell and dictate it to a teacher, who writes the words down on paper. The teacher then reads the story back multiple times, modeling appropriate fluency. Students are then invited to join in reading the story. In writing workshop, students work on independent writing pieces following the stages of the writing process. They may all be involved in different stages at different times. Trait-based writing teaches students to consider the traits of good writing, such as word choice, throughout the writing process. During modeled writing, teachers think aloud as they record their thoughts on paper or on the board.

17. C: The acronym *K.I.M.* in a K.I.M. vocabulary chart stands for Key idea, Information, and Memory clue. Under the "K" for Key idea, the student enters a vocabulary word. Under the "I" for Information, the student enters the definition of the word. Under the "M" for Memory clue, students often make a drawing or attach a picture, sometimes including written or printed captions, to remind them of the word's meaning.

18. B: *Activating* is the term experts use to identify the reading strategy whereby the reader activates prior knowledge and applies it to the new information in reading to construct meaning from it. *Inferring* is a strategy whereby the reader combines what the text states explicitly with what it does not state but implies, and combines these both with what s/he already knows to draw inferences. *Questioning* is the reading strategy whereby the reader engages in "learning dialogues" with the text, author, classmates, and teachers to ask and answer questions about the text. *Summarizing* is the reading strategy whereby the reader paraphrases or restates what s/he perceives as the text's meaning.

19. D: Research-based vocabulary instruction findings show that children need ample word repetition, but not through drilling. Multiple exposures to the same words in different contexts are more effective. Multiple and repeated exposures are important because children do not learn vocabulary through only one or two exposures to a new word. Research finds that they do not simply learn vocabulary in texts indirectly from reading; instead, teachers must give them direct instruction in the new vocabulary words they find in their texts.

20. D: When students ask themselves how the information in a text they are reading fits with what they already know, they are relating the text to their own prior knowledge, which increases their reading comprehension. Students should not only ask themselves what kinds of "expert questions" fit the subject matter of the text (A)—e.g., classification, physical, and chemical properties are typical question topics in science; genre, character, plot, and theme are typical of literature questions; sequence, cause-and-effect, and comparison-contrast questions are typical of history—but also what questions the material brings up for them personally (B). It is necessary and important for students to ask themselves continually how each text portion relates to its chapter's main ideas (C) as they read to optimize their reading comprehension and retention.

21. D: When adults employing narration to develop young children's language label present objects and current actions using new vocabulary words, this instantly puts them into natural contexts, which helps children comprehend word meanings more authentically and remember them better. When adults communicate locations and directionality to children (A), this teaches them how verbs and prepositions are used in sentence contexts. When adults describe the intensity and manner of people's actions and/or speech (B), this shows children how adverbs are used. When adults use narration of children's actions to initiate and transition to giving them verbal positive reinforcement (C), they promote young children's oral language development by introducing and illustrating sentence syntaxes for them.

22. A: Under the Individuals with Disabilities Education Act (IDEA), teachers that suspect a student may have a learning disability are required to refer the student for an initial evaluation to determine the need for special education services. Doing so is integral to creating an equitable environment in which all students receive the necessary support to learn effectively. In this situation, the fact that the student in question continues to struggle with reading comprehension and writing skills despite receiving RTI services may be indicative of a potential learning disability. Upon noticing the student's lack of progress, this teacher would have the professional responsibility to refer the student for an initial evaluation with the school special education department.

23. A: Contextual analysis skills, or the ability to look for clues within a text to decipher the meaning of unfamiliar words, are essential to vocabulary acquisition and reading comprehension. Examples of context clues include synonyms, antonyms, examples, or definitions that are embedded throughout the text and indicate the meaning of the new word. Teaching students to locate and use these clues helps them learn to make educated guesses regarding the meaning of unfamiliar terms, which increases vocabulary and improves reading comprehension skills.

24. A: Story maps are a form of graphic organizer that provides students with a visual aid to more effectively record and recall important details from a text. This resource is versatile, and can be differentiated to align with students' grade level, as well as variances in literacy skills. Story maps can be completed independently, and help students identify key components of a text, thus promoting reading comprehension and the ability to retell stories by recalling major details.

25. B: Accuracy and rate are essential components to building reading fluency. Accuracy is the ability to read and comprehend text with minimal errors, and rate is the speed at which one reads. Typically, as accuracy improves, rate also increases. Having students physically track text using their finger when reading is an effective strategy for developing both these skills. Doing so enhances students' ability to focus on individual words as they read while incorporating a kinesthetic element to strengthen connections as they develop reading comprehension skills.

26. C: The term "irregular sight words" refers to high-frequency vocabulary words that are not spelled phonetically. Recognition and understanding of these words are necessary for vocabulary acquisition, as well as the development of reading comprehension, spelling, and writing skills. However, since these words cannot be sounded out using conventional rules of phonics, students must memorize them. Therefore, repetition through a variety of instructional strategies is most effective when teaching high-frequency irregular sight words. In this situation, the teacher reviews irregular sight words daily with students using multiple activities. Doing so fosters students' recognition, understanding, and retention of such words, thus promoting reading fluency as well as the development of other necessary literacy skills.

27. B: Fluency requires good decoding skills. Fluent readers do not frequently stumble when encountering unfamiliar words; rather, they use their decoding skills and phonemic awareness to effectively associate letters and sounds. The other choices describe some of the defining characteristics of fluency.

28. C: Researchers and educators have found that reading fluency and reading comprehension have a reciprocal relationship: the more fluently a student can read, the more able the student's brain is to process the meaning of text. For example, developing automaticity of word identification enhances comprehension. Conversely, the better a student can understand the text, the more fluently she or he can read it. Therefore, while (A) and (B) are both true, each represents only half of the relationship whereas (C) indicates the relationship's mutual nature. (D) is incorrect as reading fluency and reading comprehension are interrelated components in deriving meaning from text and not separate.

29. D: The ideal group for guided reading consists of five or six students. Because students' needs and abilities vary, small and flexible groupings allow students to interact most effectively with the teacher and with each other. Reading aloud and developing fluency are major components of the guided reading experience.

30. B: Much research points to the fact that students can increase their speed, accuracy and inflection when they engage in repeated readings of various texts. By reading assigned pieces more than once, they have a chance to apply feedback which they have received so that they make fewer mistakes and read more quickly. Students will struggle if they are only exposed to phonetic rules, without working on automatic word recognition or practice activities, as is suggested in Choice "a". Applying the same logic to vocabulary, it is necessary to rule out Choice "c". Choice "d" is not a widely accepted method for building reading fluency for student readers in traditional schools.

31. B: Reading fluency refers to the speed, accuracy, and appropriate intonation with which an individual reads. As a student is beginning to learn to read, he or she will be working primarily on sounding out words (phonetics), building recognition of words (sight words), and reading with speed and appropriate vocal modulation (emotion and pauses for punctuation). A fluent reader will read at a natural pace without making many mistakes. He or she will typically pause appropriately to communicate punctuation and modulate the voice with expression to add interest to the text. Comprehension (B) is typically thought of as a reading concept that evolves in tandem with fluency, but the former is not a component of the latter.

32. C: Using context clues can help the reader determine the meanings of many unknown words quickly and also contribute to reading comprehension. Asking a classmate for the meanings of words may work in the short term, but it does not help the reader develop independent reading strategies, and there may not always be another person present while reading. Looking up the unknown words later may result in the student missing words that are critical to the meaning of the text, negatively affecting comprehension. Similarly, while skipping over the unknown words may result in sentences that appear to make sense, the missing words may play important roles in the meaning.

33. A: Introducing new vocabulary words will help students decode the words faster when they are encountered in the text, thus assisting with fluency. Recognizing the words and knowing their meanings will also build readers' confidence. Additionally, explaining the meanings of the words in advance will help students comprehend the text when they read it independently. Reading the first few pages aloud without discussion will not help students recognize or understand the vocabulary words, nor will it highlight important words beyond the first few pages. Listing what students want to learn about the topic helps to set a purpose for reading, not explain vocabulary. Predicting helps students activate prior knowledge, make connections, and stay actively engaged in the reading process.

34. C: The ability to identify letter combinations found in the spelling of many words, which emerges in the consolidated alphabetic phase of sight word recognition (Ehri, 1995), lessens the demand on the reader's memory because they recognize them as units, not single letters, and as common patterns within the orthographic system. As a result, this ability also promotes automaticity (A) and accuracy (B) of word recognition, which are essential parts of reading fluency (D).

35. D: Although all of these choices may benefit Corey to a certain extent, providing one-to-one intervention in reading fluency is most likely to improve his reading fluency. One-to-one instruction allows Corey to move at his own pace and move on to the next skill when he has mastered the previous skill. This allows the teacher to truly meet Corey's needs in reading fluency and give him complete attention during the intervention time. Answer A is incorrect because a student with a severe deficiency in reading fluency likely needs additional intervention outside the classroom. Answer B is incorrect because a small group would not allow Corey to work at his own pace and provide the individual instruction that he may need. Answer C is incorrect because modifying the material will not allow Corey to build his reading fluency skills.

36. D: In phonics, decoding refers to one's ability to recognize and correctly pronounce sounds produced by written letters and words. Encoding refers to one's ability to identify and produce written letters and words to correspond to the sounds of spoken language. These skills are reciprocal, and both are imperative for literacy development across domains, as they directly contribute to students' reading comprehension, writing, and oral language abilities. In this situation, the student shows deficiencies with both decoding and encoding, and therefore would benefit from more support to develop these skills.

37. A: It is true that many students report grammar instruction as being boring or even irrelevant. However, knowledge of correct grammar can improve students' reading fluency, comprehension, writing, speaking, and other language skills. Therefore, it is important to help students understand the importance of learning grammatical rules and how they can be applied in various contexts. All language skills are interrelated and cannot be taught separately from one another since they evolve simultaneously. A skilled teacher will make grammar interesting by conveying its importance and finding innovative ways to incorporate fun activities into instruction.

38. D: When students are unfamiliar with group discussions, teachers should not introduce these by beginning with topics below student age level (A); such topics will bore students and fail to engage them. Neither should teachers assign group discussion topics above student age levels (B), which will confuse, lose, and/or overwhelm them. They should take student cognitive, emotional, behavioral, and social levels of development into account when choosing discussion topics. For all students, and especially those inexperienced with discussion groups, teachers should explain *and* model appropriate behaviors—not just explain (C)—before beginning a discussion. These behaviors include eye contact and confirming and restating others' messages.

39. D: Having classmates offer peer reviews (A), having the teacher evaluate their work (B), and comparing their work to that of their classmates (C) are all valuable sources of feedback for students about their performance and progress in speaking and enacting through oral reports and presentations as they give different perspectives; however, video recordings of student performance (D) are the only type of completely objective feedback among these choices because they provide an exact record of what the student did. This enables students to self-monitor, make changes/improvements, and appreciate their own progress over time.

40. C: Setting clear goals, observing concrete data, and applying learning are all aspects of inquiry strategies, so choice C is correct. Each of the other choices refers to a teaching approach or set of strategies that does not involve these elements. Prewriting strategies (A) include helping students generate ideas, organize ideas, access their background knowledge, identify research topics, and use graphics to visualize ideas. Modeling strategies (B) includes teacher demonstration, giving students exemplary models of expected writing types, helping students analyze models, and inviting students to emulate effective model elements in their writing. Process writing (D) includes giving students opportunities for extended practice, peer interaction, personal responsibility, writing for authentic audiences, and self-evaluation.

41. A: One research-based writing instruction strategy teachers can use is to give students explicit instruction in combining simple sentences into compound, complex, and compound-complex sentences. This develops student ability to compose more sophisticated sentences. Computer word-processing programs are not crutches and do not interfere with independent student writing skills; on the contrary, teachers can use these as a strategy to help students engage in the processes of planning, writing, and editing more easily. A process writing approach is another research-based instructional strategy, not an incompatible one. It allows students extended practice with planning, composing, and reviewing; interacting with classmates while writing; owning writing responsibility; writing for real audiences; and self-evaluating writing. Research finds that teachers should not only provide good models of writing types and help them analyze these, but also encourage them to emulate these models in their own writing efforts.

42. C: Oral language is a vital aspect of any language arts instruction. Often, the first concepts of language are transmitted via oral and auditory processes. The first Americans also possessed a rich oral culture in which stories and histories were passed down through generations via storytelling. Inviting a guest speaker who is part of this culture helps students understand more about cultures in their world, as well as the value of oral language and storytelling. This introduction gives students a relevant personal experience with which to connect what they will be learning in class.

43. C: Sample 1's author cites evidence that is tangential to his argument, hence it is not relevant. Sample 2's author cites anecdotal evidence which is inaccurate, hence it is not factual. Sample 3's author cites evidence which is factual (accurate) and relevant (directly related), but not sufficient (an isolated example uncorroborated by any other sources). Criteria for evaluating evidence used in informational text include that the evidence be relevant, factual, and sufficient to accomplish the author's purpose (for example, proving the author's point or points and/or persuading the reader).

44. A: Coherent body paragraphs have parts that fit together well and provide a clear explanation of a single main idea, which supports the thesis. Choice A is correct because one major key to coherence is having a hierarchy of information where explanations support details that in turn support a main idea. Choice B is not correct as supporting details do not have to be organized according to importance. Choice C is not correct because there is no requirement to have a closing sentence for a paragraph. Choice D is incorrect because topic sentences do not need to reference each supporting detail, though each supporting detail should relate to the topic sentence.

45. D: To help them build strong oral language skills, adults should include questions in their conversations with young children that require them to form and express abstract concepts to answer. They should use rich vocabulary and complex sentence structures rather than simple ones. They should not just tell young children things but also ask them questions. Adults should not do most of the talking but engage young children in interactive conversations where both contribute equally.

46. C: The passage suggests that the impact of climate change on coral reefs has been challenging to understand due to intricate relationships. However, Dr. Olivia Chang's recent findings offer hope for preservation, indicating a more definitive, or *conclusive*, explanation. The other options do not fit as well: *an intricate* implies complexity; *an elusive* suggests difficulty in understanding; and *a clear* does not capture the idea of a definitive explanation.

47. C: In the passage, it describes how Winston Smith, the protagonist, encounters Party loyalists who "feign moral superiority while perpetuating the regime's cruelty." The word *sanctimonious* accurately conveys the idea of these Party loyalists pretending to be morally superior while supporting the oppressive regime.

48. A: Learning correct spelling and pronunciation of new vocabulary words develops student connections between spoken and printed language; using the new words in telling stories to the class develops student spoken narrative skills. Option B develops vocabulary and written language skills but not necessarily oral vocabulary. It also does not address spoken narrative skills or spoken-printed language connections. Option C develops oral language and narrative skills but does not address spoken-printed language connections. Option D addresses receptive vocabulary recognition and receptive connections between spoken and printed language but not expressive oral vocabulary, expressive spoken-printed language production, or spoken narrative skills.

History and Social Science

49. A: When the prices farmers receive for their crops decline in a developing country, this typically results in increased urbanization. When crop prices decline, farmers can no longer make a living from their land. As a result, they often choose to migrate to cities in search of low-wage employment in the manufacturing or service sectors.

50. D: While rising prices may hurt many members of an economy, those same rising prices may benefit other members of the same economy. For example, rising prices may help those who sell goods and services and are able to keep their costs of production low, increasing their profit margin. Meanwhile, rising prices can hurt consumers because their income is now able to purchase fewer goods and services than before.

51. C: Purchasing a DVD is a discretionary expense because it is based on personal desire rather than need. In other words, it is an expense made at the discretion of the consumer. Discretionary expenses are those over which a consumer has the most control. A comprehensive budget must include discretionary expenses as well as fixed and variable expenses. Fixed expenses, such as rent, are the same every month. Variable expenses, including groceries, school supplies, and heating oil, are always present but vary in amount over the course of a year.

52. B: Marx's focus in *The Communist Manifesto* (1848) and *Das Kapital* (1867) was on the inevitable conflict between the working class and the capitalists who own the means of production. He identified these two opposing forces as the proletariat and the bourgeoisie.

53. C: A person who has taken out a fixed-rate loan can benefit from inflation by paying back the loan with dollars that are less valuable than they were when the loan was taken out. In the other examples, inflation harms the individual or entity.

54. A: Rivers promoted the development of the ancient river valley civilizations of the world, including in the Middle East, India, and China. Rivers not only supply water for drinking and crop irrigation, but also provide fertile soil, vegetation for shade cover, food, building materials, and animal life. They additionally allow water travel to other locations. Although some peoples have settled and lived in deserts, they are among the most inhospitable climates. Forests also provide plenty of flora and fauna and exist in areas receiving enough rainfall, but rivers have been historically superior in attracting human societies. Mountains near living areas provide protective barriers; however, though some peoples live there, as in deserts, living in the mountains is difficult due to high altitudes, harsh climates, poor soil for planting, and rough terrain.

55. B: The Erie Canal opened in 1825 and created a water route between the Hudson River and Lake Erie. Water routes have historically been cheaper and easier than overland ones and the Erie Canal was originally proposed in the 1700s as a means of providing a shipping route to assist in settling the areas west of the Appalachian Mountains. The Mississippi River is to the west of the Great Lakes; its source is in Minnesota and it discharges into the Gulf of Mexico approximately 100 miles downstream of New Orleans, Louisiana. The Susquehanna River runs through New York, Pennsylvania, and Maryland and is the home of Three Mile Island, the site of the United States' largest nuclear disaster. The Lehigh River is located in eastern Pennsylvania.

56. A: In geography, location—specifically, relative location—determines things like land prices based on the characteristics of an area, which are affected by nearby regions. An example of distance (B) is that land that is close to major highways is more expensive, while land far from main thoroughfares costs less. One example of pattern (C) in geography is that where rock folds form mountains (fold regions), the rivers accordingly form trellis patterns. Another example of pattern, in geographically oriented human behavior, is that settlements in mountainous areas form mainly spreading patterns. An example of interaction (D) in geography is when an industrial city needs raw materials from a rural village for production, and the village needs the city both as a market to buy its resources and for its industrial products: their mutual interdependence creates interaction between them.

57. B: The Andes mountain range is the world's longest continental mountain range. It lies as a continuous chain of mountains along the western coast of South America.

58. B: Lines of longitude, which run north-south from pole to pole, are used to separate time zones. Houston, Texas, and Fargo, North Dakota, which are on almost the exact same line of longitude, are both in the Central Time Zone; however, they are not in the same state, do not have the same climate, and are not equidistant from the equator. To calculate distance from the equator, the latitude of the city would need to be known.

59. B: The President may veto legislation passed by Congress. The executive branch has this "check" on the legislative branch.

60. A: The 10th Amendment establishes that any power not given to the federal government in the Constitution belongs to the states or the people. The federal and local governments share many responsibilities.

61. D: Criminal cases are tried under both state law and federal law. The nature of the crime determines whether it is tried in state court or federal court.

62. B: The Presidential Succession Act lists the Speaker of the House, president pro tempore of the Senate, and secretary of state next in succession after the vice president. However, anyone who succeeds as president must meet all of the legal qualifications.

63. D: Congress did not have the authority to levy taxes under the Articles of Confederation. Without the ability to levy taxes, there was no way to finance programs, which weakened the government.

64. C: The 12th Amendment passed in 1804 gave each member of the Electoral College one vote for the president and another for the vice president. Previously, the runner-up in the presidential election became vice president.

65. B: Determining methods of carrying babies and studying the toddlers in several countries would be the best method for gathering data for this study.

66. A: A primary source is a document or object that was created at the time of an event. Primary sources include such things as original manuscripts, letters, official records, and photographs. Secondary sources, such as textbooks and encyclopedia articles, are removed by one or more steps from the original event. They offer interpretation or analysis based on primary sources.

67. B: Economics is the study of how goods and services are produced and distributed. Anthropologists and historians are also concerned with economic issues, but such issues are not necessarily the focal point of their studies. Psychologists focus on the mental activity and behavioral patterns of individuals within a society.

68. B: Southern states provided raw materials that were manufactured into commodities in Northern states. Southerners resented paying taxes to Northern states for these products (textiles, furniture, etc.).

69. C: The Mason-Dixon Line was the manifestation of a border dispute between the British colonies of Pennsylvania, Maryland, and Delaware. It effectively separated, or illustrated, a cultural divide between North and South before the Civil War.

70. A: The French and Indian War (Seven Years' War) happened from 1754–1763. The American Revolution happened from 1775–1783. The French Revolution happened from 1789–1799. The War of 1812 happened from 1812–1815.

71. A: Lyndon Johnson became president following the assassination of John F. Kennedy on November 22, 1963. The Great Society was a series of social programs implemented under the direction of Lyndon Johnson. The Great Society's goal was to eliminate poverty and racial injustice in America. The Great Society began with economic reforms including a tax cut and the creation of the Office of Economic Opportunity. From there, it grew to include the enacting of laws creating the Medicare and Medicaid systems to assist the elderly and poor with their health care costs, respectively. Educational and Housing reforms followed.

72. C: The Sugar Act of 1764 raised import duties on goods which were not of British origin, including sugar, while reducing the import tax on molasses. The Stamp Act of 1765 was a tax of paper and printed products, intended to help the British government recoup some of the costs of the French and Indian War. It was extremely unpopular with the colonists and was repealed in 1766. Lead was one of the goods taxed under the Townshend Acts, enacted in 1767, but it did not receive its own specific tax act. The Tea Act of 1773 was another unpopular tax and led to tea boycotts and was the catalyst for the Boston Tea Party.

73. B: The only true statement is the March on Versailles was made primarily by women. Therefore, an equal number of both men and women did not undertake the March on Versailles. The women took action because of the dire economic conditions from which they suffered, especially the high prices on bread and food shortages. The storming of the Bastille occurred on July 14, 1789; the March on Versailles occurred on October 5, 1789, almost three months later, not prior to it. (The date of July 14th is so famous as Bastille Day in France that generally it is familiar in other countries as well.) It is not true that the March on Versailles was not effective in accomplishing its purpose. In fact, the marchers did achieve their goal: They stormed the palace and killed several guards. La Fayette, in charge of the National Guard to control the mob, convinced the royals to move from Versailles to Paris and to stop blocking the National Assembly, and the royal family complied with these demands. The women did not march right to Versailles with no preliminaries. First, they assembled in markets around Paris and marched to the Hôtel de Ville. There they made their demands of the Paris city officials. When those officials did not give acceptable responses, the women then joined a march to the palace at Versailles. While the march to Versailles included men and weapons, some 7,000 women made up the majority of the marchers.

74. D: Power was centralized in the Incan Empire. When the invading Spaniards imprisoned Incan ruler Atahualpa and killed other Incan military leaders, the Incas were unable to mount an effective military response. Incas of lesser status simply lacked the appropriate authority. Answers A and B may be eliminated because they are factually inaccurate. The Incas had built some functional roads, which allowed the invading Spanish to access some Incan cities. Also, Pizarro's soldiers did not outnumber the Incans. The new diseases introduced by the Spanish decimated the Incan army, making D the correct answer. While the centralized power structure did create a vulnerability, the impact of disease was far more devastating.

75. A: According to Plato's Theory of Forms, nonphysical ideal forms are most good and real. The form of the Good has the highest degree of reality and goodness. Answer B can be rejected because Plato did not believe there was an ideal form of evil. Answer C can be rejected because Plato did not believe the Good formed a trinity with other forms. Answer D can be rejected because, though Plato advocated Socratic reasoning as a method for coming to know the forms, he did not believe such reasoning led to redemption from sin as Christian doctrine contemplates this notion.

76. D: The Triple Alliance allowed the city-states to conquer city-states and land by combining forces against mutual enemies. The Triple Alliance and its conquered areas are commonly thought of as the Aztec Empire. While some conquered areas did rebel against the Aztec Empire at the time the Spanish conquistadores arrived, such rebellion did not specifically concern the city-states of the Triple Alliance. Texcoco and Tlacopan did not use the Alliance as a front against Tenochtitlan. The Triple Alliance had nothing to do with the number of annual human sacrifices. This eliminates options A, B, and C.

77. B: Johann Gutenberg's printing press led to increased scientific knowledge and advancement as scientific texts were printed and dispersed throughout Europe. Because the distribution of such texts extended outside of Germany, options C and D may be eliminated. Gutenberg Bibles were printed using Gutenberg's press, and thus Gutenberg's invention was likely a factor in the Reformation of the Catholic Church. In fact, Martin Luther's Ninety-Five Theses (against the Catholic Church) were printed using a printing press. However, this reformation occurred alongside, rather than in place of, the advancement of scientific knowledge. This eliminates option A.

78. B: It is not true that the Crusades ultimately succeeded in retaking the Holy Land (Jerusalem and surrounding areas) from Muslim control. Although the Crusaders achieved temporary victories, such as capturing Jerusalem during the First Crusade (1099) and establishing short-lived Crusader states, these gains were not permanent. Over time, Muslim forces reconquered these territories, and by 1291, the last Crusader stronghold at Acre fell. While the Crusades did not achieve their main goal, they did contribute to the weakening of the Byzantine Empire, which lost territory to the Seljuks and later faced ongoing pressure from other powers. Additionally, the Crusades indirectly helped Egypt reemerge as a significant regional power in the Middle East.

Mathematics

79. B: The points in the table represent a symmetrical curve mirrored across the y-axis. This is a parabola, or a quadratic equation.

80. C: If x is a prime number and the greatest common factor of x and y is greater than 1, the greatest common factor of x and y must be x. The least common multiple of two numbers is equal to the product of those numbers divided by their greatest common factor. So, the least common multiple of x and y is $\frac{xy}{x} = y$. Therefore, the two quantities are the same.

81. C: The position of an accelerating car is changing according to a non-constant speed. Thus, the graph will show a curve with an increasing slope. The slope is increasing since it represents the velocity, and the velocity is increasing.

82. A: This graph shows a slope of 3, a y-intercept of −6, and the correct shading above the line. Using the test point (0,0), the equation $0 \geq 0 - 6$ may be written. Since $0 \geq -6$, the solution is the shaded area above the line, which contains the point (0,0).

83. C: Using the points $(-3,1)$ and $(1,-11)$, the slope may be written as $m = \frac{-11-1}{1-(-3)}$ or $m = -3$. Substituting the slope of −3 and the x- and y-values from the point $(-3,1)$, into the slope-intercept form of an equation gives $1 = -3(-3) + b$, which simplifies to $1 = 9 + b$. Subtracting 9 from both sides of the equation gives $b = -8$. Thus, the linear equation that includes the data in the table is $y = -3x - 8$.

84. C: All four answer choices are linear equations in slope-intercept form, $y = mx + b$. For a linear equation, we can arbitrarily choose any two points (x_1, y_1) and (x_2, y_2) and calculate the slope as $m = \frac{y_2-y_1}{x_2-x_1}$. Using the points $(-6,1)$ and $(-2,3)$, we find $m = \frac{3-1}{-2-(-6)} = \frac{2}{4} = \frac{1}{2}$. Substituting the slope of $\frac{1}{2}$ and the x- and y-values from the point $(-6,1)$ into $y = mx + b$ gives $1 = \left(\frac{1}{2}\right)(-6) + b$, which simplifies to $1 = -3 + b$, or $b = 4$. Thus, the linear equation that includes the data in the table is $y = \frac{1}{2}x + 4$.

85. C: Myles needs to purchase a combined total of at least 15 sandwiches and salads, so $x + y \geq 15$. Each sandwich costs \$3, each salad costs \$5, and he has a budget of \$60, so $3x + 5y \leq 60$. Therefore, the system of inequalities is:

$$\begin{cases} x + y \geq 15 \\ 3x + 5y \leq 60 \end{cases}$$

Graph the two lines. They should both be solid lines since both expressions allow equality (i.e., we have $\geq$ and $\leq$ rather than $>$ or $<$). The first inequality should be shaded above the line because he needs to buy 15 or more items, and the second inequality should be shaded below the line because he needs to spend \$60 or less. The overlapping shading occurs in the lower-right portion between the lines, which matches graph C.

86. A: The inequality will be less than or equal to, since he may spend \$100 or less on his purchase.

87. B: Notice that $x = 1$ results in a zero in the denominator, so choice C cannot be correct since $x \neq 1$. To solve, subtract $\frac{2}{x-1}$ from both sides, then cross-multiply.

$\frac{x-2}{x-1} = \frac{x-1}{x+1} + \frac{2}{x-1}$	Write out the original equation.
$\frac{x-4}{x-1} = \frac{x-1}{x+1}$	Subtract $\frac{2}{x-1}$ from both sides.
$(x+1)(x-4) = (x-1)(x-1)$	Cross multiply.
$x^2 - 3x - 4 = x^2 - 2x + 1$	Multiply the binomials on both sides.
$-3x - 4 = -2x + 1$	Subtract x^2 from both sides.
$-4 = x + 1$	Add $3x$ to both sides.
$-5 = x$	Subtract 1 from both sides.

88. B: The perimeter is equal to the sum of the lengths of the two bases, 2 and 6 units, and the diagonal distances of the other two sides. Using the distance formula, each side length may be represented as $d = \sqrt{20} = 2\sqrt{5}$. Thus, the sum of the two sides is equal to $2\sqrt{20}$, or $4\sqrt{5}$. The whole perimeter is equal to $8 + 4\sqrt{5}$.

89. A: The net of a triangular prism has three rectangular faces and two triangular faces, and the rectangular faces must all be able to connect to each other directly. This is shown in choice A.

90. C: The surface area of a rectangular prism may be calculated using the formula $SA = 2lw + 2wh + 2hl$. Substituting the dimensions of 14 inches, 6 inches, and 8 inches gives $SA = 2(14)(6) + 2(6)(8) + 2(8)(14)$. Thus, the surface area is 488 square inches.

91. B: The volume of a pyramid may be calculated using the formula $V = \frac{1}{3}Bh$, where B represents the area of the base and h represents the height of the pyramid. Since the base is a square, the area of the base is equal to 3.5^2, or 12.25 square inches. Substituting 12.25 for B and 6 for h gives $V = \frac{1}{3}(12.25)(6)$, which simplifies to $V = 24.5$. Therefore, the bottle can hold 24.5 cubic inches of lotion.

92. D: The three-dimensional shape being described must be a pyramid because it only has one base and all triangular sides. We can envision the sides meeting at the top, forming the point of the pyramid. Furthermore, a pyramid is named for the shape of its base. Here, the pyramid has a square base so we must classify it as a square pyramid.

93. D: Congruent figures have the same shape and the same size. Two squares have the same shape. If the areas are the same, they also have the same size and are congruent. Choice A is incorrect because two rectangles can have the same perimeter but not the same shape. Choice B is the incorrect because two polygons of the same shape are not necessarily the same size. Choice C is incorrect because two polygons can have the same side lengths but different shapes. Therefore, the correct answer is choice D.

94. C: Since there are 144 square inches in 1 square foot, the following proportion may be written and solved for x: $\frac{144}{1} = \frac{2,012}{x}$. $144x = 2,012$. Dividing both sides of the equation by 144 gives $x \approx 13.97$. Thus, 2,012 square inches is approximately equal to 13.97 square feet.

95. D: The area of the square is $A = s^2 = (30 \text{ cm})^2 = 900 \text{ cm}^2$. The area of the circle is $A = \pi r^2 = (3.14)(15 \text{ cm})^2 \approx 707 \text{ cm}^2$. The area of the shaded region is equal to the difference between the area of the square and the area of the circle, or $900 \text{ cm}^2 - 707 \text{ cm}^2$, which equals 193 cm^2.

96. C: The slope may be written as $m = \frac{4-0}{-3-(-4)}$, which simplifies to $m = 4$.

97. B: The first argument's reasoning is invalid; that the premises are true is irrelevant. (For example, consider the true premises "all cats are mammals" and "all mammals are warm-blooded;" it cannot be logically concluded that all warm-blooded animals are cats. The second argument's reasoning is valid, and since its premises are true, the argument is also sound. The third argument uses a false premise, and in addition the reasoning is not valid, so the argument is invalid.

98. A: Deductive reasoning moves from one or more general statements to a specific, while inductive reasoning makes a general conclusion based on a series of specific instances or observations. Whenever the premises used in deductive reasoning are true, the conclusion drawn is necessarily true. In inductive reasoning, it is possible for the premises to be true and the conclusion to be false since there may exist an exception to the general conclusion drawn from the observations made.

99. B: If Sofia had correctly used the techniques described in choice A or choice D, she would have arrived at the correct answers, $\frac{2}{4}$ and $\frac{3}{6}$. Choice C would have shown her that $\frac{2}{4}$ and $\frac{4}{8}$ are equivalent fractions of $\frac{1}{2}$. By adding equal numbers to the numerator and denominator of $\frac{1}{2}$, Sophia concluded that $\frac{2}{3}$ and $\frac{3}{4}$ were equivalent fractions.

100. B: The data set $\{67, 2, 67, 73, 85, 60, 68\}$ contains seven numbers, six of which are within 15 units of each other. The remaining piece of data, 2, is an outlier, meaning it is much greater or smaller than the rest of the data. Using the range of this data set, 83 (because $85 - 2 = 83$), would give the impression that the entire data set greatly varies, which is not the case. Using the range of this data set, 83 (because 85-2=83), would give the impression that the entire data set greatly varies, which is not the case. Using the range to describe a data set is not the most common, but in select instances, it can provide a quick glance as to how spread out the data is. However, outliers can drastically distort the range. For this type of data set, the median would be a better representation of the set because the outlier does not have as great an effect.

101. C: Since it is established that $\angle BEA \cong \angle DEA$, we can substitute $\angle BEA$ for $\angle DEA$ in the equation from Step 2.

102. D: Step 6 established that $\angle BEA$ was a right angle. According to the definition of perpendicular lines, two lines that meet at a right angle are perpendicular.

103. B: Emotional and behavioral self-regulation skills are important components of problem-solving abilities in students. Without these, students would not have the patience, persistence, and flexibility to keep trying alternative solutions if their first solution fails (D). Another characteristic of problem-solving behavior is to formulate hypotheses first and then test them for accuracy, not vice versa (A). An additional characteristic of good problem-solvers is to be willing to take reasonable risks (C).

104. B: Since $7 \geq 5$, 10.37 kg rounds to 10.4 kg when rounded to the nearest tenth. Since $4 \leq 5$, 10.44 kg rounds to 10.4 kg when rounded to the nearest tenth. Since $0 \leq 5$, 10.406 kg rounds to 10.4 kg when rounded to the nearest tenth. However, since $5 \geq 5$, 10.45 kg rounds to 10.5 kg when rounded to the nearest tenth.

105. C: To quickly solve, notice that 648 is an even number (divisible by 2), its digits add up to 18 (divisible by 3), and 8 can be divided into the figure.

106. C: The total distance traveled was 8 miles + 3.6 miles = 11.6 miles. The first $\frac{1}{5}$ of a mile is charged at the higher rate. Since $\frac{1}{5} = 0.2$, the remainder of the trip is 11.4 miles, and multiplying the distance by 5 gives the number of $\frac{1}{5}$ of a mile increments. Thus, the fare for the distance traveled is computed as $\$5.50 + 5 \times 11.4 \times \$1.50 = \$91$. The charge for waiting time is added next, which is simply $9 \times 20¢ = 180¢ = \$1.80$. Finally, add the two charges, $\$91 + \$1.80 = \$92.80$.

107. D: The percent change can be found using the following formula.

$$\% \text{ Change} = \frac{\text{new} - \text{old}}{\text{old}} \times 100$$

The old value is his current rent (750), and the new value is his new monthly rent (900).

$$\% \text{ Change} = \frac{900 - 750}{750} \times 100$$

$$\% \text{ Change} = \frac{150}{750} \times 100$$

$$\% \text{ Change} = \frac{1}{5} \times 100$$

$$\% \text{ Change} = 20$$

Since the percent change is positive, this represents a percent increase of 20%.

108. D: Begin by calculating the total rainfall in the summer and autumn months by adding all the values together. The total rainfall is 25.38 inches. Then, create a ratio comparing the rainfall in October to the total rainfall. The ratio $\frac{4.5}{25.38}$ represents the fraction of rainfall received during October. Convert the ratio to a percentage by dividing the numerator by the denominator and then multiplying by 100: $\frac{4.5}{25.38} \approx 0.177 = 17.7\%$. Therefore, about 17.7% of the rain fell during October.

109. C: The set of irrational numbers is separate from the set of rational numbers. A rational number cannot be irrational, and an irrational number cannot be rational.

110. D: The first three choices can be disproved using the numbers 2, 3, and 5, which are all prime. $3 + 5 = 8$, which is even and is not prime. $2 + 3 = 5$, which is an odd number. Therefore, none of the statements are true.

111. C: Start by setting up a proportion to solve: $\frac{1\text{ inch}}{60\text{ feet}} = \frac{10\text{ inches}}{x\text{ feet}}$. When the numbers are cross-multiplied, you get $x = 600$. Now we need to convert 600 feet to yards. There are 3 feet in 1 yard, so divide 600 by 3 to find the number of yards between the two points: $600 \div 3 = 200$. Therefore, the two points are 200 yards apart.

112. C: When ordering negative numbers, it helps to remember that the largest digit has the smallest value. That makes –5 our smallest value, followed by –3, and finally –1. Next comes 0 because 0 separates our negative numbers from our positive numbers. To compare decimals, we can insert zeros at the end of each number so that each value has the same number of digits. Here, that would look like 15.05 and 15.30. When we start comparing digits from left to right, we see that the first place value that differs is the tenths place. Because 3 is greater than 0, we know that 15.3 is greater than 15.05. Finally, our greatest number of the set is 19 because positive 19 is greater than all the other numbers in the set. That makes our ordered list –5, –3, –1, 0, 15.05, 15.3, 19.

113. B: The line through the center of the box represents the median. The median test score for English and History is the same, not the mean test score, which makes choice B the correct answer. Note that for Science, the median is a better representation of the data than the mean. There is at least one outlier (a point that lies outside of two standard deviations from the mean), which brings down the average test score. In cases such as this, the mean is not the best measure of central tendency, so choice A is not the correct answer. The median of the History scores is 87, and the 3rd quartile scores for Math is also 87, so choice C is not the answer. The median of the English scores is 86, and based on the spread of data, the mean is lower than the median, so choice D is also not correct.

114. B: Since they are not mutually exclusive events, $P(4\text{ or }E) = P(4) + P(E) - P(4\text{ and }E)$. Substituting the probability of each event gives $P(4\text{ or }E) = \frac{1}{6} + \frac{1}{2} - \frac{1}{6} = \frac{1}{2}$.

115. D: Since there are 100 homes' market times represented in each set, the median time a home spends on the market is between the 50th and 51st data point in each set. The 50th and 51st data points for Zip Code 1 are six months and seven months, respectively, so the median time a house in Zip Code 1 spends on the market is between six and seven months (6.5 months), which by the realtor's definition of market time is a seven-month market time. The 50th and 51st data points for Zip Code 2 are both thirteen months, so the median time a house in Zip Code 2 spends on the market is thirteen months. Therefore, there is a six-month difference between the median of Zip Code 1 and the median of Zip Code 2.

To find the mean market time for 100 houses, find the sum of the market times and divide by 100. If the frequency of a one-month market time is 9, the number 1 is added nine times (1×9), if the frequency of a two-month market time is 10, the number 2 is added ten times (2×10), and so on. So, to find the average market time, divide by 100 the sum of the products of each market time and its corresponding frequency. For Zip Code 1, the mean market time is 7.38 months, which, by the realtor's definition of market time, is an eight-month market time. For Zip Code 2, the mean market time is 12.74, which, by the realtor's definition of market time, is a thirteen-month market time. Therefore, the difference between the mean of Zip Code 1 and the mean of Zip Code 2 is 5 months.

The mode market time is the market time for which the frequency is the highest. For Zip Code 1, the mode market time is three months, and for Zip Code 2, the mode market time is eleven months. Therefore, the median time a house spends on the market in Zip Code 1 is less than the mean time a house spends on the market in Zip Code 1.

116. B: The probability may be written as $P(E \text{ and } H) = P(E) \times P(H)$. The probability of rolling an even number on a die is $E = \frac{3}{6} = \frac{1}{2}$. The probability of a coin landing on heads is $H = \frac{1}{2}$. Substituting the probability of each event gives $P(E \text{ and } H) = \frac{1}{2} \times \frac{1}{2} = \frac{1}{4}$.

117. D: The number of outcomes in the event is 2 (rolling a 5 or 6), and the sample space is 6 (numbers 1 to 6). Thus, the probability may be written as $\frac{2}{6}$, which simplifies to $\frac{1}{3}$.

118. D: The theoretical probability of tossing any particular number is $\frac{1}{6}$. Since she tosses a two $\frac{3}{12}$, or $\frac{1}{4}$ times, the experimental probability of tossing a 2 is greater than the theoretical probability. The experimental probability should grow closer to the experimental probability as she tosses the die more times.

119. A: Nominal data are data that are collected which have no intrinsic quantity or order. For instance, a survey might ask the respondent to identify his or her gender. While it is possible to compare the relative frequency of each response (for example, "most of the respondents are women"), it is not possible to calculate the mean, which requires data to be numeric, or median, which requires data to be ordered. Interval data are both numeric and ordered, so mean and median can be determined, as can the mode, the interval within which there are the most data. Ordinal data has an inherent order, but there is not a set interval between two points. For example, a survey might ask the respondents whether they were very dissatisfied, dissatisfied, neutral, satisfied, or very satisfied with the customer service received. Since the data are not numeric, the mean cannot be calculated, but since ordering the data is possible, the median has context.

120. D: This is a counting problem. The possible number of outfits is equal to the product of the possibilities for each category. The product of 4, 6, and 5 is 120. Thus, there are 120 outfits that she may create.

Science

121. B: Pros of solar energy include the facts that it is renewable, abundant, environmentally friendly, low maintenance, and silent. Cons of solar energy include that it is expensive and intermittent and requires a lot of space. Solar panels require rare minerals like indium and tellurium and at this point are only about 20% efficient in harvesting energy—putting them behind several other alternative methods. Other solar harvesting methods besides the photoelectric effect include concentrated solar and water heating.

122. C: The Moon is slowly moving further away from the Earth. The Moon is moving a little less than 4 cm a year away from the Earth. Since the Moon only rotates once in every orbit around the Earth, the same side is always seen from Earth. The acceleration of gravity on the surface of the Moon is approximately one-sixth of the gravitational acceleration on the surface of the Earth. Although the Moon has less than 1/80 the mass of the Earth, it also has a smaller radius, and the acceleration of gravity on the surface depends on both.

123. C: The Sun's energy is the energy source behind Earth's weather patterns, but since the Sun's energy only directly reaches a fraction of Earth's landmass, other factors play an enormous role in distributing the energy globally. The ocean absorbs the Sun's energy and transports it throughout the world, acting as the primary driving force behind global climate and weather. Wind belts, the Earth's orbit, and atmospheric conditions also play a role in driving global weather.

124. A: Chemical composition is not one of the physical properties used to classify minerals. The five major physical properties used to classify minerals are luster, hardness, cleavage, streak, and form. There is a separate classification system based on the chemical composition of minerals.

125. C: Chemicals should not be stored routinely on bench tops. Each chemical should be stored in a location for that specific type of chemical. When in use, chemicals may be temporarily kept on bench tops, but only in the quantities that are required for that particular situation. Chemicals should be returned to an appropriate location after use.

126. A: Glass is manufactured and can be recycled, but is considered a non-renewable resource. Wood is considered a renewable resource because with proper management, an equilibrium can be reached between harvesting trees and planting new ones. Cattle are managed in herds and a balance can be achieved between those consumed and those born. Soil is the result of long-term erosion and includes organic matter and minerals needed by plants. Soil found naturally in the environment is renewed. Crops can be rotated to help maintain a healthy soil composition for farming.

127. C: James Hutton is best known for proposing the theory of uniformitarianism. This geological theory, which is essentially the opposite of catastrophism, suggests that the laws and forces acting on the Earth have remained basically the same since the beginning of geologic time.

128. A: A lysosome is an organelle that is thought to be linked to the aging process and contains digestive enzymes that break down food and unneeded substances. Chromatin is the structure created by DNA and various proteins in the cell's nucleus during interphase and condenses to form chromosomes. Plastids are found in plants and algae. They often contain pigments and usually help make chemical compounds for the plant. The Golgi apparatus prepares macromolecules like proteins and lipids for transport.

129. C: Translation is the process of the tRNA bringing the correct amino acid to the ribosome according to the sequence of the mRNA. Since translation only involves RNA, the four bases are adenine (A), cytosine (C), guanine (G), and uracil (U). There is no thymine (T) used in RNA. Cytosine (C) and guanine (G) pair and adenine (A) and uracil (U) pair. A codon is the triplet sequence that represents a specific amino acid or a start/stop point. It is on the messenger RNA (mRNA). The anticodon is on tRNA and corresponds to the amino acid used by the ribosome during translation. They are complementary. UGC becomes AUG; AUG becomes CGA. The mRNA codon sequence is U G C A U G C G A if the anticodon sequence formed during translation is A C G U A C G C U.

130. B: Secondary succession occurs when a habitat has been entirely or partially disturbed or destroyed by abandonment, burning, storms, etc.

131. D: The circulatory system and gas exchange with the environment is not paired correctly. It is the respiratory system that exchanges gases with the environment by delivering oxygen to the bloodstream and releasing carbon dioxide. The circulatory system transports nutrients, gases, hormones, and blood to and away from cells. The muscle system controls movement through three types of muscle tissue. The nervous system controls sensory responses by carrying impulses away from and toward the cell body. The digestive system breaks down food for absorption into the bloodstream where it is delivered to cells for respiration.

132. A: Cardiac output is total volume of blood that is pumped by the heart over a certain period of time. This value is typically reported in the amount of liters per minute. Cardiac output is determined by the product of heart rate and stroke volume. Heart rate is the number of heartbeats per minute, and stroke volume is the amount of blood that is pumped by the left ventricle in each heartbeat or contraction. A typical heart can pump approximately 5 liters of blood per minute. As the intensity of exercise increases, the cardiac output can increase to as high as 40 liters per minute. An individual's heart rate will increase linearly until the maximum level is reached. Stroke volume, however, tends to increase to approximately 40-50% of the maximum and will then level off. Aerobic exercise helps to strengthen the heart, pump blood more efficiently, and increase stroke volume.

133. D: Stomata are openings on leaves that allow for gas exchange, which is essential for photosynthesis. Stomata are surrounded by guard cells, which open and close based on their turgidity.

134. D: Respiration produces carbon dioxide and water. The net equation of respiration is the reverse of the equation for photosynthesis. Respiration is a series of reactions that consume glucose and oxygen to release energy and produce carbon dioxide and water. Oxygen and glucose are the substances that are broken down in respiration.

135. C: In humans, diploid cells are those that contain 46 chromosomes. There are 23 pairs of chromosomes each made up of one chromosome from the father and one from the mother. In meiosis I, each chromosome replicates itself and lines up, or synapses, with its homologous chromosome, and each of the daughter cells ends up with one copy of each of the chromosomes. The two daughter cells at the end of meiosis I are haploid because they contain half of the chromosomes of the parent cell. In humans, this would be 23 chromosomes. However, each of these chromosomes are made of two sister chromatids. In meiosis II, the sister chromatids in the daughter cells separate and result in the production of the gametes. These are also haploid cells because they contain one copy of half of the genetic material of the parent cell. Four haploid cells result from meiosis. Choice A, mitosis, can be eliminated as it refers to the process of cell division where each daughter cell contains exactly the same genetic material as the parent cell. Choice B, telophase, refers to phases of both mitosis and meiosis, during which chromosomes move toward the opposite ends of the cell.

136. A: Since the atomic number is 20, which represents the number of protons in the atom, there must be an equal number of electrons in a neutral atom. Protons have a positive charge and electrons are negative. Equal numbers of protons and electrons will result in a neutral atom, or zero charge.

137. A: Most organic molecules are not highly soluble in water. A low melting point, covalent bonds, and high flammability are all characteristics of organic molecules. Organic molecules are those that contain carbon atoms, with a few exceptions. Organic molecules tend to be less soluble in water than inorganic salts. They are good at forming unique structures and there are many organic compounds. Examples of organic compounds include hydrocarbons, carbohydrates, lipids, and proteins.

138. A: Chemical compounds are formed when valence electrons from atoms of two different elements are shared or transferred. Valence electrons are the electrons located in the outermost shell of the atom, and they occupy the highest energy level. Atoms may form compounds by sharing valence electrons (covalent bonding) or by transferring electrons.

139. C: Predictions of the solubility of each chemical at 150 degrees Celsius can be made by extending the lines or curves. Since the data for KBr is relatively linear, it is reasonable to assume that the solubility may increase to about 130 g per 100 g H_2O. If the curves for $NaClO_3$ and KNO_3

continue along the same lines, then these predictions are too low. The prediction for NaCl is too high.

140. A: The sky looks blue because of Rayleigh scattering, in which air molecules scatter short-wavelength light, especially blue, much more than longer wavelengths. This scattered blue light reaches our eyes from all directions, making the sky look blue. Therefore (B) is incorrect. Glass appears transparent to us; however, it is really only transparent to the light frequencies (wavelengths) that we can see, but to ultraviolet light frequencies, which we cannot see, glass is actually opaque. Wood, metal, and other materials look opaque to us *not* because they reflect light (D) but rather because they absorb light.

141. A: The period of a simple pendulum depends on the length and the rate of acceleration due to gravity. The period is independent of amplitude (to a good approximation) for amplitudes less than about 15 degrees. The period of a pendulum is unaffected by increasing the mass.

142. C: The ideal mechanical advantage of a simple machine is determined by the ratio of input distance to output distance. Since the input distance is 1.5 m and the output distance is 0.5 m, the ideal mechanical advantage for this pulley is 3.

143. C: The vapor pressure decreases by an amount proportional to the amount of solute. Raoult's law states that the vapor pressure of a solution containing a non-volatile solute is equal to the vapor pressure of the volatile solvent multiplied by its mole fraction, which is basically the proportion of the solution that is made up by solvent. In a liquid, some of the surface particles have higher than average energy and can break away to become a gas, or evaporate. The pressure of this gas right above the surface of the liquid is called the vapor pressure. Increasing the amount of solute in a liquid decreases the number of solvent particles at the surface. Because of this, fewer solvent molecules are able to escape, thus lowering the vapor pressure.

144. B: Since the points in this scatterplot "tend" to be rising, this is a positive correlation. However, since the points are not clustered to resemble a straight line, this is a low positive correlation.

145. A: Observation includes collecting evidence, using the five senses, and writing descriptions. Classifying includes grouping items based on similarities, differences, and interrelationships. Inferring includes explaining or interpreting collected evidence. Communication is reporting to others what has been found by experimentation.

146. D: Once a hypothesis has been verified and accepted, it becomes a theory. A theory is a generally accepted explanation that has been highly developed and tested. A theory can explain data and be expected to predict outcomes of tests. A fact is considered to be an objective and verifiable observation, whereas a scientific theory is a greater body of accepted knowledge, principles, or relationships that might explain a fact. A law is an explanation of events for which the outcome is always the same. A conclusion is more of an opinion and could be based on observation, evidence, fact, laws, or even beliefs.

147. A: A good hypothesis is testable and logical, and can be used to predict future events. A good hypothesis is also simple, not complex.

148. A: Repetition is the only way to prove that an experiment is reliable. If an experiment can't be successfully repeated with the same outcome, one cannot determine that the experimental results are valid. Repetition is the key to scientific progress.

149. B: When scientists and students are able to identify patterns and find meaning in the results of their experiments, they are using the process skill of Inference. When they use the results of their experiments to formulate new hypotheses (A), they are using the process skill of Prediction. When they identify the properties of objects or situations using their senses, they are using the process skill of Observation. When they report the results of their experiments and their conclusions based on these results to others (D), they are using the process skill of Communication. These skills are required for solving both math and science problems.

150. C: Scientists make observations, gather data, and complete research over many years in order to compile knowledge that will provide insight into future disasters, such as earthquakes, storms, and global warming. Although science can be used to predict earthquakes and other natural disasters, there is currently no way of preventing them from occurring.

Practice Test #2

Reading and English Language Arts

1. Mrs. Gilbert, an English teacher, and Ms. Dudley, an Art teacher, are working together to create an integrated unit of study for their common students. The students will be studying King Tut, reading various accounts of his life, both fiction and non-fiction. Ms. Dudley will be guiding the students through various art projects related to the time period in which King Tut lived (e.g., making papyrus). Which choice provides an example of an additional project or lesson that will address visual interpretation and decoding skills?

a. The students participate in Ancient Egypt Day and can dress up as characters or historical figures from the appropriate time period.
b. The students visit a local museum exhibit on Ancient Egypt and keep a log of visual images and representations they see. The class discusses those images and their meanings during both classes.
c. The students write stories about the lives of Ancient Egyptians and draw illustrations to go along with their writing.
d. The students watch a movie about King Tut and create free-writing pieces based on what they have seen.

2. A teacher asks her students to say the word *map*. She then says, "Change the /m/ sound to a /t/ sound. What word do you have now?" Which phonemic awareness skill are students practicing?

a. Alliteration
b. Segmenting
c. Blending onset and rime
d. Phoneme substitution

3. A group of students is playing a card game at a classroom reading center. They take turns flipping over two cards and trying to create matches. Each match consists of a letter and a picture of a word that begins with that letter. For example, a student matches a card containing a letter *p* and a card displaying a picture of a pig. What concept are students practicing?

a. Encoding
b. One-to-one correspondence
c. Phoneme isolation
d. Alphabetic principle

4. Which activity would be most appropriate to teach decoding of CVCe words?

a. Covering parts of the word
b. Chunking
c. Building word families
d. Blending

5. Mr. Clark is conducting a daily phonics lesson. Today, the class is focusing on the *st* consonant blend. Students first repeatedly produce the sound the blend makes. They then search for *st* words within the classroom. Which approach to phonics instruction is Mr. Clark demonstrating?

a. Implicit
b. Explicit
c. Whole language
d. Analytical

6. Students in a second-grade classroom are exploring and building words that contain *eigh*. Which layer of orthography are they exploring?

a. Alphabet layer
b. Pattern layer
c. Meaning layer
d. Conventional layer

7. Which of the following is most accurate about the benefits of various levels of phonological awareness instruction to the development of reading skills?

a. Instruction in rhyming, onsets, and rimes appears most directly beneficial to reading development.
b. Instruction in simpler phonology skills can aid teaching more complex ones and reading development.
c. Instruction that integrates blending and segmenting appears most beneficial to reading development.
d. Instruction that integrates deleting and substituting appears most beneficial to reading development.

8. A student is stumped by an unfamiliar word. The teacher guides the student to look for parts of the word that seem familiar. The student discovers a prefix, root, and suffix, each resembling those in other words she knows. Which instructional approach does this reflect?

a. Synthetic phonics
b. Onsets and rimes
c. Structural analysis
d. Analytic phonics

9. In which of the following sentences would it be most appropriate to suggest that a first-grade student use the "sound it out" strategy to decode the underlined word?

a. The child started to <u>tear</u> the wrapping paper off the gift.
b. The <u>chain</u> on the swing was squeaky.
c. The kitten was hiding behind the <u>curtain</u>.
d. The dolphin swam across the <u>ocean</u>.

10. A first-grade teacher wants to help students compare and contrast short vowel sounds. Which activity would best assist students with this skill?

a. Segmenting words with short vowel sounds using Elkonin boxes
b. Tracing words with short vowel sounds using stencils
c. Sorting words containing short vowel sounds
d. Including words with short vowel sounds on the weekly spelling list

11. According to a large body of research, how is systematic phonics instruction most effective?

a. For the majority of K-6 students, with the exception of students having difficulty with learning to read
b. When it is provided to K–6 students as an instructional program separate from any reading instruction.
c. With pre-K–2 students but not older, and paired with phonemic awareness but not other instruction
d. In the context of comprehensive reading programs including fluency, vocabulary, and comprehension

12. During informal assessment, which of these is the best example of print awareness in a young child?

a. The child can identify the front and the back of a book.
b. The child can identify all letters in the words in a book.
c. The child can identify words but not spaces in between.
d. The child can identify and read sentences with fluency.

13. A teacher notices that her new student, Carl, has a hard time answering questions related to comprehension during class and has scored low on comprehension quizzes and worksheets. What would be the most logical first step in determining how to help Carl?

a. Encourage Carl to read all assigned texts at least twice before class to help him understand what he has read.
b. Provide Carl with story maps of what he will be reading to assist his comprehension visually.
c. Ask Carl to read aloud with his teacher individually so that she can ensure that he is reading with expected accuracy and speed (i.e., fluently).
d. Modify Carl's class work so that he is able to work on easier comprehension material until his skills are brought up to speed.

14. A student who encounters an unfamiliar word in a story is able to deduce its meaning by associating it with a synonym that appears in the preceding sentence. The strategy the student has employed is called:

a. Decoding
b. Using context clues
c. Developing fluency
d. Phonological awareness

15. When introducing new high-frequency vocabulary, a first-grade teacher uses a mapping activity in which students separate, graph, and tap out the individual phonemes of each new word while reading them aloud. This strategy is likely intended to promote which of the following?

a. Automaticity
b. Prosody
c. Orthographic mapping
d. Receptive language skills

16. As a reading strategy, ELA teachers can best give students practice in making predictions to support comprehension through which activity?

a. Predicting what or whom a book is about
b. Predicting what a novel's character will do
c. Predicting a significant event in a narrative
d. Predicting (B) and/or (C), rather than (A)

17. Which of the following instructional strategies would likely help students the most in understanding the difference between denotation and connotation and help them learn to identify the connotation of a word in context?

a. Providing example sentences in multiple choice questions asking for a word's connotation
b. Filling out a Venn diagram with sets of words that have connotations, denotations, or both
c. Assigning a reading where students identify and highlight words that have connotations
d. Giving word definitions and asking students to describe the feelings elicited by each definition

18. The first paragraph of Abraham Lincoln's Gettysburg Address is a single sentence that reads: "Four score and seven years ago our fathers brought forth, on this continent, a new nation, conceived in Liberty, and dedicated to the proposition that all men are created equal." In the two-column notes active reading strategy, which of the following phrases from this introduction would go in the main idea column?

a. "Four score and seven years ago"
b. "...our fathers brought forth... a new nation"
c. "...conceived in Liberty"
d. "...dedicated to the proposition that all men are created equal."

19. A teacher is working with a student who is struggling with reading. The teacher gives him a story with key words missing:

> The boy wanted to take the dog for a walk. The boy opened the door. The _____ ran out. The ____ looked for the dog. When he found the dog, he was very ______.

The student is able to fill in the blanks by considering:

a. Syntax. Oftentimes, word order gives enough clues that a reader can predict what happens next.
b. Pretext. By previewing the story, the student can deduce the missing words.
c. Context. By considering the other words in the story, the student can determine the missing words.
d. Sequencing. By putting the ideas in logical order, the student can determine the missing words.

20. The first-grade teacher wants her class to understand that stories have a certain order. She reads them a story, then orally reviews how each event that happened in the story caused the next event to happen. To reinforce the lesson, the teacher should:

a. Give each child a piece of drawing paper that has been folded in half and then in half again, creating four boxes, along with a piece that has not been folded. The teacher should then ask the students to draw a cartoon about the story. Each of the first four boxes will show the events in order. The second page is to show how the story ends.
b. Give each child a piece of drawing paper and ask the students to draw the most important scene.
c. Give each child a piece of drawing paper and ask the students to draw the story's beginning on the front of the page and ending on the back.
d. Give each child a piece of drawing paper that has been folded in half and then in half again, creating four boxes, along with a piece that has not been folded. The teacher should then ask the students to draw a cartoon about anything they want. She reminds them to put their story cartoons in proper order.

21. Which statement is most accurate regarding children who have good reading comprehension?

a. They read material which is familiar within their existing knowledge.
b. They are skilled at decoding, so they do not need good vocabularies.
c. They can summarize what they read and predict what will come next.
d. They comprehend text without needing to use the sentence structure.

22. While reading a work of fictional literature, a third-grade teacher asks students to circle words that describe the main character in order to determine the character's motives throughout the story. This strategy is likely intended to develop which of the following skills?

a. Literal reading comprehension
b. Inferential reading comprehension
c. Critical reading comprehension
d. Evaluative reading comprehension

23. After having students read an informational text on the life cycle of plants, a third-grade teacher noticed that some individuals struggled to understand key vocabulary in the passage. Which of the following strategies would likely best help these students improve their comprehension?

a. Assigning comprehension questions corresponding to the text
b. Having students complete a KWL chart
c. Demonstrating how to look up unfamiliar vocabulary in the dictionary
d. Having students create a semantic map

24. A fourth-grade class is reading an informational text about the role of local, state, and national government in daily life. As they read, the teacher instructs students to highlight unfamiliar vocabulary words, circle important information, and write down questions about parts they do not understand. Which of the following skills does this promote?

a. Phonological processing
b. Structural analysis
c. Critical analysis
d. Contextual analysis

25. After a reading fluency check, a first-grade teacher has noticed that a student is struggling to distinguish between open and closed syllables when reading aloud. Which of the following interventions would likely best support the student's development of this skill?

a. Reviewing how to blend and segment syllables
b. Having the student sound out words letter by letter
c. Providing direct instruction on the beginning, middle, and final phonemes in words
d. Having the student practice forming words with letter tiles and reading them aloud

26. When reading grade-level texts, a third-grade student struggles to recognize both new and familiar vocabulary words. The student reads slowly, and often has trouble deriving meaning from what he has read. Based upon this information, this student appears to have difficulty with which of the following skills?

a. Irregular sight word recognition
b. Prosody
c. Phonemic awareness
d. Automaticity

Refer to the following for question 27:

Valeria is a bright sixth-grader who struggles with reading fluency. She comes from a predominantly Spanish-speaking home and has only lived in the United States for two years. Her teacher plans to use the guided oral reading strategy to help increase Valeria's reading skills. She also plans to use Valeria's scheduled media time to help work on her fluency.

27. Which of the following computer activities/games would be most beneficial to use during Valeria's media time?

a. Valeria can select from a variety of high-interest texts and read aloud what she sees on the screen.
b. Valeria can hear high-frequency sight and vocabulary words in her headphones and get points for "zapping" (clicking) the correct matching word on her screen.
c. Valeria can practice typing in a keyboarding program to build her speed and accuracy in writing reports and papers.
d. Valeria can surf a limited and pre-approved number of internet sites to read on subjects of her choosing.

28. Which of these is correct regarding children's reading fluency?

a. Sounding choppy when reading out loud indicates a lack of fluency.
b. Fluency is only an issue for children when they are reading out loud.
c. Reading aloud without expression is no issue as long as it is accurate.
d. Reading fluency is measured by reading speed, but not by accuracy.

29. Which exercise would be best for building fluency in young students?

a. Allowing students to draw pictures that illustrate the texts they read if they are unable to write their responses
b. Using daily games and lessons to reinforce phoneme-identification skills
c. Placing the students into groups to read aloud to one another
d. Reading to the students every day from a variety of texts

30. In monitoring a group of elementary-age students' reading fluency, which of the following students may need extra or specialized instruction?

a. A student who reads an unfamiliar text more slowly than he reads a familiar text.
b. A student reading an independent-level text, finding approximately 1 in 25 words difficult to read.
c. A student reading an instructional-level text, finding approximately 1 in 5 words difficult to read.
d. A student who scores a 70% on a comprehension test.

31. During a reading assessment, which of the following student behaviors reflects a weakness in strategy?

a. The student tries to read every word, with many errors.
b. The student pays attention to the punctuation in a text.
c. The student understands the main idea, but not details.
d. The student takes a holistic approach to reading words.

32. A student is able to decode most words fluently and has a borderline/acceptable vocabulary, but his reading comprehension is quite low. He can be helped with instructional focus on:

a. Strategies to increase comprehension and to build vocabulary
b. Strategies to increase comprehension and to be able to identify correct syntactical usage
c. Strategies to improve his understanding of both content and context
d. Strategies to build vocabulary and to improve his understanding of both content and context

33. Corey is a third-grade student with a specific learning disability in the area of reading fluency. Which of the following assessments would be most appropriate in determining his eligibility for special education services?

a. Wechsler Preschool and Primary Scale of Intelligence
b. Wechsler Individual Achievement Test
c. Wechsler Intelligence Scale
d. Wechsler Intelligence Scale for Children

34. Regarding teaching strategies to improve reading fluency, teachers can encourage students to read independently by providing books with suitable difficulty levels that students find interesting. Which is true about these additional strategies?

a. Timed exercises should be avoided for creating undue pressure
b. Repetition is a very effective technique to build reading fluency
c. Readers' theatre is good for showing progress but not making it
d. Reading in pairs assists reading comprehension but not fluency

35. What statement is accurate regarding research findings about methods for teaching reading fluency?

a. Assisted reading approaches have been found highly effective for fluency.
b. Repeated reading and assisted reading approaches are mutually exclusive.
c. Assisted reading methods work equally well one-on-one and in regular classrooms.
d. Reading while listening is more efficient but unrelated to assisted reading.

36. A first-grade student often leaves out the ending sounds when reading regular high-frequency sight words aloud. Which of the following strategies would best help this student improve her decoding skills?

a. Having the student practice sounding out words using letter tiles
b. Incorporating rhyming games and songs into instruction
c. Giving the student a list of spelling words to practice each week
d. Having the student trace and practice writing high-frequency sight words

37. Which of the following would *not* be used as instruction on writing conventions?

a. Practice correcting sentences with incorrect punctuation.
b. Re-writing work that is difficult to read due to word spacing and handwriting.
c. Brainstorming details to support the main concepts in an essay.
d. Checking spelling and using a dictionary and thesaurus to make sure that words are used correctly.

38. When teachers assign students to small groups for collaborative writing, which of these applies?

a. Teachers should only set individual performance expectations for individual, not group work.
b. Teachers should expect student groups to self-manage, and not interfere by giving structure.
c. Classmates in collaborative groups should give each other positive feedback, not corrections.
d. Classmates in collaborative groups should give each other constructive and positive feedback.

39. Which of the following is most accurate about the relationship between the physics of thinking and speaking as these inform classroom instruction in listening actively?

a. Because thinking outpaces speech, students' minds wander, so listening is less effective than reading.
b. The disparity between speaking and thinking speeds is conducive to active listening via summarizing.
c. The process of listening is an inherently social interaction; the process of learning is not equally social.
d. The process of learning is essentially a reciprocal one, but the process of listening is not as reciprocal.

40. In writing instruction, what does the process writing approach entail?

a. Hypothetical audiences for written work
b. Students work on their own throughout.
c. Personal responsibility for written work
d. Writing is evaluated only by the teacher.

41. Which of these accurately reflects research findings about effective writing instruction methods?

a. Procedural strategies like mnemonics, graphic organizers, outlines, and checklists aren't very useful.
b. Studies show teaching cognitive strategies is helpful only to students of certain ages and ability levels.
c. Students need explicit instruction, modeling, think-alouds, and scaffolding to learn how to write well.
d. Teaching self-regulation improves only student awareness of their writing strengths and weaknesses.

42. Which of the following sentences demonstrates subject-verb agreement?

a. "The beautiful shores of Hawaii is where I call home."
b. "Neither Harriet nor her sister are going to visit him."
c. "The people of the Iroquois Nation are in agreement."
d. "Only one of these islands have a civilized population."

43. Which of the following is true of the introduction to a written piece?

a. It is best to write it first.
b. It is best to write it last.
c. It should reinforce the points made in the piece.
d. It is the least important part of a piece of writing.

44. When asking a research question, which of the following should a researcher do first?

a. Search the literature for knowledge gaps related to the topic
b. Search the literature for definitive answers to that question
c. Search the literature for additional research needs or openings
d. Search the literature for consensus or controversy on the topic

45. Among instructional techniques to develop oral communication skills, which one would incorporate "CROWD" and "PEER" prompts?

a. Dialogic Reading
b. Think-Pair-Share
c. Choral Response
d. Inside/Outside Circle

46. Which choice completes the text with the most logical and precise word or phrase?

Literature, as a cornerstone of the humanities, often serves as a reflection of society's values, beliefs, and cultural norms. Classic works of literature like George Orwell's *1984* or Harper Lee's *To Kill a Mockingbird* delve into complex social and moral issues. These novels not only entertain but also challenge readers to ________ ethical dilemmas, justice, and human nature. The humanities, through the study of literature and other artistic forms, provide us with a deeper understanding of the human experience and the complexities of the world around us.

a. obfuscate
b. contemplate
c. elude
d. resolve

47. Which of the following activities would incorporate the best use of technology to increase students' oral language skills?

a. Students visit the school computer lab to work on math and science activities with software that utilizes voice-recognition technology in an interactive process.
b. Students use an internet program and computer camera to converse with English-speaking students in other countries.
c. Students can visit the classroom's Language Lab, in which there are tape recorders and CD players. Students can use these players to listen to novels, poetry, and other literary works on tape.
d. A teacher videotapes a class discussion about a story and replays it for the students to watch and discuss.

48. In developing elementary-age students' oral communication skills, which is most appropriate for 2nd-grade students?

a. Being able to communicate one's experiences verbally
b. Being able to adapt stories for different audiences
c. Being able to summarize stories aloud for others
d. Being able to read stories aloud to classmates

History and Social Science

49. Which statement about factors related to the growth of the US economy between 1945 and 1970 is NOT correct?

a. The Baby Boom's greatly increased birth rates contributed to economic growth during this time.
b. The reduction in military spending after World War II contributed to the stronger US economy.
c. Government programs and growing affluence nearly quadrupled college enrollments in 20 years.
d. Increased mobility and bigger families caused fast suburban expansion, especially in the Sunbelt.

50. In economic terms, which of the following is considered investment?

a. Buying a new home computer
b. Construction of a new manufacturing plant
c. Purchase of a college education
d. Selling finished goods to a customer

51. Which of the market structures is most efficient?

a. Perfect competition
b. Monopolistic competition
c. Oligopoly
d. Monopoly

52. Who was the economist focused on the potential for populations to grow faster than available food supplies?

a. Adam Smith
b. John Stuart Mill
c. Thomas Malthus
d. Friedrich Engels

53. Which of the following will result if two nations use the theory of comparative advantage when making decisions of which goods to produce and trade?

a. Each nation will make all of their own goods.
b. Both nations will specialize in the production of the same specific goods.
c. Each nation will specialize in the production of different specific goods.
d. Neither nation will trade with one another.

54. Which of the following statements about the equator is true?

a. It intersects four continents.
b. It is to the north of both horse latitudes.
c. It is located at 0° longitude.
d. It is not very windy.

55. Which of the following landmasses is *not* part of the Ring of Fire?

a. Japan
b. Cascade Mountains in Washington
c. Andes Mountains in South America
d. Mount Kilimanjaro

56. The Mojave Desert is located in which country?

a. Afghanistan
b. Morocco
c. Australia
d. United States

57. Which of the following locations would be considered a modern cultural hearth?

a. New York City
b. Baghdad
c. Auckland
d. Edmonton

Refer to the following for question 58:

A first-grade teacher is planning a geography unit focused on how the weather impacts the way that people live. This unit will focus on how weather differs in the regions near the poles, the tropical regions, and the mid-latitudes.

58. What should the teacher tell students that the main reason that tropical regions near the Equator tend to experience relatively constant year-round temperatures is?

a. They are usually located near the ocean.
b. The angle at which sunlight hits them remains relatively constant throughout the year.
c. They are located along the "Ring of Fire."
d. They do not have seasons.

59. Gun control, strong environmental laws, social programs, and opposition to the death penalty are what kind of issues?

a. Compassion issues
b. Activism
c. Regional issues
d. Religious issues

60. The primary expense for most state and local governments is:

a. Emergency medical services
b. Transportation services
c. Police and fire departments
d. Education

61. How long can members of the Federal Judiciary serve?

a. Four years
b. Eight years
c. For life
d. Six years

62. The president serves as commander-in-chief. What are the president's two limitations in that role?

a. The president cannot declare war or make rules governing the military.
b. The president cannot enforce blockades or declare war.
c. The president cannot enforce quarantines or make rules governing the military.
d. The president cannot enforce blockades or quarantines.

63. In order to be accepted, amended, or rejected completely, a newly introduced bill is first given to what type of committee?

a. Full committee
b. Conference committee
c. Subcommittee
d. Senate committee

64. What is the main purpose of the census?

a. To monitor illegal immigration
b. To apportion seats in the House of Representatives
c. To help determine federal income tax rates
d. To reapportion seats in the United States Senate

65. Which of the following is correct regarding common types of graphs?

a. A pie chart shows differences in quantities over time.
b. A bar graph can compare quantities but not over time.
c. A line graph clarifies how amounts change over time.
d. A number column makes patterns and trends clearer.

66. What kind of chart would be best for representing the major events of World War I?

a. Timeline
b. Bar graph
c. Pie chart
d. Political map

67. Consider the map below. Shaded areas indicate water use, with darker areas indicating heavier use. On the basis of the map, which of the following is the best inference regarding the areas where there is no shading?

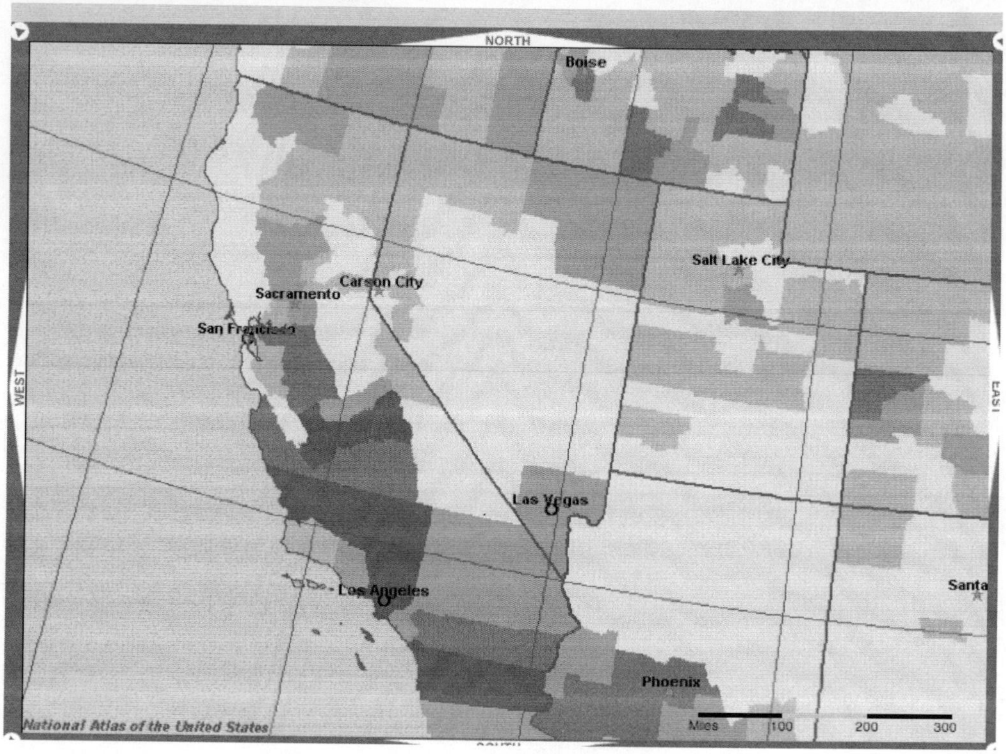

Map source: http://www.nationalatlas.gov/natlas/Natlasstart.asp

a. They are less inhabited.
b. They are more desert-like.
c. Residents are better at conservation.
d. Residents require less water per capita.

68. Of the following, who was NOT a dispatch rider notifying Americans of British troop movements reported by American surveillance in 1775?

a. Paul Revere
b. William Dawes
c. John Parker
d. Samuel Prescott

69. Which of the following is NOT true regarding the Virginia Companies?

a. One of these companies, the Virginia Company of Plymouth, made its base in North America.
b. One of these companies, the Virginia Company of London, made its base in Massachusetts.
c. One company had a charter to colonize America between the Hudson and Cape Fear rivers.
d. One company had a charter to colonize America from the Potomac River to north Maine.

70. Which invention had a major role in communication during the Civil War?

a. Morse Code
b. Telephone
c. Radio
d. Computer

71. Which of the following is NOT a true statement regarding the Louisiana Purchase?

a. Jefferson sent a delegation to Paris to endeavor to purchase only the city of New Orleans from Napoleon.
b. Napoleon, anticipating US intrusions into Louisiana, offered to sell the US the entire Louisiana territory.
c. The American delegation accepted Napoleon's offer, though they were only authorized to buy New Orleans.
d. The Louisiana Purchase, once it was completed, increased the territory of the US by 50% overnight.

72. Which of these is true concerning the French Revolution, America, and Europe?

a. When France's revolution spread and they went to war with other European countries, George Washington allied with the French.
b. During the time period around 1792, American merchants were trading with countries on both sides of the war.
c. American traders conducted business with various countries, profiting the most from the British West Indies.
d. The Spanish navy retaliated against America for trading with the French by capturing American trading ships.

73. Which of the following is NOT considered among the causes of the French Revolution?

a. Famines causing malnutrition and starvation
b. War debt, court spending, and a bad monetary system
c. Resentment against the Catholic Church's rule
d. Resentment against the Protestant Reformation

74. What effect did the Crusades have on Europe's Jewish population?

a. Entire European Jewish communities were killed during the First Crusade.
b. Persecution of Jewish people declined as the Crusaders focused on Muslims.
c. Most Jewish traders and merchants profited through Crusades-related business.
d. To avoid persecution, some Jewish-only battalions fought in each Crusade.

75. Which list is in the correct chronological order?

a. Great Papal Schism, Norman Conquest, French Revolution
b. Great Papal Schism, French Revolution, Norman Conquest
c. Norman Conquest, Great Papal Schism, French Revolution
d. French Revolution, Norman Conquest, Great Papal Schism

76. The French and Indian War ended in 1763. Which subsequent British policy regarding the American colonies was most important to the American Revolution?

a. Increasingly limited oversight of the colonies in order to focus on Canadian territories
b. A determination that the colonies should help pay for the War
c. The Proclamation of 1763 limiting the location of new American colonies
d. Increasing the colonies' dependence on the British military

77. Which statement best describes the role of the Catholic Church in medieval Western Europe?

a. Powerful and wealthy, the Church was important to both poor and rich people.
b. The Church concerned itself mainly with the poorer members of medieval society.
c. Weakened by infighting about Church doctrine, the Church struggled to wield power.
d. The Catholic Church served as a neutral force between competing political leaders.

78. Which of the following empires still existed following the armistice ending World War I?

a. The Austro-Hungarian Empire
b. The Ottoman Empire
c. The German Empire
d. The British Empire

Mathematics

79. Which type of function is represented by the table of values below?

x	y
−2	0.25
−1	0.5
0	1
1	2
2	4

a. Linear
b. Quadratic
c. Cubic
d. Exponential

80. If a, b, and c are even integers and $3a^2 + 9b^3 = c$, which of these is the largest number which must be factor of c?

a. 2
b. 3
c. 6
d. 12

81. A car slows down with constant deceleration. Which of the following accurately describes the graph of its position with respect to time?

a. It is a line with a positive slope.
b. It is a line with a negative slope.
c. It is a curve with an increasing slope.
d. It is a curve with a decreasing slope.

82. Jamal is placing an order for ink cartridges and reams of paper. Each ink cartridge costs \$7.50. Each ream of paper costs \$3. He intends to spend less than \$45. Which of the following graphs represents the possible combinations of paper and ink that he may purchase, if the x-axis represents ink cartridges and the y-axis represents reams of paper?

a.
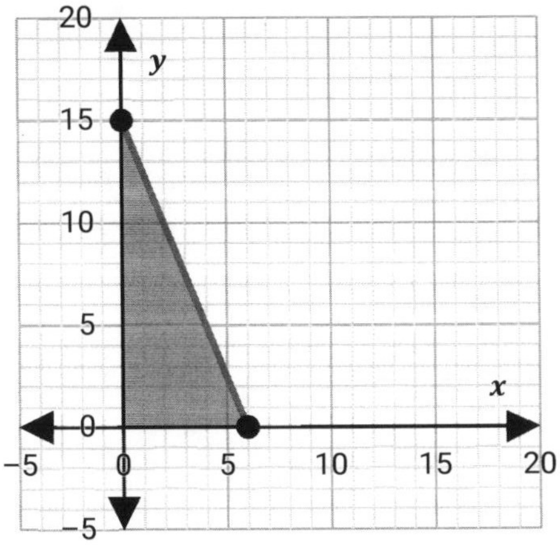

b.
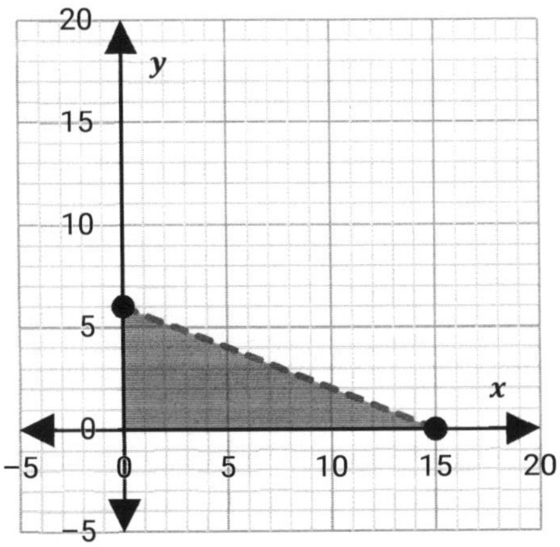

c.
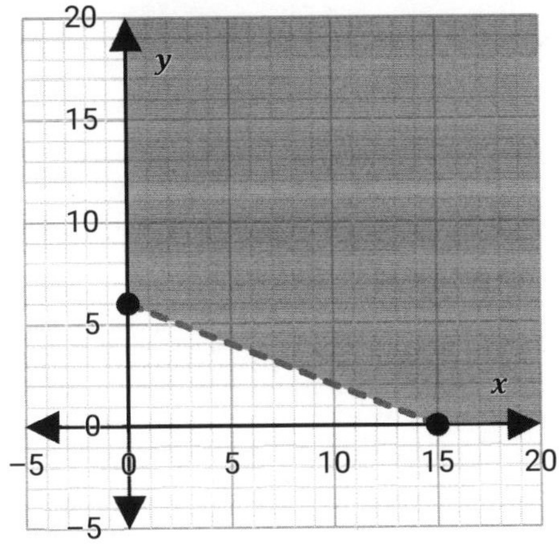

d.
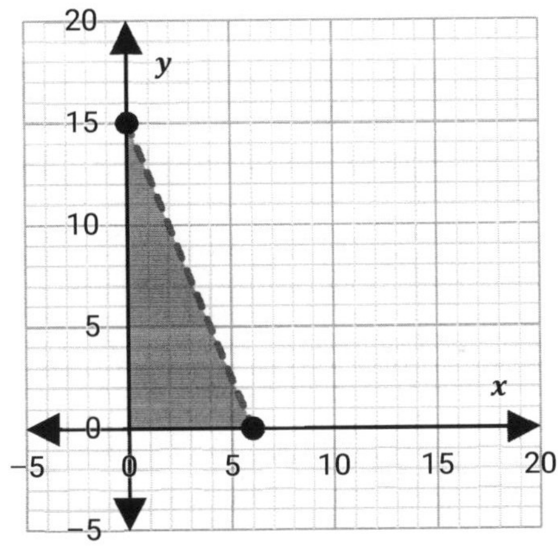

83. Which of the following equations is a linear equation?

a. $y = x^2 + 4$
b. $y = \frac{2}{x^3}$
c. $2x - 3y = 5$
d. $x = (y + 2)^2$

84. Which of the following formulas may be used to represent the sequence 8, 13, 18, 23, 28, ...?

a. $a_n = 5n + 3; n \in \mathbb{N}$
b. $a_n = n + 5; n \in \mathbb{N}$
c. $a_n = n + 8; n \in \mathbb{N}$
d. $a_n = 5n + 8; n \in \mathbb{N}$

85. Claus has \$20 to spend at the local fair. The entrance fee is \$2. 50, and tickets for the booths are \$2 each. Which of the following inequalities represents the number of tickets x that Claus can afford with his \$20?

a. $2.50x + 2x \leq 20$
b. $2.50 + 2x \leq 20$
c. $2x \leq 20 + 2.50$
d. $2.50 + 2x \geq 20x$

86. Two companies offer monthly cell phone plans, both of which include free text messaging. Company A charges a \$25 monthly fee plus five cents per minute of phone conversation, while Company B charges a \$50 monthly fee and offers unlimited calling. At what total duration of monthly calls do both companies charge the same amount?

a. 500 hours
b. 8 hours and 33 minutes
c. 8 hours and 20 minutes
d. 5 hours

87. Solve the system of equations.

$$3x + 4y = 2$$
$$2x + 6y = -2$$

a. $\left(0, \frac{1}{2}\right)$
b. $\left(\frac{2}{5}, \frac{1}{5}\right)$
c. $(2, -1)$
d. $\left(-1, \frac{5}{4}\right)$

88. Which of these is NOT a net of a cube?

a. b. c. d.

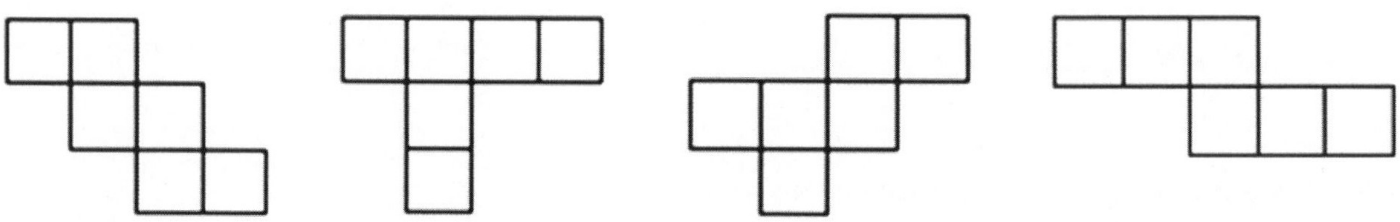

89. A room has a length of 12 feet, a height of 9 feet, and a width of 10 feet. How many square feet are there to paint, including the walls, floor, and ceiling?

a. 425
b. 636
c. 898
d. 1,080

90. Natasha designs a square pyramidal tent for her children. Each of the sides of the square base measures x ft, and the tent's height is h feet. If Natasha were to increase by 1 ft the length of each side of the base, how much more interior space would the tent have?

a. $\frac{x^2h+2xh+h}{3}$ ft^3
b. $\frac{2xh+h}{3}$ ft^3
c. $\frac{x^2h+3}{3}$ ft^3
d. 1 ft^3

91. Aidan has a plastic container in the shape of a square pyramid. He wants to fill the container with chocolate candies. If the base has a side length of 6 inches and the height of the container is 9 inches, how many cubic inches of space may be filled with candies?

a. 98
b. 102
c. 108
d. 112

92. You wish to determine the area of a regular pentagon, and all you know is the length of one side. What additional information is sufficient for you to be able to compute the area?

a. The length of all the other sides
b. The width of the pentagon
c. The length of the apothem
d. No other information needed

93. How many diagonals are in a dodecagon?

a. 12
b. 24
c. 54
d. 108

94. A large L-shaped field is 400 m long on its longest side and 150 m wide at its widest point. The opposite parallel sides are only $\frac{1}{5}$ as long. The total perimeter of the field is:

a. 6,000 m
b. 900 m
c. 1,200 m
d. 1,100 m

95. Which of the following transformations has been applied to ΔABC?

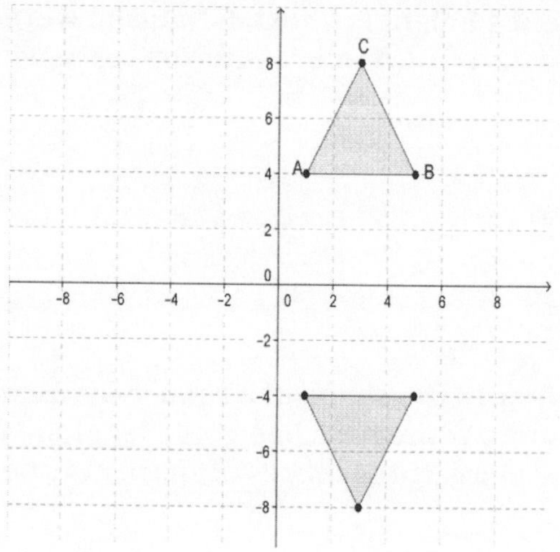

a. Translation
b. Rotation of 90 degrees
c. Reflection
d. Dilation

96. What is the length of the hypotenuse in the triangle shown below?

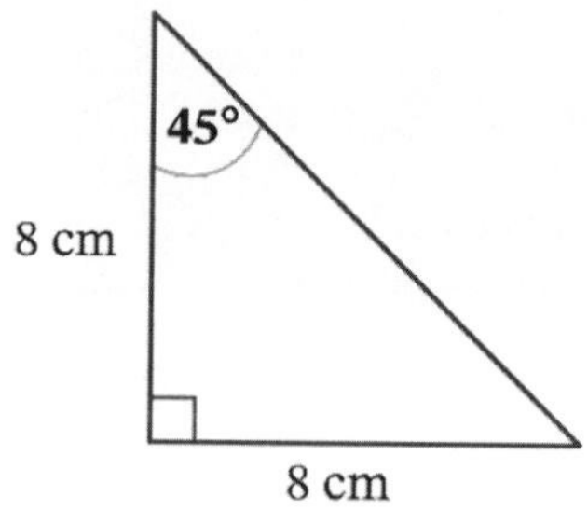

a. 4 cm
b. $8\sqrt{3}$ cm
c. 16 cm
d. $8\sqrt{2}$ cm

97. Given that premises "all *d* are *a*," "all *c* are *d*," and "no *b* are *a*" are true and that premise "all *b* are *a*" is false, determine the validity and soundness of the following arguments:

Argument I: All d are a. All c are d. Therefore, all a are c.
Argument II: All d are a. All b are a. Therefore, all b are d.
Argument III: All d are a. No b are a. Therefore, no b are d.

a.

	Invalid	Valid	Sound
Argument I		X	
Argument II	X		
Argument III		X	X

b.

	Invalid	Valid	Sound
Argument I	X		
Argument II		X	X
Argument III		X	

c.

	Invalid	Valid	Sound
Argument I		X	X
Argument II	X		
Argument III		X	X

d.

	Invalid	Valid	Sound
Argument I	X		
Argument II		X	
Argument III		X	X

98. Mr. Carver is teaching his students about deductive reasoning and states the premises listed below. Which of these students has reached a valid conclusion?

Premise 1	All primates are mammals.
Premise 2	All lemurs are primates.

a. Mia states, "All primates are lemurs."
b. Carlos states, "All lemurs are mammals."
c. Xavier states, "All whales are mammals."
d. Gavin states, "All monkeys are primates."

99. A class is multiplying whole numbers by fractions. Four of the students correctly responded that $10 \times \frac{3}{5} = 6$. Their teacher asks each student to give his or her reasoning. The students' responses show that each student arrived at his or her answer in a different way. Read the following student explanations and indicate which explanations demonstrate mathematically valid reasoning. Select all that apply.

Student responses	Valid	Invalid
A: "I made $\frac{3}{5}$ into the decimal 0.3 and then multiplied it by 10 and multiplied that by 2."		
B: "I divided 10 by 5, which is 2, and then multiplied it by 3."		
C: "I multiplied 10 by 3, which is 30, and then divided it by 5."		
D: "I drew 10 rectangles and split them all into fifths and colored three fifths in all of them and then regrouped the colored ones to see how many I had."		

100. Which answer choice is a valid direct proof that the sum of two odd integers, $x + y$, is even?

a. Because they are odd, $x = 2a + 1$ and $y = 2b + 1$. The expression $x + y$ can then be written as $(2a + 1) + (2b + 1) = 2a + 2b + 2 = 2(a + b + 1)$. Because this final expression clearly has a factor of 2, $x + y$ must be even.

b. Assume $y = 13$ and $x = 11$. $13 + 11 = 24$. 24 is even, therefore $x + y$ is even.

c. Let $x + y = z$, let $z = 2c$, $x = 2a + 1$, and $y = 2b + 1$. $2a + 1 + 2b + 1 = 2c$ which is the same as $2a + 2b = 2c - 2$, therefore $x + y$ is even.

d. If $x + y = z$, where z is even, then $x + y$ must be even.

Refer to the following for questions 101–102:

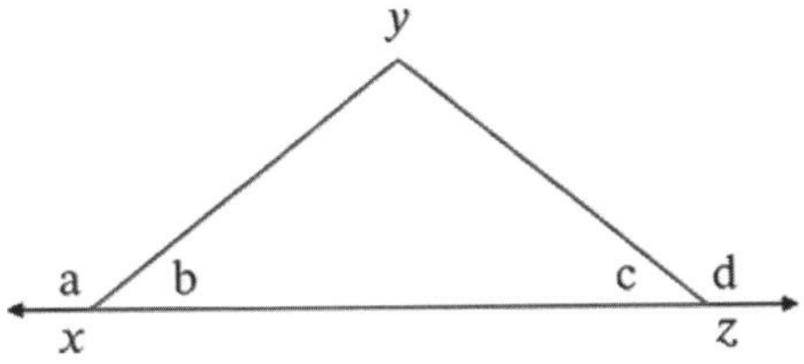

Given: $\angle a \cong \angle d$
Prove: ΔXYZ is isosceles

Statement	Reason
1. $\angle a \cong \angle d$	Given
2. $m\angle a + m\angle b = 180°; m\angle c + m\angle d = 180°$	Linear pair angles are supplementary
3. $m\angle a + m\angle b = m\angle c + m\angle d$	Substitution
4. $m\angle a = m\angle d$	Congruent angles have equal measures
5. $m\angle b = m\angle c$	__________
6. $\angle b \cong \angle c$	Congruent angles have equal measures
7. __________	If two angles of a triangle are congruent, the sides opposite them are congruent
8. ΔXYZ is isosceles	An isosceles triangle has two congruent sides

■

101. Which of the following justifies step 5 in the proof?

a. Linear pair angles are supplementary
b. Subtraction property of equality
c. Definition of supplementary angles
d. An isosceles triangle has two congruent angles

102. Step 7 in the proof should contain which of the following statements?

a. $\overline{XY} \cong \overline{ZY}$
b. $\overline{XZ} \cong \overline{XZ}$
c. $\overline{XY} \cong \overline{XZ}$
d. $\angle YXZ \cong \angle YZX$

103. Antonio is using place value to determine the value of each digit in the number 35.64. He explains his thinking using the drawing below. How would you describe Antonio's current understanding of place value?

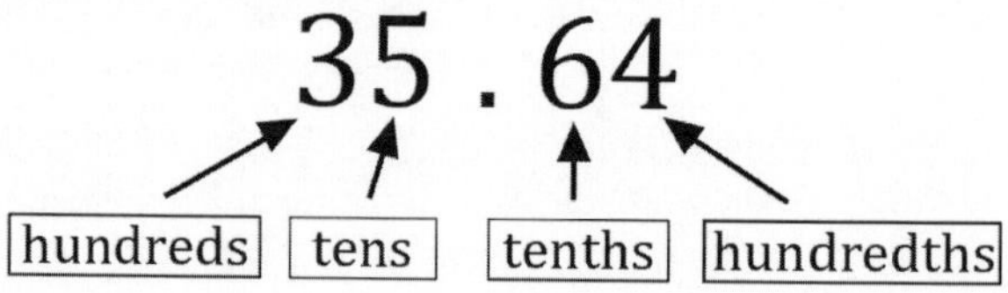

a. Antonio is very close to mastery of place value. His only error is that the decimal point should be moved one place to the right. Other than that, his work is correct.
b. Antonio has some awareness of the role of the decimal point. He seems to understand that values larger than one whole are located to the left of the decimal and that values less than one whole are located to the right of the decimal; however, Antonio has misidentified the place value of some of the digits.
c. Antonio seems to have a strong understanding of place value because each digit is labeled correctly.
d. Antonio has incorrectly labeled all place values. A review of the lesson is necessary.

104. If 52% of 25 people polled in a coffee survey preferred Brand A and 48% preferred Brand B, which of the following inferences is a logical conclusion?

a. At least 52% of shoppers will prefer Brand A over Brand B.
b. The majority of shoppers will prefer Brand A over Brand B.
c. The majority of shoppers will prefer Brand B over Brand A.
d. The number of shoppers who prefer Brand A may be similar to the number of shoppers who prefer Brand B.

105. Which shows four factors of 12?

a. 0, 1, 2, 4
b. 1, 2, 3, 4
c. 12, 24, 36, 48
d. 0, 12, 24, 36

106. In a town of 35,638 people, about a quarter of the population is under the age of 35. Of those, just over a third attend local K–12 schools. If the number of students in each grade is about the same, how many fourth graders likely reside in the town?

a. Fewer than 100
b. Between 200 and 300
c. Between 300 and 400
d. More than 400

107. Robert buys a car for $24,210. The price of the car has been marked down by 10%. What was the original price of the car?

a. $25,900
b. $26,300
c. $26,900
d. $27,300

108. Which of the following accurately describes the set of integers?

a. The set of counting numbers
b. The set of counting numbers, plus zero
c. The set of numbers that may be written as the ratio of $\frac{a}{b}$, where $b \neq 0$
d. The set of counting numbers, zero, and the negations of the counting numbers

109. In the number 1,492.738, what is the place value of the number 3?

a. Tenths
b. Hundredths
c. Thousandths
d. Ten-thousandths

110. Which of the following illustrates the additive inverse property?

a. The sum of a and 0 is a.
b. The sum of a and $-a$ is 0.
c. The sum of a and a is $2a$.
d. The sum of a and any variable x is $a + x$.

111. Coach Weybright's 6th-grade basketball team has played 36 games this season. The ratio of wins to losses is 2 : 1. If x represents the number of wins, which of the following proportions can be used to determine the number of wins?

a. $\frac{x}{36} = \frac{2}{1}$
b. $\frac{x}{2} = \frac{1}{36}$
c. $\frac{x}{3} = \frac{36}{2}$
d. $\frac{x}{36} = \frac{2}{3}$

112. Jason decides to donate 1% of his annual salary to a local charity. If his annual salary is $45,000, how much will he donate?

a. $4.50
b. $45
c. $450
d. $4,500

113. Which of the following statements is NOT true?

a. In most cases of a skewed distribution, the mean is pulled towards the longer tail.
b. In most cases of a skewed distribution, the mean is pulled towards the area with a higher frequency of scores.
c. In a normal distribution, the mean, median, and mode are the same value.
d. The area under a normal curve is 1.

114. Quentin sets aside 10% of his monthly salary to save for a car. If his monthly salary is $2,450, how much will he set aside each month?

a. $2.45
b. $24.50
c. $245
d. $2,450

115. A bag contains 16 coins, each with a different date. If 3 coins are pulled from the bag without replacement, how many possibilities exist for the set of coins pulled?

a. 650
b. 48
c. 560
d. 6

116. Lewis rolls a die and tosses a coin. What is the probability he gets a number less than 3 and heads?

a. $\frac{1}{6}$
b. $\frac{1}{4}$
c. $\frac{1}{3}$
d. 1

117. In a pack of 20 jelly beans, there are two licorice- and four cinnamon-flavored jelly beans. What is the probability of choosing a licorice jelly bean followed by a cinnamon jelly bean?

a. $\frac{2}{5}$
b. $\frac{8}{20}$
c. $\frac{2}{95}$
d. $\frac{1}{50}$

118. A magician has a hat that holds two rabbits. One rabbit is black and the other is white. In his last 16 performances he has randomly pulled the black rabbit from the hat 16 times. What is the probability that he will randomly pull the white rabbit from the hat in his next performance?

a. 0.5
b. 1
c. $\frac{1}{17}$
d. 0

119. For which of the following data sets would the mean be an appropriate measure of center to use?

a. 7, 15, 20, 24, 27, 28, 31, 36, 41, 50
b. 6, 7, 8, 8, 9, 9, 10, 20, 34, 50
c. 5, 18, 30, 42, 43, 44, 46, 48, 49, 50
d. 8, 10, 12, 13, 14, 16, 20, 22, 24, 2200

120. Given the two-way frequency table below, which of the following best represents *P*(Blue or Felt tip)?

	Felt tip	Ballpoint	Total
Black	3,114	5,283	8,397
Blue	1,756	2,459	4,215
Total	4,870	7,742	12,612

a. 55%
b. 60%
c. 65%
d. 70%

Science

121. The majority of weather phenomena occur in which part of the Earth's atmosphere?

a. Troposphere
b. Stratosphere
c. Hydrosphere
d. Ionosphere

122. The distance from the earth to the sun is equal to which of the following?

a. One astronomical unit
b. One light-year
c. One parsec
d. One arcsecond

123. Which of the following apparent colors of stars indicates the coolest temperature?

a. Orange red
b. Yellow orange
c. Yellow white
d. Blue white

124. When the accumulation of snow and ice exceeds ablation, which of the following occurs as a direct result?

a. An iceberg breaks free from a glacier.
b. A glacier gradually forms.
c. A glacier slowly erodes.
d. A lake forms within a glacier.

125. Which of the following is true of a volcano that is thought to be dormant?

a. It will probably never erupt again, and it is quite safe for people to live near its base.
b. It is expected to erupt some time again in the future, but danger is not imminent.
c. It is expected to erupt soon, and evacuation should be commenced.
d. It is a shield volcano that is erupting, but people living near the volcano should not expect their lives to be significantly disrupted.

126. What drives weather systems to move west to east in the mid-latitudes?

a. The prevailing westerlies
b. The prevailing easterlies
c. The trade winds
d. The doldrums

127. What is the best use for a barometer?

a. Measuring temperature
b. Measuring atmospheric pressure
c. Observing remote objects
d. Viewing objects too small for the naked eye to see

128. Which of the following are formed when the plasma membrane surrounds a particle outside of the cell?

a. Golgi bodies
b. Rough endoplasmic reticulum
c. Secretory vesicles
d. Endocytic vesicles

129. A bacterial mini-chromosome used in recombinant DNA technology is called a

a. Centromere
b. Telomere
c. Plasmid
d. Transposon

130. Which of the following is true of the enzyme telomerase?

a. It is active on the leading strand during DNA synthesis
b. It requires a chromosomal DNA template
c. It acts in the $3' \rightarrow 5'$ direction
d. It adds a repetitive DNA sequence to the end of chromosomes

131. In humans, more than one gene contributes to the trait of hair color. What is this an example of

a. Pleiotropy
b. Polygenic inheritance
c. Codominance
d. Linkage

132. In a strenuously exercising muscle under anaerobic conditions, NADH begins to accumulate in high concentration. Which of the following metabolic processes will be activated to reduce the concentration of NADH?

a. Glycolysis
b. The Krebs cycle
c. Lactic acid fermentation
d. Oxidative phosphorylation

133. Which of the following is an example of the alternation of generations life cycle?

a. Asexual reproduction of strawberries by runners
b. Annual plants that live through a single growing season
c. Ferns that have a large diploid and a diminutive haploid stage
d. Insects that have distinct larval and adult stages

134. Plant A undergoes C4 photosynthesis. What type of environment would the plant most likely live in?

a. Plant A lives in a very cold environment.
b. Plant A lives in a very hot environment.
c. Plant A lives in a marine environment.
d. Plant A lives in a dark environment that lacks solar energy.

135. Before they can be used by the body as fuel, complex carbohydrates must be converted into:

a. Glucose
b. Amino acids
c. Lipids
d. Folic acid

136. Which of the following is true of different isotopes of the same element?

a. It has a different number of protons than its element.
b. It has a different number of electrons than its element.
c. It has a different charge as compared to its element.
d. It has a different number of neutrons than other isotopes of the same element.

137. A gas at constant volume is cooled. Which statement about the gas must be true?

a. The kinetic energy of the gas molecules has decreased.
b. The gas has condensed to a liquid.
c. The weight of the gas has decreased.
d. The density of the gas has increased.

138. Which of the following conditions and chemical pairs is an example of a buffer?

a. Homeostasis; $H_2CO_3/HCO_3{}^-$
b. Water has a neutral pH; $(H_3O)^+/OH^-$
c. Copper can be electroplated onto tin; Cu^+/Sn^{2+}
d. Aluminum hydroxide is not soluble; Al^{3+}/OH^-

139. A uranium isotope is represented by the symbol $^{238}_{92}U$. How many neutrons does an atom of this isotope contain?

a. 92
b. 330
c. 238
d. 146

140. For electricity to flow and move, it requires which of these?

a. A generator and an insulator
b. A generator and a conductor
c. A conductor and an insulator
d. Electricity needs all of these.

141. Which of the following statements about isotopes of an element is true?

a. They have the same number of nucleons.
b. They have the same number of neutrons, but different numbers of protons.
c. They have the same number of protons, but different numbers of neutrons.
d. They have a different number of electrons.

142. Which of the following statements about energy is false?

a. Mechanical energy is always conserved in an isolated system.
b. Total energy is always conserved in an isolated system.
c. Energy is never created or destroyed.
d. Matter can be transformed into energy

143. What unit describes the loudness of a sound?

a. Hertz (Hz)
b. Decibels (dB)
c. Meters (m)
d. Meters per second (m/s)

144. Which of the following describes the process skill of concluding?

a. Explaining or interpreting observations
b. Making a determination based on the results of a controlled experiment
c. Reading an instrument during an experiment
d. Listing similarities and differences between two objects

Refer to the following for question 145:

A chemistry experiment is performed to determine the effect of a nonvolatile solute on the boiling point of water. Three trials are performed in which 10 mg, 20 mg, and 30 mg of salt are added to 500 mL of distilled water. Each solution is heated on a hot plate, and the elevated boiling points are recorded.

145. What is the purpose of conducting this experiment?

a. To test a hypothesis
b. To collect data
c. To identify a control state
d. To choose variables

Refer to the following for question 146:

A student is conducting an experiment using a ball that is attached to the end of a string, forming a pendulum. The student pulls the ball back so that it is at an angle to its resting position. As the student releases the ball, it swings forward and backward. The student measures the time it takes the ball to make one complete period. A period is defined as the time it takes the ball to swing forward and back again to its starting position. This is repeated using different string lengths.

146. The student formed the following hypothesis:

Lengthening the string of the pendulum will increase the time it takes the ball to make one complete period.

What correction would you have the student make to the hypothesis to make it follow the classical hypothesis model?

a. Turn it into an "if/then" statement.
b. Change "will increase" to "increases."
c. Switch the order of the sentence so that the phrase about the period comes first, and the phrase about the string's length is last.
d. No corrections are needed.

Refer to the following for question 147:

A sixth-grade science teacher tells her students that they will have a seismologist studying plate tectonics come to class. She has a group of early-intermediate English learners in her class. The seismologist will discuss what causes earthquakes, the effects of earthquakes, and any questions students might have on the topic.

147. One student wants to know what causes the shaking that occurs with an earthquake. What answer would the seismologist likely give to that student?

a. Static deformation
b. Seismic waves
c. Compression waves
d. Continental drift

148. Which of the following is NOT true about Louis Pasteur?

a. He made the first rabies vaccine.
b. He discovered the medical use for penicillin.
c. His experiments advanced the germ theory of disease.
d. He created the first polio vaccine.

Refer to the following for question 149:

State Coyote Population, 1900-2010

Year	Population	Year	Population
1900	5,000	1960	50,000
1910	11,000	1970	70,000
1920	30,000	1980	50,000
1930	75,000	1990	40,000
1940	100,000	2000	20,000
1950	65,000	2010	8,000

149. In reference to the above table, if the state allowed hunting in only the highest populated years, what conclusions below would not have affected the continued decrease in population numbers from 1970 to 2010?

a. Scarcity of food sources
b. Migration to another area
c. The prohibition of coyote hunting
d. Reduction of shelter

150. A researcher is studying the response of bacteria to a certain chemical. In three experiments, the bacteria swim towards the chemical, and in one experiment the bacteria swim away from it. What would be the most appropriate next step for the researcher?

a. Report only the first three experiments.
b. Report all the experiments, but refrain from making any conclusions.
c. Repeat the experiment several more times and apply a statistical analysis to the data.
d. Repeat the experiment, adding a new chemical to determine its effect on the bacteria.

Answer Key and Explanations for Test #2

Reading and English Language Arts

1. B: Ancient Egypt provides a rich backdrop for a myriad of literacy skills. Students can develop their visual literacy skills in a number of ways, even using material and studies that date back thousands of years. In Choice A, students are creating visual images with costume and dress, but no method for decoding those messages is stated in the answer choice. Drawing illustrations focuses on the same skill: creation of visual images, but no decoding or discussion of those images. In Choice D, students could build their visual literacy skills if they were to discuss the visual images or representations in the film, but this activity is not included in the answer choice. In the correct answer, (B), students are exposed to various representations and exhibits regarding the material in question and then have a chance to discuss and uncover meaning in what they have seen, with the guidance of the teachers.

2. D: Phonemes are the smallest units of sound in words. In this activity, students are replacing one phoneme with another, which is known as phoneme substitution. Alliteration refers to a series of words in which most words begin with the same sound. Segmenting refers to breaking a word down into its individual sounds, or phonemes. Onset and rime blending involve blending the beginning sound of a word with the rest of the word.

3. D: Alphabetic principle is the understanding that each letter makes a predictable sound. Students are practicing the alphabetic principle by matching the letter to a word that begins with the sound that letter makes. Encoding is the process of translating phonemes to graphemes, or recording sounds using letters. One-to-one correspondence is the understanding that each printed word corresponds with one spoken word. Phoneme isolation is the identification of the beginning, middle, or ending sound in a word.

4. C: Word families are an effective strategy for teaching CVCe words. Once students have determined the sound made by the last three letters using knowledge of the silent *e* rule, they can identify other rhyming words within the same family by changing the first letter. This increases the number of words they can easily decode. Because these words have a silent letter that affects the vowel sound, covering parts of the word, chunking, and blending are not as effective.

5. B: Explicit phonics instruction uses a part-to-whole approach. Mr. Clark's students first learn the *st* blend in isolation before applying it to whole words. Implicit phonics instruction, also referred to as whole language or analytical phonics, uses a whole-to-part approach. Students recognize whole words by sight before breaking them down into individual phonemes.

6. B: The pattern layer of orthography involves looking at groups of letters within words that form patterns. Therefore, exploring and building words that all contain *eigh* involves the pattern layer. The alphabet layer involves letter/sound relationships. The meaning layer involves the relationships between word meanings and their spellings. Conventional spelling refers to spelling words accurately.

7. C: Researchers have found that instruction in simpler phonological skills like rhyming, onsets, and rimes may not have any direct benefits for reading development (A); however, they find that teaching these simpler skills first nevertheless can make it easier to teach the more complex ones *without* directly benefiting reading development (B). Researchers have also found that the phonological awareness instruction that appears most beneficial to subsequent reading development integrates blending and segmenting (C), not deleting and substituting (D).

8. C: Synthetic phonics (A) involves blending individual phonemes into words. Onsets and rimes (B) involve identifying the part of a syllable or word before the vowel (onset) and the part including and following the vowel (rime), which enables decoding many words in the same family. Structural analysis (C) involves identifying component word parts to determine meaning and pronunciation. Analytic phonics (D) involves identifying letter-sound correspondences in words already known or learned.

9. B: The word *chain* contains a common consonant digraph, *ch*; and two vowels together, *ai*, which make the /ā/ sound. Recognizing these patterns will make the word easy to sound out. In choice A, the two vowels in *tear* do not make the /ē/ sound, as would likely be expected. The sound produced by *ain* in *curtain* makes it more difficult for a first grader to sound out, as does the sound of the *c* in *ocean*.

10. C: Word sorts assist students with comparing and contrasting features of words. While completing the sort, students must analyze each word to determine and categorize its vowel sound and determine how each word is similar to and different from other words in the set. Segmenting words using Elkonin boxes helps students break words into individual phonemes, but it doesn't assist with comparing and contrasting. Tracing words may help students practice short vowel spelling patterns, but it doesn't assist with comparing and contrasting either. Including words with short vowel sounds on the weekly spelling list will mainly assist with learning spelling patterns.

11. D: According to the National Reading Panel (NRP, 2000), multiple and replicated research studies conducted over time confirm that systematic phonics instruction is most effective when taught as part of a comprehensive reading program that also includes phonemic awareness, vocabulary, reading fluency, and reading comprehension. Hence teaching phonics separately or only with phonemic awareness are incorrect. The research also finds this instruction effective for both K-6 students and students having difficulty with learning to read.

12. A: One good indication of print awareness in a young child during informal assessment is that the child can identify the front and back of a book. Another is that the child can identify one letter in a word in the book, not all letters in words (B). Another is that the child can identify both words in a book, and the spaces between them (C). Print awareness in a young child does not mean the child can read sentences fluently (D), or even words yet: awareness of print concepts is a prerequisite for learning to read.

13. C: Many factors can affect a student's ability to understand what he or she is reading. Building comprehension skills is an ongoing process and can be made difficult if a student lacks the appropriate level of reading fluency. If he or she cannot read accurately or with enough speed, he or she will have much more trouble with comprehension than the average student. It is important to identify any decoding or vocabulary problems that might be affecting comprehension first; if those can be solved, comprehension skills may naturally increase as reading fluency increases.

14. B: Context clues are words or phrases that appear in proximity to an unfamiliar word and can be used to deduce its meaning. Context clues include synonyms, antonyms, illustrations and definitions.

15. C: Orthographic mapping refers to a process that occurs when the reader uses knowledge of letter-sound correspondence to recognize and recall the spelling, pronunciation, and meaning of written words. This process is necessary to build the word recognition skills and automaticity necessary for developing reading fluency. When introducing new vocabulary, teachers can stimulate orthographic mapping by having students separate the words into individual sounds to demonstrate the phonemic-graphemic relationship. This strategy helps students commit new words to memory, thus promoting vocabulary acquisition and sight word recognition. Further, having students tap out each phoneme as they read it aloud adds a kinesthetic element, thus strengthening connections for greater understanding.

16. D: Predicting what (like a quest or a war) or whom (such as a prince or three animals) a book is about is a common practice of students who fall back on the easiest answer to a teacher's request to make predictions. It is more useful for teachers to challenge students to try to predict what a character in a novel will do or a significant event that may occur in a story. Teachers can explain to students that they can make predictions by looking for clues in book titles, front-cover illustrations, and illustrations inside a book before even reading it. They can also have students read just one passage from a book, and then have them predict what will occur next.

17. A: An effective way to teach students the difference between denotation and connotation is to provide example sentences and have students choose a given word that best expresses the connotation of a highlighted word in each sentence. For example, to show the connotation of the word *challenge*, an example sentence "This is one of the many challenges that must be faced in order to solve the problem" could be given, and students could choose whether the connotation suggested by "challenges" in this case was "threats," "obstacles," "criticisms," or "setbacks." This instructional strategy is summarized in choice A, which is the correct answer. Since words generally have denotations and may or may not have connotations depending on their use, a Venn diagram would be misleading, and choice B is incorrect. Choice C is also incorrect, as highlighting words in a passage would not require students to distinguish between denotations and connotations, nor even to identify the exact connotations of words in context. Choice D would not be logical, since not all words have an emotional connotation, and the definition alone will be of little use for determining the connotations of a specific use of a word.

18. B: In the two-column notes active reading strategy, main ideas are noted in one of two columns while details are noted in the other column. The phrase "our fathers brought forth… a new nation" (B) would be considered the main idea and go in the main idea column. "Four score and seven years ago" (A), "conceived in Liberty" (C), and "dedicated to the proposition that all men are created equal" (D) are all details related to the central idea of a newly created nation.

19. C: By considering the other words in the story, the student can determine the missing words. The student is depending on the information supplied by the rest of the story. This information puts the story into context.

20. A: The teacher should give each child a piece of drawing paper that has been folded in half and then in half again, creating four boxes, along with a piece that has not been folded. The teacher should then ask the students to draw a cartoon about the story. Each of the first four boxes will show the events in order. The second page is to show how the story ends. When a child is able to visually see the way a familiar story has unfolded, that child can find causal or thematic connections in the action that increases her comprehension of the story overall. Asking the class to draw a single picture or to draw the beginning and end doesn't sufficiently demonstrate the importance of order to meaning. While some first-graders may be able to create their own cartoon stories that demonstrate a logical series of events, many first-graders are not yet ready to organize thought into a linear progression.

21. C: Research finds that children with good reading comprehension are able to summarize the text they have read and make predictions based on it. Rather than only reading text familiar within their existing knowledge (A), they are able to make connections or associations of new material to the knowledge they already have that is pertinent to the text. They are not only skilled at decoding words, but they also have good vocabularies, which *is* necessary (B) because it is exceedingly hard for readers to comprehend text if they are unable to define many of the words in it. Readers with good comprehension also do show skills in using the sentence structure (D) in the text they read to aid their reading comprehension. Many cues in sentence syntax and grammar help them rule out some meanings and confirm others.

22. B: Reading comprehension refers to one's ability to read and understand a text. This skill can be categorized into three levels with increasing degrees of complexity. Literal reading comprehension refers to the ability to read and understand the basic meaning of words and sentences in a text. Inferential reading comprehension requires individuals to employ higher-order thinking skills by using contextual clues to determine what is implied by the author's use of literary techniques. Evaluative, or critical, reading comprehension occurs when readers connect a text to their own background knowledge and experiences to formulate personal thoughts and opinions on what they have read. In this situation, the teacher asks students to circle descriptive language that may indicate the motives of the main character. Students are tasked with using evidence from the text to support their thoughts and ideas about this topic, promoting the development of inferential reading comprehension skills.

23. D: Vocabulary acquisition is a necessary component in the development of reading comprehension skills. When engaging with a new text, students may struggle to understand unfamiliar terms, impeding their ability to comprehend the text as a whole. Semantic mapping is an analysis strategy intended to help students develop word-learning skills by having them categorize the features of new vocabulary using a graphic organizer. This activity allows students to visualize the characteristics of and relationship between new words associated with a particular concept, thus strengthening overall understanding, and ultimately, reading comprehension. In this situation, having students complete a semantic map of words associated with the life cycle of plants would be beneficial in improving their comprehension of the informational text.

24. C: Critical analysis skills are necessary for effectively reading, analyzing, and interpreting texts across genres and content areas. The ability to read critically enhances students' overall connection to and comprehension of a text, so it must be taught explicitly. In this situation, the teacher is asking students to engage in a close reading of an informational text by marking it with various symbols as they read. This strategy helps students focus intently on the text, promoting their ability to think critically about it and ultimately strengthening their understanding of the information presented.

25. D: Distinguishing between syllable types is essential to developing the decoding skills necessary to facilitate reading comprehension, spelling, and writing abilities. Closed syllables are ones that include the short vowel sound followed by a consonant, whereas open syllables end with a long vowel sound. Students that struggle to recognize the difference will likely require additional support to ensure proper literacy development. Having these students practice forming words with letter tiles and reading them aloud provides a multisensory approach to develop this skill. This activity allows students to visualize, verbalize, and physically manipulate letters to strengthen their understanding of the different sounds produced by these two syllable types.

26. D: Automaticity refers to one's ability to quickly recognize and understand written words. This skill is fundamental to the development of reading fluency, and is cultivated by frequent exposure to new vocabulary, printed words, and patterns of phonics. Students that struggle with automaticity typically have trouble recognizing written words, reading at a grade-level-appropriate pace, and comprehending what they have read. Difficulty with automaticity in reading may result from numerous factors, such as limited phonics knowledge or exposure to printed language, weak decoding skills, or a learning disability. As this skill is integral to language and literacy development, struggling students must receive necessary interventions and support.

27. B: Reading fluency refers to the speed, inflection and accuracy with which students read, either orally or silently. In order to read fluently, students must be able to decode, or break down into segments, words that adhere to the common rules of the English alphabet. For those words that are generally not easily decoded, students must build their vocabulary of "sight words," which should be recognized without the need to decode. In (A), students may or may not be reading fluently or accurately, since the computer program does not monitor how the student reads. In (C), keyboarding practice bears no direct relationship to reading fluency. In (D), again, the computer is simply a source for text, but does not build any specific fluency skill. In (B), students are exposed to sight words and vocabulary in a fun way. Using a computer program allows for an unlimited supply of relevant words and for accurate scoring.

28. A: When a child's reading out loud sounds choppy and awkward, this is a sign that the child lacks reading fluency. To read fluently, children must not only sound fluent when reading aloud (B), but also read quickly, smoothly, and effortlessly when reading silently to achieve good comprehension and time-efficiency. When reading aloud, fluent readers not only read the words accurately, but also supply the appropriate expression (C) for the meanings in the text. Reading fluency is measured by *both* speed *and* accuracy (D) in reading.

29. B: Reading fluency combines accuracy, speed, and inflection while reading aloud. As children are learning to read, they work on all of these skills simultaneously with writing, thinking, viewing, listening, and comprehension. By using daily games or specific lessons, a teacher can directly affect students' ability to read the individual sounds in words (phonemes). As students identify more sounds correctly, they will read more accurately. Practicing reading aloud can increase fluency, but only if the child's reading partner is able to correct and encourage him or her to read more accurately. By reading aloud to the students, a teacher models correct speed and inflection, but this will affect the students' skills less directly than lessons and games in phonetics.

30. C: Generally speaking, students will read more slowly when introduced to texts and material that is new; speed increases with each subsequent reading. Hence, answer A) describes a normal child's reading pattern. When reading material independently, a student should not find more than approximately 1 in 20 words to be "difficult to read." Therefore, answer "b" is incorrect. Answer "d" refers to a comprehension test, which is not specifically related to the monitoring of fluency skills. This answer can be ruled out based upon its irrelevance. However, a student reading instructional-level material should find no more than 1 in 10 words difficult to read. Therefore, a student finding 1 in 5 questions difficult on an instructional-level test may need extra help or a text more appropriate for his age level.

31. D: Making at least the attempt to read every single word, even with many errors (A), is a strategic strength that gives students decoding practice and, even without success every time, enables their potential. Attending to punctuation in text (B) is a strength, since punctuation can significantly affect meaning (e.g., "Let's eat, Grandma" vs. "Let's eat Grandma"). Even without understanding all details, getting the gist of text meaning (C) is also a strength. However, holistic word reading (D) misses plural or verb tense endings and other morphological changes affecting meaning, reflecting a strategic weakness.

32. A: The student should receive instruction focused on just the areas in which he is exhibiting difficulty, which are comprehension and vocabulary. Improved vocabulary will give him greater skill at comprehending the meaning of a particular text. Strategies focused on enhancing comprehension together with a stronger vocabulary will provide the greatest help.

33. B: For students with specific learning disabilities, achievement tests are beneficial in gathering information about where the student may be deficient. Achievement tests such as the Wechsler Individual Achievement Test correspond with the categories associated with specific learning disabilities. This information is valuable in assessment of where students need improvement and potential strategies for instruction. Answer A is incorrect because this kind of assessment would be more appropriate for a younger student who is new to school. Answer C is incorrect because this assessment is typically used for those students who are at least 16 years old. Answer D is incorrect because this kind of assessment is an intelligence test rather than an achievement test.

34. B: The only true choice is (B): Repetition is very effective for building reading fluency. The teacher can have the student read a passage aloud repeatedly until s/he achieves the desired fluency, and then progress to a harder selection. Timing this exercise also promotes fluency, which includes speed as well as accuracy; therefore (A) is incorrect: Timed exercises should not be avoided in remediating fluency problems. Teachers can also use timing by giving students "speed drills" for individual words. A non-timed exercise can be having a student repeatedly read a familiar book out loud, giving feedback and direction as needed. Another technique is a readers' theatre; it is not true that this is good for showing progress but not making progress (C). The practice and feedback component of this exercise aids with improvement, even as it showcases progress in fluency. It is not true that reading in pairs increases comprehension but not fluency (D); partner/paired reading promotes both.

35. A: A number of researchers have found that assisted reading methods achieve significant improvements in students' reading fluency. Methods using repeated readings can be both unassisted and assisted (B). Assisted reading methods, because of the need for one-on-one instruction, have been found more workable in tutoring, but they are too time-intensive to be incorporated successfully in traditional classrooms (C). Reading while listening takes less time by being adapted using recordings for instruction of a group rather than individual students. It is thus more efficient than assisted reading, but it is not unrelated (D) because it was adapted from assisted reading.

36. A: The ability to isolate individual phonemes is essential to building the degree of phonemic awareness necessary for oral language and reading comprehension development. While activities such as rhyming games, chants, and songs help young children acquire this skill, such activities often present new words in their entirety, which proves difficult for some students. When decoding regular high-frequency sight words, students may recognize and correctly pronounce the root of the word, but often ignore modifiers such as prefixes or suffixes, leading to errors in pronunciation. Having struggling students practice sounding out words using letter tiles lets them visualize and physically manipulate each letter, strengthening their understanding of letter-sound relationships.

37. C: There are six generally accepted traits of writing: ideas, word choice, sentence fluency, conventions, organization and voice. Writing conventions refer to aspects of writing that make the text easy to read. These conventions include spelling, punctuation, grammar, spacing and titles. Each choice in this question refers to some aspect of writing conventions except choice C. This choice refers to an aspect of the "ideas" trait, and working on supporting details and their relationship to main concepts would not fall under the writing conventions category.

38. D: According to research-based writing instruction strategies, when teachers assign students to small collaborative writing groups, they should set individual performance expectations for within-group as well as individual work. Teachers should also support student groups by providing them with structure. Classmates in collaborative writing groups should give each other both positive feedback for reinforcement and constructive feedback for correction as well.

39. B: Typical speech is roughly 125 words per minute, while typical thinking is estimated at roughly 500 words per minute. This natural disparity does not make listening less effective than reading. While the slower rate of speech and the faster rate of thought does allow students' minds to wander, teachers can have students make use of this time by instructing them to summarize mentally the speech they hear as an active listening technique. This enables students to process, consider, and manipulate heard information and make richer, more creative decisions about it. Listening and learning share the common characteristics of being both social and reciprocal.

40. C: In the process writing approach, elements include having students write for authentic audiences (A), interact with other students throughout the writing process (B), take personal responsibility for their written work (C), and self-evaluate their writing (D).

41. C: Research studies have found that explicit instruction, teacher modeling, teacher think-alouds, and scaffolding (graduated, faded support) are all effective methods of writing instruction for all students. Research also shows that procedural strategies including mnemonic devices, graphic organizers, outlining, and checklists are helpful to students for planning and revision of writing. Studies find that teaching cognitive strategies helps students of all ages and ability levels, not just some. Teaching self-regulation not only improves student awareness of their writing strengths and weaknesses, but it also makes their writing work more strategic, empowers them to adapt the strategies they learn as they need, and increases their generalization and maintenance of the writing strategies they have learned.

42. C: The verb in option A should be plural "are" to agree with subject "shores," not singular to agree with modifier "Hawaii." Because both subjects "Harriet" and "sister" in option B are singular and so is the construction "Neither… nor," the verb should be singular "is," not plural "are." The verb is correctly plural "are" to agree with subject "people" in option C, not with singular noun "Nation" in the modifying prepositional phrase. The verb should be singular "has" in option D to agree with subject "one," not with modifying plural noun "islands."

43. B: In most cases, it is best to write the introduction last. Although it is the first part of the finished work, the introduction provides a synopsis for what is in the entire document. Until the writing is complete, the writer cannot reflect on the work as a whole. Writing the introduction prior to the body runs the risk that what follows may not completely conform to the ideas expressed in the introduction. An introduction usually should not reinforce ideas made in the piece, as the body portion of a work is the best place to flesh out ideas. Answer D is incorrect because an introduction frames the rest of the work; it is an incorrect generalization that the introduction, body, or conclusion are always the most or least important parts.

44. B: The first thing a researcher should look for in a review of the existing literature related to a specific research question is whether that question has already been definitively answered. If so, the researcher should ask a different research question. If the question has not already been answered conclusively, then the researcher can look for gaps in knowledge about the topic that searching the literature reveals; review the literature to find what needs and opportunities for further research other researchers have identified; examine the literature to discern whether there is consensus, controversy, or both; and if so, what those opinions are about the topic. These considerations help inform the direction for research.

45. A: In Dialogic Reading, the teacher reads books with individual students/small groups, incorporating "CROWD" prompts for sentence **C**ompletion; text **R**ecall questions; **O**pen-ended text picture questions; **Wh**- picture questions; and **D**istancing text/pictures to student experiences. In Dialogic Reading, the teacher also uses "PEER" prompts, **P**rompting student text discussion; **E**valuating responses; **E**xpanding responses; and **R**epeating prompts on higher levels. Think-Pair-Share lets students rehearse responses with partners who help with corrective feedback and elaboration to prepare for whole-class interaction. Choral response involves unison student responses upon teacher cues after teacher questions, signals, and wait time. Inside/Outside Circle involves students pairing up, conversing, and rotating partners.

46. B: To *contemplate* means to think deeply or consider something carefully. In the context of the passage, the word *contemplate* fits because it conveys the idea that literature encourages readers to think deeply and critically about complex issues. It aligns with the passage's message that literature serves as a reflection of society's values and beliefs and encourages readers to engage with these topics on a thoughtful level.

47. B: Oral language skills incorporate speaking, listening, and knowledge of conventional language. In choice A, students would be limited to a very specific vocabulary in order to work with the science and math programs, and would not have opportunities to increase their knowledge of language. In choice C, students are practicing their listening skills, but are not required to speak or think critically about what they have heard. Choice D does involve technology and class discussions; however, the benefit of watching the discussion on tape is relatively unclear. In choice B, students not only have a chance to build their speaking and listening skills, but also increase their knowledge of other cultures and ways of speaking.

48. C: According to communication experts, kindergarten students should be given instructional activities including communicating their experiences verbally (A), practicing good listening skills, recognizing nonverbal communication, and learning about emotions. First-graders should learn to read aloud to their classmates (D), tell their own stories in greater depth, demonstrate more changes in vocal quality to express emotions and meanings, and become more aware of language choices. Second-graders should be able to summarize stories aloud (C), maintain conversations with peers and others, respond to others' emotions, identify relationships between roles and language choices, and learn to role-play peer pressure, bullying, and other difficult situations. Third-graders should learn to understand communication's role in different cultural groups and settings, discuss gender roles, identify positive and negative characteristics in speeches, practice leading small groups, engage in group discussions, and adapt stories for different audiences (B).

History and Social Science

49. B: There was not a reduction in military spending after the war. Although the manufacturing demand for war supplies and the size of the military decreased, the government had increased military spending from $10 billion in 1947 to more than $50 billion by 1953—a more than fivefold increase. This increase strengthened the American economy. Other factors contributing to the strengthened economy included the significantly higher birth rates during the Baby Boom from 1946 to 1957, which stimulated the growth of the building and automotive industries by increased demand. Government programs, such as the GI Bill (the Servicemen's Readjustment Act of 1944), other veterans' benefits, and the National Defense Education Act all encouraged college enrollments, which increased by nearly four times. Additionally, larger families, increased mobility and low-interest loans offered to veterans led to suburban development and growth as well as increased home construction. Improvements in public health were also results of the new affluence; the rate of infant deaths decreased significantly, and as a result, from 1946–1957, the American life span rose from 67 to 71 years. Moreover, Dr. Jonas Salk developed the polio vaccine in 1955, which virtually wiped out poliomyelitis, preventing many deaths and disabilities in children.

50. B: Any expenditure that will increase a firm's future productivity is considered investment. Of the items listed, only the construction of a new plant matches the definition.

51. A: Perfect competition is a theoretical type of market more so than one actually found in real life. That's because it is the most efficient, operating where P = MR = MC.

52. C: Formulated in the early 19th century, Malthus's theory that population increase would ultimately outpace increases in the means of subsistence did not anticipate technological advances in food production and birth control; nevertheless, the theory was highly influential in the formulation of subsequent economic and social policies.

53. C: When a nation follows the theory of comparative advantage, it specializes in producing the goods and services it can make at a lower opportunity cost and then engages in trade to obtain other goods.

54. D: Around the world, the area around the equator is known for a relative lack of wind. Indeed, the equatorial belt is sometimes called the doldrums because the constant warm water encourages the air to rise gently. To the north and south, however, there are trade winds that can become quite violent. The equator only intersects three continents: Asia, Africa, and South America. It is in between the north and south horse latitudes, which are belts known for calm winds. Finally, the equator is located at 0° latitude, not longitude, though the 0° line of longitude does intersect the equator.

55. D: Mount Kilimanjaro is not part of the Ring of Fire, a circle of volcanoes that stretches around the Pacific Ocean. The Ring of Fire extends from islands east of Australia through Indonesia, Japan, the Aleutian Islands connecting Russia to Alaska, and down the western coast of the Americas. It includes such famous volcanoes as Mount Saint Helens and Krakatoa. Over 90 percent of earthquakes and over 80 percent of volcanic eruptions occur along the Ring of Fire.

56. D: The Mojave Desert is located in the United States.

57. A: Of the four answer choices, New York City is the most likely to be considered a modern cultural hearth. A cultural hearth is an area from which cultural trends emanate. Geographers suggest that there were seven original cultural hearths, including Mesoamerica and the Indus River Valley. The modes of living that originated in these areas emanated out into the rest of the world. These days, the cultural hearths tend to be the cities and countries with the most economic power. Of the four answer choices, New York City is clearly the wealthiest and the most influential. The styles and trends that originate in New York City find their way into communities all around the world.

58. B: Tropical regions near the Equator tend to experience relatively constant temperatures year-round because the angle at which sunlight hits them remains relatively constant throughout the year. In regions that are farther north or south, the angle at which sunlight hits them changes much more drastically due to the changing angle of the Earth's axis relative to the Sun. This results in greater variations in the length of daylight and in temperatures. Tropical regions do have seasons (usually a "wet" season and a "dry" season), but temperature fluctuations are less pronounced than those in regions farther from the Equator.

59. A: Compassion issues, such as gun control, strong environmental laws, social programs, and opposition to the death penalty, show a wide gender gap, as women are more likely to support compassion issues.

60. D: Free public education has been a US tradition since the 18th century. State constitutions govern the educational issues of each state, although federal, state, and local governments all work together on educational issues.

61. C: Article III judges are appointed for life and can retire at 65. They can only be removed from their posts by impeachment in the House and conviction in the Senate. Having judges serve life terms is meant to allow them to serve without being governed by the changing opinions of the public.

62. A: The president of the United States serves as commander-in-chief, but the writers of the Constitution, who feared how authority was used by monarchs, limited the president's power in this role. The president cannot declare war or make rules governing the military, although presidents have traditionally authorized the use of force without war being declared.

63. C: A bill is usually first reviewed by the appropriate subcommittee. The subcommittee can accept the bill, amend the bill, or reject the bill. If the subcommittee accepts or amends the bill, they send it to the full committee for review. Expert witnesses and testimony are all part of committee review.

64. B: Article I of the Constitution mandates the taking of a census every ten years. The purpose was to be sure that each state was proportionately represented in Congress according to its population as specified in the Constitution. Census data is also used to allocate federal funding for various programs and for shaping economic policies. Individual data collected by the US Bureau of the Census is kept confidential for seventy-two years and does not affect income tax rates. Every state has two seats in the Senate regardless of population.

65. C: A line graph makes clearest how quantities vary across periods of time, by drawing a line connecting each data point so we can see how many/much of something there was each second, minute, hour, day, week, month, year, etc. A pie chart (A) is excellent for clearly visualizing different percentages or proportions, by dividing a "pie" (circle) into "slices" representing what part of the whole each amount represents; however, pie charts do not show change across time the way line graphs do. But a bar graph (B) *can* compare quantities over time: for example, each bar could show the amount of rainfall in a given month. A column of numbers (D) is not a type of graph, and it does not make patterns and trends as clear visually as graphs do.

66. A: A timeline would be the best way to represent the major events of World War I. Timelines place events in chronological order, with the distance between the events correlated to their interval on the line. A timeline can run in any direction. A thematic map or a flow-line map might also be good at representing this subject, but a political map is restricted to borders and cities; therefore, it would not be able to suggest the changes caused by the war. Bar graphs and pie charts are used to depict quantities and proportions rather than sequences of events.

67. A: The most reasonable inference based on the data given by the map is that the areas with no shading (which represent areas of low water use) are less inhabited than areas with shading. Note that the areas with no shading also have no listed cities; cities on the map are surrounded by shaded areas. Because the map does not give any information regarding how much water is required per capita, option D can be rejected. The map gives no indication regarding residents' prowess at conservation efforts (positive or negative). This eliminates option C. Additionally, there is no indication from the map that any land is more desert-like. In fact, some of the lightly-shaded area is adjacent to the ocean. Therefore, option B can be rejected.

68. C: Paul Revere and William Dawes were both dispatch riders who set out on horseback from Massachusetts to spread news of British troop movements across the American countryside around the beginning of the War of Independence. John Parker was the captain of the Minutemen militia, who were waiting for the British at Lexington, Massachusetts. Samuel Prescott, a young physician, joined Paul Revere and William Dawes along their route.

69. B: The Virginia Company of London was based in London, not Massachusetts. It had a charter to colonize American land between the Hudson and Cape Fear rivers. The other Virginia Company was the Virginia Company of Plymouth, which was based in the American colony of Plymouth, Massachusetts. It had a charter to colonize North America between the Potomac River and the northern boundary of Maine. Both Virginia Companies were joint-stock companies, which had often been used by England for trading with other countries.

70. A: Samuel Morse invented a code of dots and dashes that became known as Morse Code, and in 1844 the first message was transmitted over a telegraph line. Morse code played an important role in communications during the Civil War.

71. D: The Louisiana Purchase actually increased the US's territory by 100% overnight, not 50%. The Louisiana territory doubled the size of the nation. It is true that Jefferson initially sent a delegation to Paris to see if Napoleon would agree to sell only New Orleans to the United States. It is also true that Napoleon, who expected America to encroach on Louisiana, decided to avoid this by offering to sell the entire territory to the US It is likewise true that America only had authority to buy New Orleans. Nevertheless, the delegation accepted Napoleon's offer of all of Louisiana. Due to his belief in strict interpretation of the Constitution, Jefferson did require approval from Congress to make the purchase. When his advisors characterized the purchase as being within his purview based on the presidential power to make treaties, Congress agreed.

72. B: In 1792, when the French Revolution turned into European war, American traders conducted business with both sides. It is not true that Washington allied with the French at this time. Washington issued a Proclamation of Neutrality in 1792 when the French went to war with European countries. While they did trade with both sides, American merchants profited the most from the French West Indies, not the British West Indies. The Spanish navy did not retaliate against America for trading with the French. Though Spain was an ally of Britain, it was the British who most often seized American ships and forced their crews to serve the British navy. Edmond-Charles Genêt, or Citizen Genêt, a French ambassador to the United States during the French Revolution, defied Washington's policy of neutrality by encouraging the American people to support the French. Washington was embarrassed by this violation. He did not agree with it.

73. D: Resentment against the Protestant Reformation was not a cause given for the French Revolution. Many causes have been cited for the war. Famines caused malnutrition and even starvation among the poorest people. Escalating bread prices contributed greatly to the hunger. Louis XV had amassed a great amount of debt from spending money on many wars in addition to the American Revolution. Military failures as well as a lack of social services for veterans exacerbated these debts. In addition, the Court of Louis XVI and Marie Antoinette spent excessively and obviously on luxuries even while people in the country were starving, and France's monetary system was outdated, inefficient, and thus unable to manage the national debt. Much of the populace greatly resented the Catholic Church's control of the country. However, there was not great resentment against the Protestant Reformation; there were large minorities of Protestants in France, who not only exerted their influence on government institutions, but undoubtedly also contributed to the resentment of the Catholic Church.

74. A: The Crusades' biggest impact upon Europe's Jewish population was that entire Jewish communities were killed during the First Crusade. This is the only option that accurately describes historical effects of the Crusades on the Jewish population. Rather than diminishing anti-Jewish sentiment, the Crusades seemed to inflame it, eliminating option B. One specific example of Crusades-era anti-Semitism is that many Jewish people were excluded from particular trades, and thus did not profit from the Crusades. This fact eliminates option C. Finally, there were no Jewish-only battalions during the Crusades, eliminating option D.

75. C: The Norman Conquest was the English historical period beginning in 1066. It began with the defeat of Anglo-Saxon King Harold II. With this defeat, the customs, laws, and language of the Normans was introduced in England. The Great Papal Schism was the division in the Roman Catholic Church from 1378–1417 when two rival popes emerged.

The French Revolution was the prolonged political and social struggle between 1789 and 1799 in France. It encompassed the regicide of the king, Louis XVI, and the queen, Marie-Antoinette, included the Reign of Terror, the establishment of the First Republic, and led to the rise of Napoleon Bonaparte as Emperor of France, leading Europe to war.

76. B: The cost of the French and Indian War was high, and after the war, Great Britain sought to have the American colonies help pay for the war through measures such as higher taxes. This led to colonial resentment, in part because the colonists lacked representation in the British government. Option A can be rejected because, rather than limiting oversight on the American colonies, Great Britain reasserted its authority there. The Proclamation of 1763, although it did limit the location of new American colonies, was modified in response to colonial demands prior to the American Revolution. This eliminates choice C. Option D can be rejected because the French and Indian War (in which American colonists participated) actually decreased colonial dependence on the British military.

77. A: The Catholic Church was both powerful and wealthy in medieval Europe. It affected the lives of both the rich and poor; for example, wealthy families often donated to monasteries in exchange for prayers on the donors' behalf. This eliminates option B. Because of these donations, some monasteries became quite wealthy. Rather than being a neutral force, the Catholic Church wielded political power. In medieval times, some claimed that rulers derived their authority to rule from the Catholic Church itself. These facts eliminate options C and D.

78. D: Only the British Empire existed following the armistice ending WWI. The Austro-Hungarian Empire, the Ottoman Empire, and the German Empire were all among the Central powers that lost the war. As empires capitulated, armistices and peace treaties were signed and the map of Europe was redrawn as territories formerly occupied by Central powers were partitioned. For example, the former Austro-Hungarian Empire was partitioned into Austria, Hungary, Czechoslovakia, Yugoslavia, Transylvania, and Romania. The Treaty of Lausanne (1923) gave Turkey both independence and recognition as successor to the former Ottoman Empire after Turkey refused the earlier Treaty of Sèvres (1920), and Mustafa Kemal Ataturk led the Turkish Independence War. Greece, Bulgaria, and other former Ottoman possessions became independent. The Lausanne

Treaty defined the boundaries of these countries as well as the boundaries of Iraq, Syria, Cyprus, Sudan, and Egypt.

Mathematics

79. D: Looking at the values of our function—call it $f(x)$—we may notice a pattern:

$$f(-2) = 0.25 = 2^{-2}$$
$$f(-1) = 0.5 = 2^{-1}$$
$$f(0) = 1 = 2^{0}$$
$$f(1) = 2 = 2^{1}$$
$$f(2) = 4 = 2^{2}$$

From this, we can see that $f(x) = 2^x$, which is an exponential function.

80. D: Since a and b are even integers, each can be expressed as the product of 2 and an integer. So, if we let $a = 2x$ and $b = 2y$, then $3(2x)^2 + 9(2y)^3 = c$.

$$3(4x^2) + 9(8y^3) = c$$
$$12x^2 + 72y^3 = c$$
$$12(x^2 + 6y^3) = c$$

Since c is the product of 12 and some other integer, 12 must be a factor of c. Incidentally, the numbers 2, 3, and 6 must also be factors of c since each is also a factor of 12.

81. D: The position of a decelerating car is changing according to a non-constant speed. Thus, the graph will show a curve rather than a line. The slope is decreasing since it represents the velocity, which is decreasing.

82. D: The situation may be modeled by the inequality $7.5x + 3y < 45$. Isolating the y-term gives $3y < -7.5x + 45$. Solving for y gives $y < -2.5x + 15$. Thus, the y-intercept will be 15, the line will be dotted, and a test point of (0,0) indicates the shading should occur below the line.

83. C: A linear equation is an equation of the first degree. That means that the highest exponent of any term or variable is one, so it follows that an exponent cannot be variable. Choice C is a linear equation. Choices A and D are quadratic equations. Choice B is neither linear nor quadratic. Therefore, the correct answer is choice C.

84. A: The sum of 3 and the product of each term number and 5 equals the term value. For example, for term number 4, the value is equal to $5(4) + 3$, or 23.

85. B: Claus has \$20 to spend, so the amount he spends must be less than or equal to ($\leq$) \$20. The entrance fee of \$2.50 is only charged once, so it should not be multiplied by x. The cost of a ticket multiplied by x represents the cost of buying x tickets. The entrance fee plus the cost of the tickets is Claus's total cost: $2.50 + 2x \leq 20$.

86. C: The expression representing the monthly charge for Company A is $\$25 + \$0.05m$, where m is the time in minutes spent talking on the phone. Set this expression equal to the monthly charge for

Company B, which is \$50. Solve for m to find the number of minutes the two companies charge the same amount.

$$\begin{aligned} \$25 + \$0.05m &= \$50 \\ \$0.05m &= \$25 \\ m &= 500 \end{aligned}$$

Notice that the answer choices are given in hours, not in minutes. Since there are 60 minutes in an hour, $m = \frac{500}{60}$ hours $= 8\frac{1}{3}$ hours. One-third of an hour is 20 minutes, so m is 8 hours and 20 minutes.

87. C: A system of linear equations can be solved by using matrices or by using the graphing, substitution, or elimination (also called linear combination) method. The elimination method is shown here:

$$\begin{aligned} 3x + 4y &= 2 \\ 2x + 6y &= -2 \end{aligned}$$

In order to eliminate x by linear combination, multiply the top equation by 2 and the bottom equation by −3 so that the coefficients of the x-terms will be additive inverses.

$$\begin{aligned} 2(3x + 4y &= 2) \\ -3(2x + 6y &= -2) \end{aligned}$$

Then, add the two equations and solve for y.

$$\begin{aligned} 6x + 8y &= 4 \\ \underline{-6x - 18y} &\underline{= 6} \\ -10y &= 10 \\ y &= -1 \end{aligned}$$

Substitute −1 for y in either of the given equations and solve for x.

$$\begin{aligned} 3x + 4y &= 2 \\ 3x + 4(-1) &= 2 \\ 3x - 4 &= 2 \\ 3x &= 6 \\ x &= 2 \end{aligned}$$

The solution to the system of equations is $(2, -1)$.

88. B: A cube has six square faces. The arrangement of these faces in a two-dimensional figure is a net of a cube if the figure can be folded to form a cube. If choice B is folded, the bottom square in the second column will overlap the fourth square in the top row, so the figure does not represent a net of a cube. The other figures represent three of the eleven possible nets of a cube.

89. B: The surface area of a rectangular prism may be calculated using the formula $SA = 2lw + 2wh + 2hl$. Substituting the dimensions of 12 feet, 9 feet, and 10 feet gives $SA = 2(12)(10) + 2(10)(9) + 2(9)(12)$. Thus, the surface area is 636 square feet.

90. B: The volume of Natasha's tent can be found by using the volume formula for a square pyramid, $V = \frac{1}{3}Bh = \frac{1}{3}s^2h$, where B is the area of the base, s is the side length of the square base, and h is the height of the pyramid. Therefore, the volume of her tent is $\frac{x^2h}{3}$. If she were to increase the length of each side of the square base by 1 ft, the tent's volume would be $\frac{(x+1)^2h}{3} = \frac{(x^2+2x+1)(h)}{3} = \frac{x^2h+2xh+h}{3} = \frac{x^2h}{3} + \frac{2xh+h}{3}$. Notice this is the volume of Natasha's tent, $\frac{x^2h}{3}$, increased by $\frac{2xh+h}{3}$.

91. C: The volume of a pyramid may be calculated using the formula $V = \frac{1}{3}Bh$, where B represents the area of the base and h represents the height. Since the base is a square, the area of the base is equal to 6^2, or 36 square inches. Substituting 36 for B and 9 for h gives $V = \frac{1}{3}(36)(9)$, which simplifies to $V = 108$ cubic inches.

92. D: Since the pentagon is regular, all the sides are equal, and the shape is convex. Because of this, there are enough constraints to determine the area as a function of the side length of the pentagon.

93. C: To find the number of diagonals in a polygon, use the formula $\frac{n(n-3)}{2}$, where n is the number of sides on the polygon. A dodecagon has 12 sides, so substitute 12 for n and simplify.

$$\frac{12(12-3)}{2} = \frac{12(9)}{2} = \frac{108}{2} = 54$$

Therefore, a dodecagon has 54 diagonals.

94. D: The perimeter is the total length of the outside edge of the field. Because the sides of the field are orthogonal and parallel, the indented sides do not change the length of the boundaries of the field, only their relative positions.

95. C: The original triangle was reflected across the x-axis. When reflecting across the x-axis, the x-values of each point remain the same, but the y-values of the points will be opposites.

$$(1,4) \to (1,-4) \quad (5,4) \to (5,-4) \quad (3,8) \to (3,-8)$$

96. D: The triangle is a 45-45-90 right triangle. Thus, if each leg is represented by x, the hypotenuse is represented by $x\sqrt{2}$. Thus, the hypotenuse is equal to $8\sqrt{2}$ cm.

97. D: The first argument's reasoning is invalid; that the premises are true is irrelevant. (For example, consider the true premises "all mammals are animals" and "all cats are mammals;" it cannot be logically concluded that all animals are cats.) The second argument's reasoning is valid, but since one of its premises is false, the argument is not sound. The third argument's reasoning is valid, and since its premises are true, the argument is also sound.

98. B: If all primates are mammals, and all lemurs are primates, then all lemurs are mammals. All primates are not lemurs. Since neither whales nor monkeys are mentioned in the premises, they cannot be included in the conclusion. The conclusion can only be based on the information given in the premises. Therefore, the correct answer is choice B.

99. B, C, D: Choices B and C both use correct order of operations to solve the problem. Choice D is an accurate visual representation of the problem. In choice A, the student inaccurately converted $\frac{3}{5}$ to the decimal 0.3 and did not explain why he or she multiplied by 2 at the end.

100. A: A direct proof starts with a set of certainties and states a series of logical facts to prove a separate statement. Once $x + y$ is expressed in a valid format that clearly has a factor of 2 (as does $2(a + b + 1)$), it is certain that the sum of these two integers is even. Choice B contains a direct assumption and is therefore incorrect. Choice C begins to make valid point but skips to the conclusion without clear explanation. Choice D makes no proof at all and simply restates the original information.

101. B: Since it has been established that $m\angle a + m\angle b = m\angle c + m\angle d$ and $m\angle a = m\angle d$, we can conclude that $m\angle b = m\angle c$ because of the subtraction property of equality, which states that subtracting equal amounts from each side of a balanced equation will keep it balanced.

102. A: Because Step 6 established that $\angle b \cong \angle c$, we can conclude that the sides opposite these congruent angles are congruent, or $\overline{XY} \cong \overline{ZY}$.

103. B: Most of the work provided by Antonio is correct; however, the place value for the 5 and the 3 are not labeled correctly. The 5 should be labeled "ones," and the 3 should be labeled "tens." Other than that, the work is correct.

104. D: If 52% of the sample group prefer Brand A, this is very close to half, and it is not logical to claim that either brand has a majority (answer choices B and C) when only 25 people were polled and results are fairly inconclusive (we can calculate that 13 liked Brand A and 12 liked Brand B). We cannot presume that 52% or more of all shoppers will prefer it (answer choice A), because there can be margin of error in either direction.

105. B: Factors are numbers that when multiplied together provide the result. Zero is not a factor of any number. The numbers 1, 2, 3, and 4 are all factors of 12.

106. B: The population is approximately 36,000, so one-quarter of the population consists of about 9,000 individuals under age 35. A third of 9,000 is 3,000, which is the approximate number of students in grades K–12. Since there are thirteen grades, divide 3,000 by 13. There are about 230 students in each grade. So, the number of fourth graders is between 200 and 300.

107. C: The original price may be represented by the equation $24{,}210 = x - 0.10x$ or $24{,}210 = 0.9x$. Dividing both sides of the equation by 0.9 gives $x = 26{,}900$.

108. D: The set of integers is represented as $\{\dots, -3, -2, -1, 0, 1, 2, 3, \dots\}$. The numbers 1, 2, 3, ... are counting numbers, or natural numbers. Thus, the set contains the counting numbers, zero, and the negations of the counting numbers.

109. B: To the right of a decimal point, the first number is in the tenths position, and the second number is in the hundredths position. This means that the number 3, which is the second number to the right of the decimal point, is in the hundredths position.

110. B: The additive inverse property states that the sum of a number and its negative value is 0.

111. D: This problem can be represented using the proportion $\frac{number\ of\ wins}{total\ games} = \frac{number\ of\ wins}{total\ games}$. If the ratio of wins to losses is 2 : 1, then the ratio of wins to total games is 2 : 3. The proportion to determine the number of wins is $\frac{x}{36} = \frac{2}{3}$.

112. C: The amount he donates is equal to 1% of $45,000. To calculate this value, multiply the two numbers. To multiply a percentage by another number, first convert the percentage to a decimal by changing the percentage sign to a decimal point and moving the decimal point two places to the left. Therefore, $1\% = 0.01$. Now the two numbers can be multiplied: $0.01 \times \$45{,}000 = 1 \times \$450 = \$450$. Thus, he donates \$450.

113. B: The mean is pulled towards the longer tail of a skewed distribution in most cases. It is not pulled towards the area with the higher frequency of scores. When outliers are added to an otherwise symmetric distribution, the mean shifts towards those outliers. For example, if a runner typically finishes a race in about 5 minutes and has one bad day in which she takes 20 minutes, that single outlier could significantly increase her mean time.

114. C: The amount he saves is equal to $0.1 \times \$2{,}450$. Thus, he saves \$245.

115. C: The number of possible combinations of r items from a set of n items can be calculated by the expression $\frac{n!}{r!(n-r)!}$, or in this case, $\frac{16!}{3!\times 13!} = \frac{16\times 15\times 14\times 13!}{3!\times 13!} = \frac{16\times 15\times 14}{3\times 2\times 1} = 560$. As an alternative to remembering this formula, we can approach the problem logically. There are 16 possibilities for the first coin, 15 for the second, and 14 for the third, yielding $16 \times 15 \times 14 = 3{,}360$ possibilities. But since the order doesn't matter, we must divide by the number of possible ways to order 3 coins: $3{,}360 \div (3 \times 2 \times 1) = 560$.

116. A: The probability may be written as $P(N \text{ and } H) = P(N) \times P(H)$. Substituting the probability of each event gives $(N \text{ and } H) = \frac{1}{3} \times \frac{1}{2}$, which simplifies to $\frac{1}{6}$.

117. C: To find the probability of an event, divide the number of favorable outcomes by the total number of outcomes. When there are two events in which the first depends on the second, multiply the first ratio by the second ratio. In the first part of the problem, the probability of choosing a licorice jelly bean is two out of twenty possible outcomes, or $\frac{2}{20}$. Then, because one jelly bean has already been chosen, there are four cinnamon beans out of a total of 19, or $\frac{4}{19}$. By multiplying the two ratios and dividing by a common denominator, one arrives at the final probability of $\frac{2}{95}$.

118. A: The events, if truly random, are independent of each other. There is therefore an equal probability of pulling the black rabbit or the white rabbit from the hat each time. The probability is 0.5.

119. A: Data sets B and C are asymmetrical: data set B is skewed toward lower values, and data set C is skewed toward higher values. This makes the mean a poor measure of center. Data set D is mostly symmetrical but has a large outlier. The mean is very sensitive to outliers and is not an appropriate measure of center for data sets that include them. Data set A is roughly symmetrical and has no outliers; the mean would be an appropriate measure of center here.

120. B: The probability may be written as $P(Blue \text{ or } FT) = P(Blue) + P(FT) - P(Blue \text{ and } FT)$. Substituting the probabilities, the following may be written: $P(Blue \text{ or } FT) = \frac{4{,}215}{12{,}612} + \frac{4{,}870}{12{,}612} - \frac{1{,}756}{12{,}612}$, which simplifies to $P(Blue \text{ or } FT) = \frac{7{,}329}{12{,}612}$, or approximately 60%.

Science

121. A: The majority of weather phenomena occur in the Earth's troposphere. The troposphere is the lowest layer of the atmosphere, extending from Earth's surface up to roughly 8–15 kilometers in altitude. It contains the majority of the mass of Earth's atmosphere and 99 percent of its water vapor.

122. A: The average distance from the earth to the sun is equal to one astronomical unit (AU). An AU is equal to 93 million miles and is far smaller than a light-year or a parsec. A light-year is defined as the distance light can travel in a vacuum in one year, and is equal to roughly 63,241 AU. A parsec is the parallax of one arcsecond and is equal to 2.0626×10^5 astronomical units.

123. A: Orange red stars have temperatures less than 3,700 K. Yellow orange stars range between 3,700 and 5,200 K. Yellow white stars range between 5,200 and 6,000 K. Blue white stars range between 10,000 and 30,000 K.

124. B: When the accumulation of snow and ice exceeds ablation, a glacier will gradually form. Ablation is the sloughing off of ice and snow through melting, evaporation, sublimation, and wind erosion. When snow and ice accumulate faster than ablation occurs, a glacier will form and continue to gain mass until the rate of ablation overtakes the rate of accumulation.

125. B: A volcano that is thought to be dormant is expected to erupt some time again in the future, but danger is not imminent. Dormant volcanoes are expected to erupt again in the future because they still show signs of internal volcanic activity. Extinct volcanoes are not expected to erupt again because they show no signs of activity. Active volcanoes are either erupting or about to erupt.

126. A: The prevailing westerlies drive weather systems to move west to east in the mid-latitudes. The direction refers to that which the wind is coming from. The polar easterlies that travel from the northeast occur between 90-60 degrees north latitude. The ones from the southeast are between 90-60 degrees south latitude. The trade winds refer to those occurring near the equator in the tropics moving east. The doldrums are also in the tropics, but they refer to an area of low-pressure where frequently the winds are light and unpredictable.

127. B: A barometer is an instrument for measuring atmospheric pressure, used especially in weather forecasting.

128. D: Endocytosis is a process by which cells absorb larger molecules or even tiny organisms, such as bacteria, that would not be able to pass through the plasma membrane. Endocytic vesicles containing molecules from the extracellular environment often undergo further processing once they enter the cell.

129. C: Plasmids are small circular pieces of DNA found in bacteria. Plasmids are widely used in recombinant DNA technology. They are cut with restriction enzymes and DNA of interest is ligated to them. They can then easily be used to transform bacteria.

130. D: Each time a cell divides, a few base pairs of DNA at the end of each chromosome are lost. Telomerase is an enzyme that uses a built-in template to add a short sequence of DNA over and over at the end of chromosomes—a sort of protective "cap". This prevents the loss of genetic material with each round of DNA replication.

131. B: When more than one gene contributes to a trait, inheritance of that trait is said to be polygenic. This type of inheritance does not follow the rules of Mendelian genetics. Pleiotropy is the opposite, which one gene contributes to two or more unrelated traits. Codominace is a non-Mendelian inheritance where both alleles are expressed in a heterozygote individual, rather than the dominant allele being expressed and the recessive being masked. Gene linkage occurs between two genes that are located near each other on a chromosome and are usually inherited together.

132. C: Lactic acid fermentation converts pyruvate into lactate using high-energy electrons from NADH. This process allows ATP production to continue in anaerobic conditions by providing NAD^+ so that ATP can be made in glycolysis.

133. C: Alternation of generations means the alternation between the diploid and haploid phases in plants.

134. B: Photosynthesis converts carbon dioxide into sugars that plants use. Three types of photosynthesis are C3, C4, and CAM. C3 is used by most plants. C4 plants live in areas with high temperatures and high light exposure. C4 first forms a four-carbon sugar instead of the three-carbon sugar formed by C3. Also, the stomata of C4 plants are faster at absorbing carbon dioxide and do not have to open as long, so less water is lost by transpiration. A C4 plant, such as saltbush, corn, or some grasses, would live in a very hot environment rather than a cold, marine, or dark environment. Plants that use the CAM (Crassulacean Acid Metabolism) type of photosynthesis also use water more efficiently as their stomata are closed during the day and open at night. Desert cacti are examples.

135. A: The body's main fuel is the simple sugar glucose. Complex carbohydrates provide the body with sustained energy by slowly breaking down into glucose.

136. D: Isotopes are variations of an element that have different numbers of neutrons. The various isotopes of an element have the same numbers of protons and electrons. For example, carbon has three naturally occurring isotopes: carbon-12, carbon-13 and carbon-14 (which is radioactive). Isotopes of an element differ in mass number, which is the number of protons and neutrons added together, but have the same atomic number, or number of protons.

137. A: The kinetic energy of the gas molecules is directly proportional to the temperature. If the temperature decreases, so does the molecular motion. A decrease in temperature will not necessarily mean a gas condenses to a liquid. Neither the mass nor the density is impacted, as no material was added or removed, and the volume remained the same.

138. A: Homeostasis involves the balancing of many biochemical systems and processes. Several of them include buffers as a means of expanding the range of stable conditions. In this instance, part of blood pH maintenance is controlled with the carbonic acid, H_2CO_3, and bicarbonate ion, HCO_3^-, buffer. While water, even when neutral, has a small amount of hydronium ions $(H_3O)^+$and hydroxide ions, OH^-, present, they do not act as a buffer (B). Electroplating copper onto tin is a redox reaction (C). The lack of solubility of aluminum hydroxide does not make it a buffer (D).

139. D: Since the atomic number of this isotope is 92, the atom contains 92 protons. Since the mass number is 238, the atom contains 238 protons and neutrons. Since the difference between 238 and 92 is 146, the atom contains 146 neutrons.

140. B: Electricity requires an energy source such as a generator to make it flow. It needs a conductor as a medium through which it can travel from place to place. An insulator (A and C)is a material that *blocks* the conduction of electricity. Insulation is used to prevent electricity from going where we do not want it to go—for example, into our bodies. Therefore, (D) is incorrect.

141. C: Protons and neutrons are both considered nucleons. The number of nucleons in a nucleus is called the mass number. Isotopes of the same element have different mass numbers. But since they are the same element, they must have the same atomic number, which is equal to the number of protons. Thus, only the number of neutrons changes, since electron's mass is so low that it doesn't have much effect on the mass number of an element. Unless they are also ionized, they would have the same number of protons and electrons.

142. A: The total energy of an isolated system is always conserved. However, the mechanical energy may not be, since some mechanical energy could be converted into radiation (light) or heat (through friction). According to Einstein's famous equation $E = mc^2$, where E is energy, m is mass, and c is the speed of light, energy can be converted into mass, and vice versa (like in nuclear reactions). This does not affect the conservation of energy law, however, since the mass is considered to have an energy equivalent. This equation does not tell anything about the mechanical energy of a particle; it just shows how much energy would be generated if the mass was converted directly into energy.

143. B: The loudness of a sound is related to the amplitude of the wave and is measured in decibels (dB). Wave frequency is measured in hertz (Hz). Wavelength is measured in meters (m). Wave velocity is measured in meters per second (m/s).

144. B: Making a determination based on the results of a controlled experiment is a description of concluding. Inferring can be described as explaining or interpreting observations. Reading an instrument during an experiment is one type of quantitative observation. Comparing includes noting similarities and differences.

145. A: Experiments are conducted in order to test a hypothesis. Collecting data (B), identifying a control state (C), and choosing variables (D) are steps in conducting an experiment designed to test a hypothesis.

146. A: A formalized hypothesis written in the form of an if/then statement can then be tested. A statement may make a prediction or imply a cause/effect relationship, but that does not necessarily make it a good hypothesis. In this example, the student could rewrite the statement in the form of an if/then statement such as, "If the length of the string of the pendulum is varied, then the time it takes the ball to make one complete period changes." This hypothesis is testable, and doesn't simply make a prediction or a conclusion. The validity of the hypothesis can then be supported or disproved by experimentation and observation.

147. B: The shaking that is observed during an earthquake is a direct result of seismic waves. Seismic waves are vibrations that travel through earth when rock slippage along a fault occurs. There are two types of seismic waves: body waves and surface waves. Body waves can either be primary, or P waves, and secondary, or S waves. P waves move more quickly than S waves and create motion that radiates directly outward from the point of origin. S waves produce a shearing, or side-to-side, motion. The other type of seismic wave is a surface wave, which causes much of the shaking felt at Earth's surface.

148. D: French chemist Louis Pasteur (1822–1895), considered one of the founders of bacteriology, developed a process of heating and cooling food products like milk and wine that reduces the number of pathogenic microbes to a level that will not cause sickness when ingested. This process is named pasteurization after him. Pasteur also made the first vaccines against both rabies and anthrax. All three of these accomplishments were incredible breakthroughs in preventing fatal diseases. Pasteur's experiments advanced the germ theory of disease, which when first proposed, met strong resistance from those who did not believe microorganisms cause sickness. His work supported its acceptance and colleague Robert Koch's proof of it in 1890. However, Pasteur did not create the first polio vaccine.

149. C: Although no data is shown that reflects the years in which hunting licenses were sold, the prohibition of hunting would allow a population to increase its numbers. The coyote's populations would suffer without adequate food sources or shelter, and migration would reduce it as well.

150. C: By repeating the experiment, the researcher could determine whether the instance of the bacteria swimming away from the chemical was simply due to chance. Observing the same results would allow the researcher to make conclusions with more certainty, and statistical analysis would help determine the significance of the data. Researchers must report all data (A), and reaching a conclusion is a vital part of any experiment (B). Adding a new chemical would completely change the experiment, so it would not be helpful (D).

Practice Test #3

Reading and English Language Arts

1. Some of the students in Mr. Smith's fourth-grade class cannot decode words well enough to read fluently in class. He knows they are well behind grade level and that he needs to provide them with activities that will allow them to be successful, building skills and confidence at the same time. Which activity would be best for this purpose?

a. Enlist the parents' help by sending home a weekly list of sight words that the students can practice and memorize, decreasing the need to decode when they read.
b. Show the students how to create words out of movable alphabet tiles or magnetic letters, building (encoding) words as they sound them out.
c. Provide the children with early childhood readers that contain only very simple words so that the children will not feel badly as they read.
d. Allow those children having trouble to stop each time they reach a challenging word and sound it out carefully, recording it to a list that will be studied for homework.

2. Phonological awareness activities are:

a. Oral
b. Visual
c. Tactile
d. Semantically based

3. A third-grade student has difficulties with decoding and struggles to read grade-level texts independently. Which statement is likely to be true based on this information?

a. The student will benefit from additional implicit phonics instruction.
b. The student will also struggle with phonological awareness.
c. The student will also struggle with fluency and comprehension.
d. The student likely has a language processing disorder and requires further evaluation.

4. A kindergarten teacher asks students to say the word *cart*. She then tells students to take away the /t/ sound and tell her what they get. Which type of phonemic awareness activity are students practicing?

a. Onset and rime manipulation
b. Segmenting
c. Phoneme isolation
d. Phoneme deletion

5. During assessment, a young child is able to identify and differentiate typical English-language speech sounds. This best reflects which type of awareness?

a. Phonic
b. Phonetic
c. Phonemic
d. Alphabetic

6. A teacher asks her students to say /ake/. She then tells students to add different consonant sounds to the beginning of /ake/ to see which real and nonsense words they can form. Which component of phonological awareness are students practicing in this activity?

a. Syllabification
b. Onsets and rimes
c. Phoneme isolation
d. Segmentation

7. On a continuum, which of these represents the most complex level of phonological awareness?

a. Segmenting words into their individual syllables and blending individual syllables into words
b. Phonemic awareness, i.e., understanding words consist of phonemes and manipulating these
c. Segmenting words into their onsets and rimes and blending onsets and rimes into full words
d. Segmenting sentences, i.e., understanding speech consists of separate words, and rhyming songs

8. A first-grade teacher schedules 10 minutes each day for sight word practice. This daily practice will most likely improve students' reading proficiency by building which skill?

a. Decoding
b. Automaticity
c. Phonemic awareness
d. Phonological awareness

9. A student is reading a fictional book and has difficulty decoding the word *maple*. Which spelling pattern could the teacher explain to help the student decode this word and similar words in the future?

a. Vowel digraph pairs
b. R-controlled vowels
c. Closed syllables
d. Open syllables

10. Which instructional practice would NOT be helpful for young children to understand phonics and decode words?

a. Incidental exposure to implicit phonics in instruction
b. Systematic, explicit, and direct instruction in phonics
c. Teaching main ideas or strategic integration in reading activities
d. Giving reading and writing activities to apply phonics

11. What is most accurate about using formal and informal assessments of student alphabetic knowledge and skills?

a. Individual student skills can only be analyzed via informal assessment.
b. In order to plan instruction, teachers must utilize formal assessments.
c. Teachers can monitor daily progress with formal or informal assessment.
d. Individual student skills can only be analyzed using formal assessment.

12. Ms. Walters is planning her first-grade literacy block for the upcoming school year. Currently, she has reading group time scheduled, where she plans to focus on individualized phonological awareness and phonics skills, decoding, and comprehension. Students will also reread some familiar texts for fluency practice and complete some phonological awareness and phonics-based word workstations. Ms. Walters also has time set aside for the whole class to read and analyze texts together to focus on comprehension skills, and they will write regularly in their journals. Which additional component of reading instruction, that is not already addressed through her plans, should Ms. Walters add to best support her students?

a. Phoneme blending
b. High-frequency word instruction
c. Identification of story elements
d. Using the alphabetic principle to spell words

13. Learning to construct a reading response would be most beneficial in enhancing which language skill?

a. Oral presentation
b. Comprehension
c. Fluency
d. Learning a second language

14. If a student is reading a text aloud at an "instructional level," he or she should:

a. Find no more than one in five words difficult to read.
b. Find no more than one in ten words difficult to read.
c. Comprehend the majority, if not all, of what he or she reads.
d. Be able to instruct or teach other students to read and understand the text.

15. Which of the following factors most strongly correlates with early childhood students' degree of success in building reading comprehension and writing skills?

a. Cultural background
b. Personal interest in reading
c. Oral language development
d. Socioeconomic status

16. Which of the following is the cognitive or learning objective of an assignment that asks students to "describe," "explain," "summarize," "restate," "classify," or "review" material they have read?

a. Knowledge recall
b. Application
c. Comprehension
d. Evaluation

17. In a paired reading strategy for identifying the main idea in informational text, two students silently read a selection. Then, taking two-column notes of main ideas and supporting details, they take turns with the following steps. Which choice sequences these steps in the correct order?

a. The pair develops main idea consensus, a student paraphrases the main idea, a student explains agreement or disagreement, they take turns finding supporting details
b. A student paraphrases the main idea, a student explains agreement or disagreement, the pair develops main idea consensus, they take turns finding supporting details
c. They take turns finding supporting details, a student explains agreement or disagreement, a student paraphrases the main idea, the pair develops main idea consensus
d. A student explains agreement or disagreement, they take turns finding supporting details, the pair develops main idea consensus, a student paraphrases the main idea

18. Concerning student self-monitoring strategies in reading, which statement is true?

a. If students do not comprehend something, they should identify what and locate it in the text.
b. Students should only employ self-monitoring techniques when working with texts they understand well.
c. Self-monitoring is generally considered ineffective for students who struggle with reading.
d. If students do not comprehend something, previewing text by looking ahead makes it worse.

19. A teacher wants to work on her students' listening comprehension in addition to their reading comprehension since she understands that the skills are interrelated. She has a series of short stories that she thinks the students will enjoy. Which of the following would be the best supplement to typical written comprehension exercises?

a. Preview the content and then read the stories aloud to the students. Assess listening comprehension through verbal and written questions.
b. Ask the students to choose one story each to read aloud to a small group. Encourage the students to discuss what they have learned afterward.
c. Assign each student a story to read and require them to write a report on it. Each student should then present his or her report based on what he or she has learned to the class.
d. Have the students read stories aloud to the class, and create mock tests based upon the main ideas which they identify.

20. A fourth-grade teacher had her students write haiku in order to promote the students' __________.

a. reading comprehension
b. vocabulary
c. word identification skills
d. confidence

21. Which of these is true of how the instructional strategy of Expanded Book Reading enhances literacy development and reading comprehension?

a. Teachers should avoid summarizing books in advance for students.
b. Teachers should not have children predict a book's possible content.
c. Teachers can informally assess comprehension via student retelling.
d. Teachers cannot use this strategy with literacy across the curriculum.

22. A kindergarten teacher has noticed that one student is struggling with sight word recognition and decoding skills, and is beginning to fall behind the rest of the class. The teacher is concerned that this may impede the student's development of reading comprehension skills. Which of the following interventions would be most appropriate in this situation?

a. Providing individual instruction with a reading resource teacher
b. Implementing Response to Intervention (RTI) services
c. Contacting the student's parents to address the concerns
d. Developing an Individualized Education Program (IEP) to address the student's learning needs

23. Which of the following teacher actions is most effective for fostering greater depth of preschoolers' comprehension of word meanings?

a. Focusing on one definition for a new vocabulary word
b. Introducing new concepts separately from new words
c. Limiting added information to simplify comprehension
d. Giving multiple definitions and examples of new words

24. A third-grade teacher is planning a lesson in which students will independently read an informational text. Prior to beginning the lesson, the teacher will review new vocabulary words and add them to the class word wall. As students read the text, they will fill out a guided summary frame. Afterward, students will discuss their summaries with a table partner. These strategies are likely intended to promote students' skills in which of the following areas?

a. Irregular sight word recognition
b. Using text features to locate information
c. Comprehension of academic language
d. Understanding the relationship between written and spoken language

25. A first-grade teacher reviews high-frequency sight words with students each day by having them recite the words aloud from the class word wall, trace them on dotted lines, and practice writing the words independently. These strategies are likely intended to develop which of the following skills?

a. Phonemic awareness
b. Text comprehension
c. Orthographic processing
d. Phonological processing

26. Which of the following is true regarding children's reading fluency?

a. The lack of reading fluency is always due to word-decoding deficits.
b. Children's motivation to read is unaffected by their reading fluency.
c. Some children need only more reading practice to develop fluency.
d. Fluency has equal impact on school performance at all grade levels.

27. Of the following statements, which is true about the relationship of reading fluency, word decoding, and reading comprehension?

a. Developing fluency in reading has no relationship to speed and automaticity with decoding words.
b. Students should have strong word recognition foundations established before fluency instruction.
c. Reading fluency shows faster information processing speed, but has no impact on comprehension.
d. Slower, less automatic word decoding decreases reading fluency, but it increases comprehension.

28. Which of these techniques for building reading fluency is NOT necessarily a repeated reading activity?

a. Tape-assisted reading
b. Readers theater
c. Partner reading
d. Self-correction

29. A fourth-grade teacher wants to evaluate students' automaticity when reading aloud. Which of the following techniques would be most effective in assessing this skill?

a. Timing students as they individually read aloud from a grade-level text
b. Assigning corresponding comprehension questions to complete after reading
c. Having students circle high-frequency sight words in a vocabulary list
d. Asking students to orally recall major details from a reading passage

30. When assessing error patterns in a student's reading, which is most detrimental to reading proficiency?

a. Substitution of "control" for "contrariness"
b. Substitution of "resistant" for "recalcitrant"
c. Substituting a noun, not a verb, for a noun
d. Substituting for errors informed by context

31. Which of the following options best demonstrates a kinesthetic activity to build sight word recognition?

a. Circling sight words found in a magazine article
b. Building sight words with letter tiles
c. Reading books containing numerous sight words
d. Hopping along sight words written in chalk

32. Students in the transitional stage of reading development would benefit most from instruction in which area?

a. Sight word practice
b. Identifying the theme of abstract texts
c. Analyzing morphology to determine word meanings
d. Letter/sound correspondence

33. Which of these is true about young children's preferred conversation topics and how teachers can use conversation to facilitate vocabulary acquisition and sentence completion?

a. When children speak in incomplete sentences, teachers should not extend these.
b. Young children would rather talk about other people than talk about themselves.
c. Young children prefer to talk about new things that they have not yet experienced.
d. When children misuse words, teachers can recast them showing the correct usage.

34. Brady is a second-grade student working on reading fluency. Which of the following would be the best example for a demonstration of learning at the end of the lesson?

a. Asking Brady to read a story and answer questions
b. Asking Brady to listen to a short reading passage
c. Asking Brady to read a timed short reading passage
d. Asking Brady to read a list of words with assistance

35. Which of the following would be the best example of a learning objective that is appropriately challenging for a third-grade student with a disability in reading fluency?

a. The student will be able to identify 25 letters in one minute.
b. The student will be able to identify 25 letter sounds in one minute.
c. The student will be able to read 50 sight words in one minute.
d. The student will be able to read 100 words in one minute.

36. In addition to speed, which of the following is a component of reading fluency?

a. Suitable intonations when reading aloud
b. Lack of obvious effort when reading
c. Accuracy of word decoding
d. These are all components

37. If a teacher assigns students to pairs for cooperative writing partnerships, which of the following should their activities include?

a. One student should write, and the other should review the work.
b. Each partner in a pair takes turns being the writer and the reviewer.
c. Each student should provide only positive feedback to the other.
d. Each student should give only constructive feedback to the other.

38. Regarding research-based instructional strategies for collaborative student writing groups, what is correct about developing and setting goals?

a. Setting specific goals for writing undermines student motivation.
b. Only the teachers should develop writing goals for the students.
c. Teachers should expect students to develop their writing goals.
d. Both the teachers and the students may develop writing goals.

39. What do research studies find about student collaboration relative to effective writing instruction?

a. Cooperative learning does not apply to teaching writing.
b. Cooperative learning is an effective practice for writing.
c. Cooperative learning needs no structure from teachers.
d. Cooperative learning needs structure, not expectations.

40. Based on research evidence, what do experts recommend to effectively instruct students in writing strategies?

a. Teachers should demonstrate strategies and then assign independent student practice.
b. Teachers should explain strategies and let students practice them without any models.
c. Teachers should model strategies, then guide practice, then give independent practice.
d. Teachers should first give students guided practice in strategies and then model them.

41. Which of the following statements correctly describes research findings regarding effective writing instruction techniques?

a. Teacher modeling and think-alouds are effective.
b. Providing students with scaffolding can slow learning.
c. Exposing students to the processes of writing is sufficient.
d. Implicit and embedded instruction is better than explicit instruction.

42. Of the following writing examples, which one reflects an error in grammar?

a. "She is without a doubt the very best freind I have ever had in my life."
b. "He said we should wait two hours, we waited two hours and returned."
c. "A great animal lover, his pets included dogs, cats, horses, and chickens."
d. "They were traveling South at first, but later in the trip they went West."

43. When is it most appropriate for students to write in casual language at their own age level?

a. To share a certain experience with their readers
b. To get parental permission for a desired activity
c. To write something for their classmates to read
d. To write a story that younger children can read

44. Which of the following is a valid guideline for writers of research papers to follow when integrating ideas from another source into their writing?

a. Use quotes to make the most important points.
b. Quote lengthy segments of text to show full context.
c. Focus discussion on the sources rather than original ideas.
d. Use quotes in a way that flows with the writer's own statements.

45. A prekindergarten teacher uses a combination of verbal cues and nonverbal gestures to signal various transitions in the classroom throughout the school day. This strategy is beneficial in developing students' speaking and listening skills because it:

a. Provides multiple means of understanding
b. Aligns communication with students' developmental levels
c. Demonstrates that communication occurs in a variety of ways
d. Strengthens their understanding of parts of speech and types of sentences

46. Which choice completes the text with the most logical and precise word or phrase?

The Industrial Revolution, a transformative period in the 18th and 19th centuries, had far-reaching implications for the humanities. Mechanization and urbanization fundamentally reshaped the fabric of society, triggering tumultuous changes that reverberated across all aspects of life. In response, artists and writers endeavored to capture the human experience within this transformation. Visionaries like J.M.W. Turner, sought to portray the stark beauty and chaos of industrial landscapes through their art, while authors such as Charles Dickens delved into the heart of the social and moral challenges faced by the working class. These creative works not only documented the era's ________ but also raised questions about the impact of industrialization on humanity's relationship with nature, labor, and society.

a. insignificance
b. stagnation
c. upheaval
d. tranquility

47. Every year, students prepare with excitement for Historical Characters Day. Each student is expected to choose a character who was influential in years past and compose a report on why he was important. The students are permitted to dress up as their respective characters on the day on which the reports are turned in. This year, the teachers want to incorporate an aspect of this anticipated event that will more directly increase their students' oral communication skills. Of the options they have brainstormed, which of the following would be most helpful?

a. Ask the students to read their reports aloud to the class.
b. Require that the reports be memorized so that students can make better use of voice modulation and eye contact while presenting.
c. Require the students to write why they chose their character and three interesting things they learned on a set note cards, and present what they have written to the class.
d. Hold an election for the student with the most realistic costume and require students to give supporting evidence for their votes.

48. A fourth grade class will begin a unit next week in which students will be building oral language concepts through a variety of readings, projects, and discussions. Which of the following genres would be most appropriate to use for reading text and class discussion?

a. Fiction
b. Folk tale
c. Biography
d. Science fiction

History and Social Science

49. A caste system is BEST described as

a. a primarily social phenomenon that has no economic consequences.
b. a system that discriminates mainly based on race, but permits upward social mobility.
c. a system wherein individuals' social, economic, and political destinies are determined at birth by group membership.
d. equivalent to the modern-day class system.

50. Proponents of legislating greater societal income equity support all of the following EXCEPT:

a. Impose a progressive income tax
b. Impose high estate or inheritance taxes
c. Impose a gift tax
d. Impose high sales taxes

51. Which of the following would NOT happen if the FOMC uses Treasury Bills to pursue a contractionary monetary policy?

a. The money supply decreases
b. The international value of the American dollar increases
c. The price of US goods to foreigners increases
d. Lower interest rates

52. Which of the following are true of the demand curve?

I. It is normally downward sloping
II. It is normally upward sloping
III. It is influenced by the law of diminishing marginal utility
IV. It is unaffected by the law of diminishing marginal utility

a. I and III only
b. I and IV only
c. II and III only
d. II and IV only

53. Which of the following is NOT correct regarding assumptions of mercantilism?

a. The money and the wealth of a nation are identical properties.
b. In order to prosper, a nation should try to increase its imports.
c. In order to prosper, a nation should try to increase its exports.
d. Economic protectionism by national governments is advisable.

54. Among the following, which is correct regarding some essential geography concepts?

a. An example of absolute location is urban vs. rural land prices.
b. Relative location equals the latitude and longitude of a place.
c. Product and land prices are affected by geographical distance.
d. Achievability relates to surface conditions and never changes.

55. Which of the following are the leading producers of petroleum in Latin America?

a. Argentina and Bolivia
b. Mexico and Guatemala
c. Brazil and Venezuela
d. Colombia and Uruguay

56. Which map describes the movement of people, trends, or materials across a physical area?

a. Political Map
b. Cartogram
c. Qualitative Map
d. Flow-line Map

57. The physical geography of a region most directly affects which of the following?

a. The religious beliefs of the native population
b. The family structure of the native population
c. The dietary preferences of the native population
d. The language spoken by the native population

58. Which of the following are NOT included in a geographical definition of Southeast Asia?

a. Myanmar, Laos, Cambodia, and Thailand
b. Vietnam, the Malay Peninsula, and Brunei
c. East Malaysia, Indonesia, and the Philippines
d. These are all geographical parts of Southeast Asia.

59. What are the first ten amendments to the Constitution more commonly known as?

a. The Civil Rights Act
b. Common law
c. The Equal Protection clause
d. The Bill of Rights

60. Who established the precedent for the two-term limit for the US presidency?

a. Abraham Lincoln
b. Alexander Hamilton
c. George Washington
d. Thomas Jefferson

61. How are members of the Federal Judiciary chosen?

a. They are elected by voters.
b. They are appointed by the president and confirmed by the House of Representatives.
c. They are chosen by a committee.
d. They are appointed by the president and confirmed by the Senate.

62. The Supreme Court has nine members. How is this number determined?

a. It is outlined in the Constitution.
b. Congress determines the number.
c. The President determines the number.
d. The Court decides on the number.

63. Who may write a bill?

a. Anyone
b. A member of the House
c. A Senator
d. Any member of Congress

64. How is a tie broken in the Senate?

a. The president pro tempore casts the deciding vote.
b. The Speaker of the House votes.
c. They vote again.
d. The vice president votes.

65. Of these materials, which can teachers use to help students develop chronological thinking?

a. Only history books can be used for this.
b. Biographies can also serve this function.
c. Historical literature can be used for this.
d. These are all good chronology materials.

66. Which type of chart is best at representing the cycle of demographic transition?

a. Pie chart
b. Political map
c. Line graph
d. Flow-line map

67. Consider the graph below. Which of the following is true?

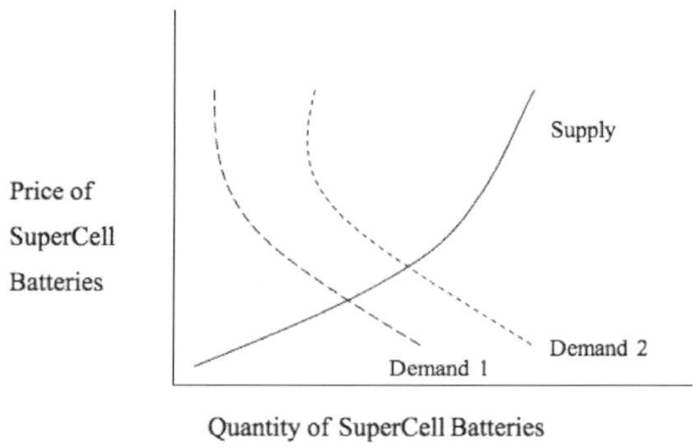

a. The price has decreased with a shift in supply.
b. The equilibrium point has remained constant.
c. The price has risen with a shift in demand.
d. There a double coincidence of wants.

68. Unlike slaves, who were considered to be the property of their masters, which of the following was true regarding most indentured servants in colonial times?

a. They received wages for their labor
b. They were generally treated kindly by their employers
c. They were highly educated
d. They voluntarily entered into servitude

69. Which of the following statements is false regarding the Puritans?

a. In terms of their theology, the Puritans were considered Calvinists.
b. Many Puritans agreed with radical views that criticized the Swiss Calvinists.
c. Many of those identified as Calvinists opposed the Puritans.
d. The Restoration and the Uniformity Act reunified the Puritan movement and the Church of England.

70. After the Civil War, urban populations increased. This growth was likely due to:

a. An increased reliance on agriculture
b. The Industrial Revolution
c. Prohibition
d. Slavery persisting in some areas

71. The Trail of Tears was:

a. The forced removal of British soldiers after the American Revolution
b. The forced evacuation of Cherokee peoples into Oklahoma
c. The forced evacuation of freed slaves from the South after the Civil War
d. The tears of Betsy Ross while she sewed the first American flag

72. The writers of *The Federalist Papers* published under the pen name "Publius." Who were the authors?

a. James Madison, John Jay, and Alexander Hamilton
b. George Washington, Thomas Jefferson, and James Madison
c. Alexander Hamilton, Benjamin Franklin, and Thomas Jefferson
d. Benjamin Franklin, John Jay, and Thomas Jefferson

73. Which of these is NOT true relative to the rise of Fascism in Europe?

a. Fascism was opposed to nationalism and to patriotism.
b. Fascism was opposed to Marxism and the bourgeoisie.
c. Fascism purported to be an alternative to Bolshevism.
d. Fascism had some things in common with Bolshevism.

74. Which of the following is the best example of a factor resulting from Europe's Commercial Revolution that contributed to the 1700s' Industrial Revolution?

a. The rediscovery of concrete
b. New advances in making iron
c. The steam engine's invention
d. Increases in population growth

75. Which statement best describes the role played by the French economy in causing the 1789 French Revolution?

a. France's very large national debt led to heavy tax burdens on the French peasantry.
b. Nearly seventy percent of annual national expenditures financed luxuries for the French nobility.
c. Reforms in the guild system allowed many peasants to rise to the middle class.
d. The king's attempt to curtail free trade led skilled journeymen to rebel against the monarchy.

76. A group that grew in numbers as a result of the Industrial Revolution was:

a. Small farmers.
b. Unskilled workers.
c. Skilled craftsmen.
d. The rural population.

77. Which of the following is true of social changes and the Industrial Revolution in Europe in the 18th and early 19th centuries?

a. They gave rise to a new middle-class
b. They improved working conditions
c. They were the result of urbanization
d. They were caused by the labor unions

78. During World War I, which group joined with the Central Powers after it formed?

a. Austria-Hungary
b. Germany
c. Ottoman Empire
d. Italy

Mathematics

79. Aaron goes on a run every morning down the straight country road that he lives on. The graph below shows Aaron's distance from home at times throughout his morning run. Which of the following statements is (are) true?

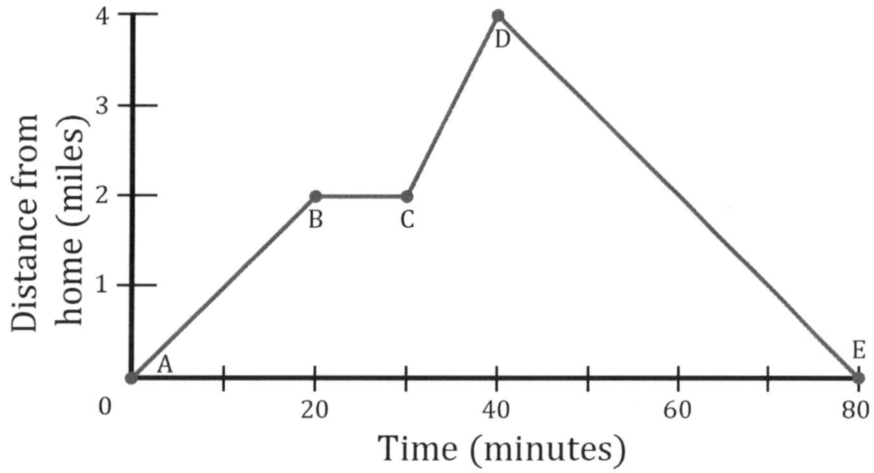

I. Aaron's average running speed was 6 mph.
II. Aaron's running speed from A to B was the same as from D to E.
III. Aaron ran a total distance of four miles.

a. I only
b. II only
c. I and II
d. I, II, and III

80. Carlos spends $\frac{1}{8}$ of his monthly salary on utility bills. If his utility bills total \$320, what is his monthly salary?

a. \$2,440
b. \$2,520
c. \$2,560
d. \$2,600

81. Which of the following is the graph of the equation $y = -4x - 6$?

a.

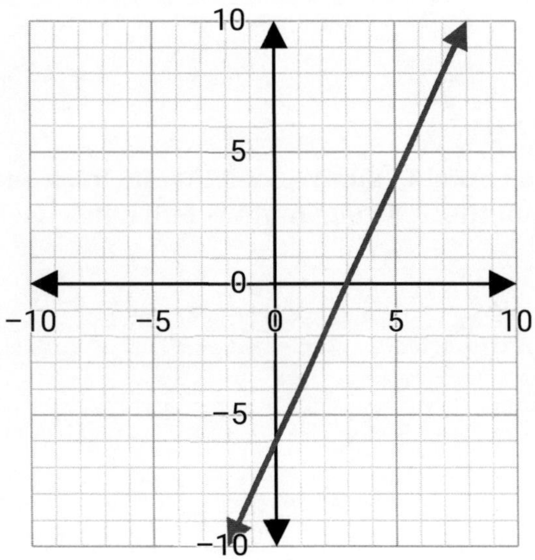

b.

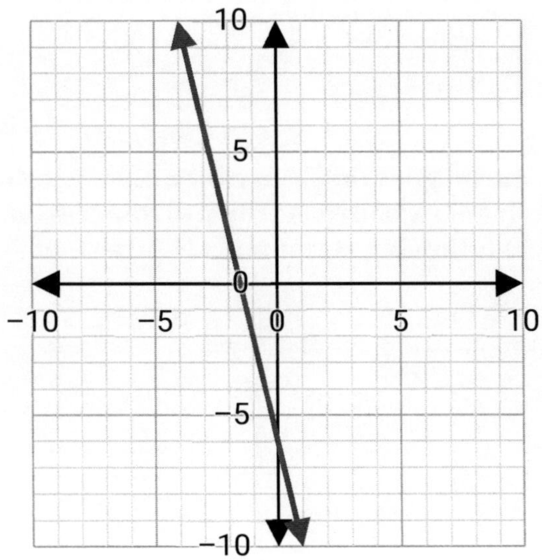

c.

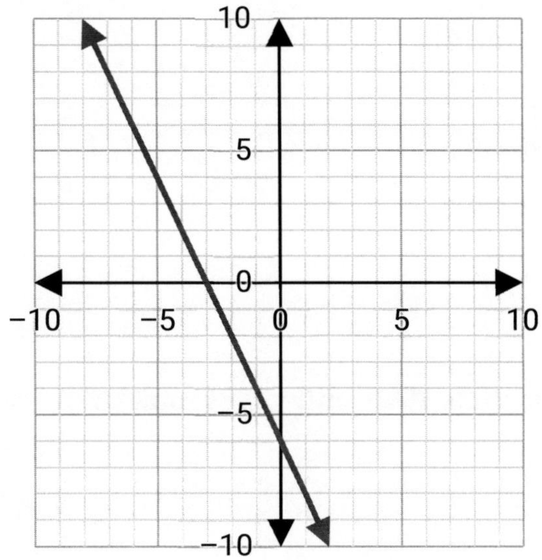

d.

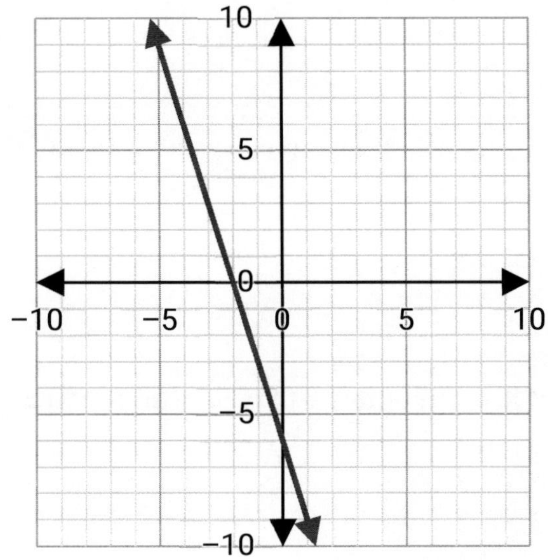

82. What is the correct solution for x in the following system of equations?

$$\begin{cases} x - 1 = y \\ y + 3 = 7 \end{cases}$$

a. $x = 6$
b. $x = 5$
c. $x = 4$
d. $x = 8$

83. On his morning run, a jogger records his distance from his front door in meters as a function of time in seconds. If x represents time in seconds, which of the following equations represents the jogger's distance from his front door as a function of time?

Time	0	3	4	6	7
Distance	5.2	25.0	31.6	44.8	51.4

a. $y = 3x + 25$
b. $y = 25.0x + 5.2$
c. $y = 18.4x + 3$
d. $y = 6.6x + 5.2$

84. Zeke drove from his house to a furniture store in Atlanta and then back home along the same route. It took Zeke three hours to drive to the store. By driving an average of 20 mph faster on his return trip, Zeke was able to save an hour of driving time. What was Zeke's average driving speed on his round trip?

a. 24 mph
b. 48 mph
c. 50 mph
d. 60 mph

85. What equation is graphed below?

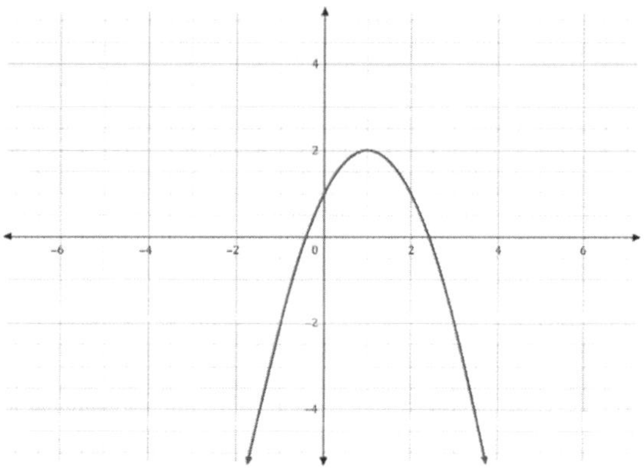

a. $y = -2x^2 - 2x + 1$
b. $y = -x^2 + 2x + 1$
c. $y = -x^2 - 2x + 2$
d. $y = -\frac{1}{2}x^2 - x + 2$

86. Robert needs to buy milk and bread. Each gallon of milk costs \$3. Each loaf of bread costs \$2. He intends to spend at least \$20. Which of the following graphs represents the possible combinations of gallons of milk and loaves of bread that he may purchase?

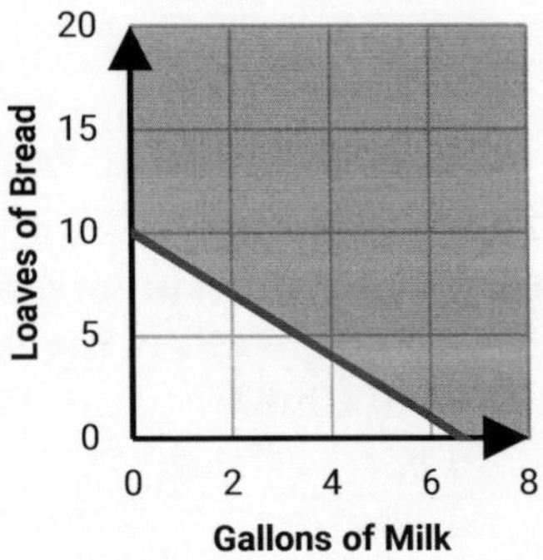

a.

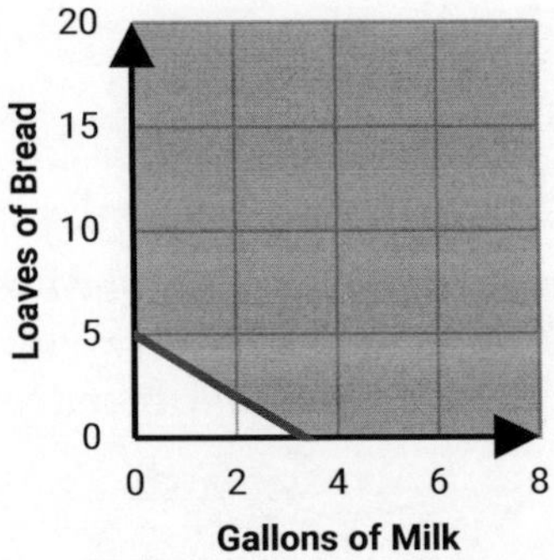

b.

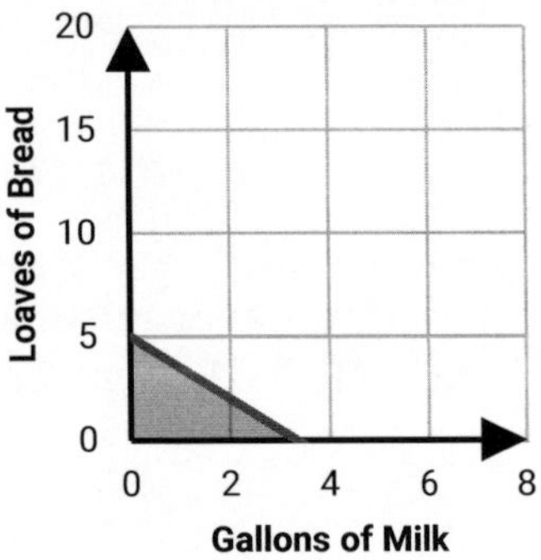

c.

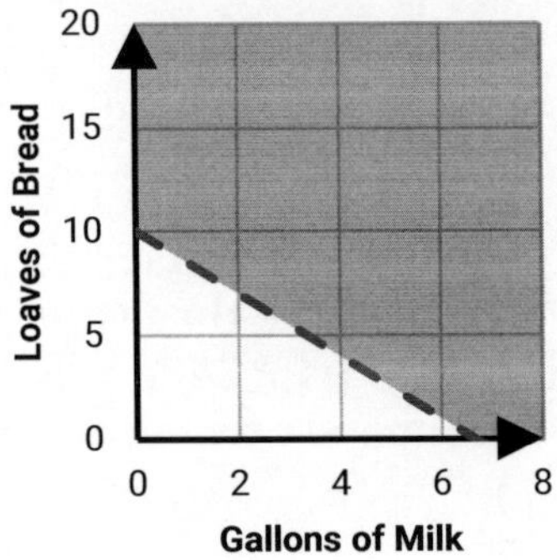

d.

87. If $f(x) = \frac{x^3-2x+1}{3x}$, what is $f(2)$?

a. $\frac{1}{3}$
b. $\frac{1}{2}$
c. $\frac{5}{6}$
d. $\frac{5}{2}$

88. For which of these does a rotation of 120° about the center of the polygon map the polygon onto itself?

a. Square
b. Regular hexagon
c. Regular octagon
d. Regular decagon

89. Which of the following descriptions best fits a hexagonal prism?

a. 8 faces, 18 edges, 12 vertices
b. 6 faces, 18 edges, 12 vertices
c. 8 faces, 16 edges, 8 vertices
d. 6 faces, 14 edges, 10 vertices

90. A cube inscribed in a sphere has a volume of 64 cubic units. What is the volume of the sphere in cubic units?

a. $4\pi\sqrt{3}$
b. $8\pi\sqrt{3}$
c. $32\pi\sqrt{3}$
d. $256\pi\sqrt{3}$

91. A can has a radius of 1.5 inches and a height of 3 inches. Which of the following best represents the volume of the can? Use 3.14 for π.

a. 17.2 in^3
b. 19.4 in^3
c. 21.2 in^3
d. 23.4 in^3

92. Eric has a beach ball with a radius of 9 inches. He is planning to wrap the ball with wrapping paper. Which of the following is the best estimate for the number of square feet of wrapping paper he will need? Use 3.14 for π.

a. 4.08
b. 5.12
c. 7.07
d. 8.14

93. The two prisms shown below are similar. What is the measurement of x?

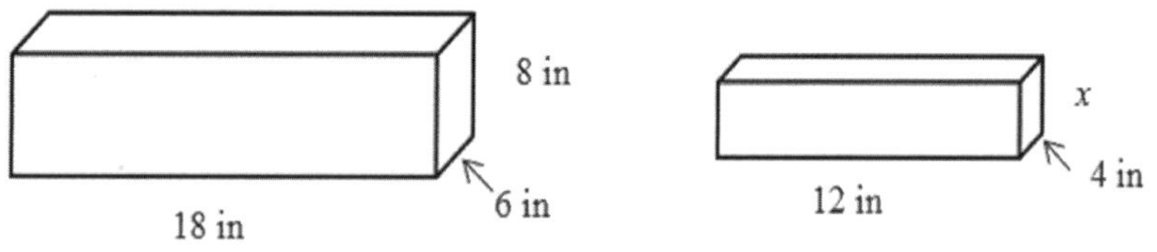

a. $4\frac{3}{4}$ in
b. $5\frac{1}{3}$ in
c. $5\frac{2}{3}$ in
d. $5\frac{3}{4}$ in

94. The total perimeter of an L-shaped field is 800 feet. The longest side is 300 feet, and the longest width is 100 feet. Each of the shorter sides is 50 feet. What is the total area of the field?

a. 17,500 square feet
b. 22,500 square feet
c. 30,000 square feet
d. 45,000 square feet

95. Which of the following steps were applied to ΔABC?

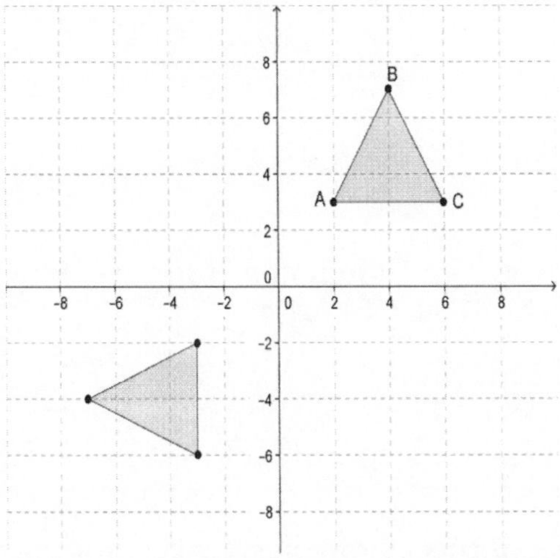

a. Reflection across the x-axis and counterclockwise rotation of 90 degrees about the origin
b. Reflection across the x-axis and counterclockwise rotation of 180 degrees about the origin
c. Reflection across the x-axis and counterclockwise rotation of 270 degrees about the origin
d. Reflection across the y-axis and counterclockwise rotation of 180 degrees about the origin

96. Which of the following theorems proves the congruence of the triangles below?

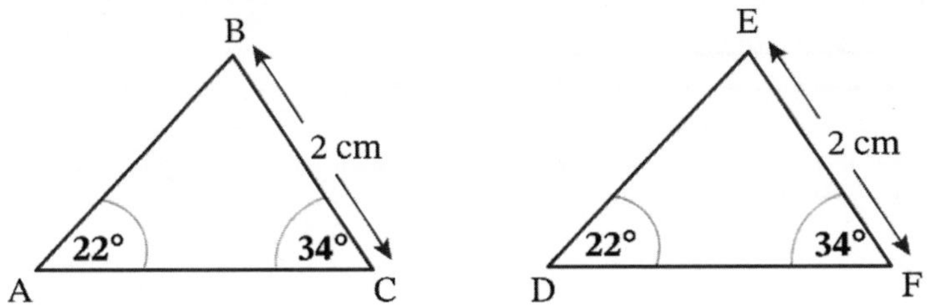

a. ASA
b. AAS
c. SAS
d. SSS

97. Which of these statements is (are) true for deductive reasoning?

I. A general conclusion is drawn from specific instances.
II. If the premises are true and proper reasoning is applied, the conclusion must be true.

a. Statement I is true
b. Statement II is true
c. Both statements are true
d. Neither statement is true

98. Mr. Orr asks his class to use inductive reasoning to determine the pattern in this sequence of numbers. Which number is next in this series?

2, 5, 10, 17, __

a. 22
b. 24
c. 25
d. 26

99. Which of these adult behaviors is most conducive to developing children's reasoning skills?

a. When adults analyze children's thought processes and then explain them to the children
b. When adults ask children questions, allow them time to think, and listen to their answers
c. When adults tell children why something exists/is a certain way and discuss it with them
d. When adults classify objects or concepts into groups to demonstrate logic to the children

100. James is running laps on his school's track. 4 laps on the track are equal to 1 mile. This summer, James has run 86 laps on the track. How many miles has James run this summer?

Frances has shown her work below. How would you describe her understanding of the problem?

$$\begin{array}{r} 21 \\ 4\overline{)86} \\ -8 \\ \hline 06 \\ -4 \\ \hline 2 \end{array} \qquad \boxed{\text{21 miles}}$$

a. Frances needed to bring down one more 0 on the last step of the long division algorithm. The last step should be dividing 20 by 4, getting 5. The final answer should be 215 miles. Frances is approaching mastery.
b. Frances is very close to mastery. However, she forgot to include the remainder in her answer. The answer should be 21 r2. This means James ran $21\frac{2}{4}$ miles, or in simplest form, $21\frac{1}{2}$ miles.
c. Frances has successfully divided 86 by 4. However, Frances needed to use multiplication to solve this problem, not division. The correct answer is $86 \times 4 = 344$ miles.
d. Frances needed to subtract 4 from 86. The final answer is 82, not 21. Frances has misconceptions regarding which operations to implement when solving word problems.

101. Mrs. Davis is working with a 3rd grade student named Julie. Mrs. Davis has asked Julie to use base ten blocks to model the number 246. Describe Julie's error.

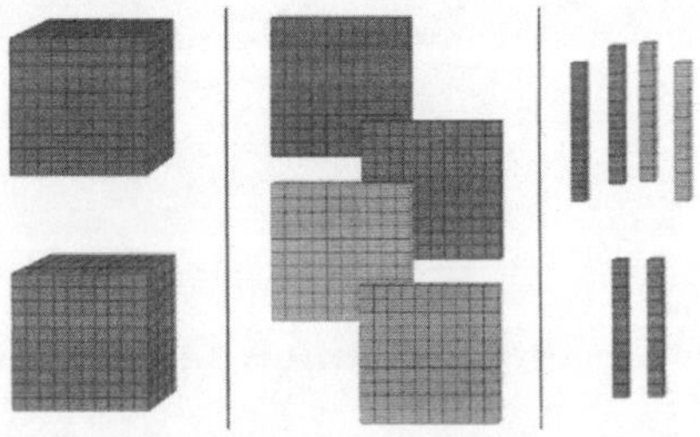

a. Julie has incorrectly represented the place value for the digit 2, within the number 246. Julie has modeled 2 thousands instead of 2 hundreds. All other digits are modeled correctly.
b. Julie's model represents 2,406 instead of 246.
c. Julie's only error is that her model is missing 6 ones. Once 6 ones are added to the model, it will be a correct representation of the number 246.
d. Julie has incorrectly represented the place value for the digits 2, 4, and 6 within the number 246. Julie has modeled 2 thousands, 4 hundreds, and 6 tens, which is the number 2,460.

102. Mr. Erikson's class has a test on dividing fractions tomorrow. The class is reviewing the strategy of "Keep, Change, Flip." One of Mr. Erikson's students has solved $\frac{3}{4} \div \frac{1}{5}$ as illustrated below. Which choice best describes the student's understanding of "Keep, Change, Flip?"

$$\frac{3}{4} \div \frac{1}{5} \rightarrow \frac{4}{3} \times \frac{1}{5} \rightarrow \frac{4}{15}$$

a. The student's work is correct. The student has mastered "Keep, Change, Flip."
b. The student's work is partially correct. The student's mistake is that their answer should be simplified. $\frac{4}{15}$ is not in simplest form.
c.
The student has successfully implemented the "Keep, Change, Flip" strategy, but when multiplying $\frac{4}{3}$ and $\frac{1}{5}$, he or she multiplied straight across instead of "cross multiplying." The student should have multiplied 4 by 5 and 3 by 1, for a product of $\frac{20}{3}$.

$$\frac{4}{3} \times \frac{1}{5} = \frac{20}{3}$$

d. The student has one misconception regarding "Keep, Change, Flip." The student's work indicates that he or she is "flipping" the wrong fraction. The student's computation seems accurate, but he or she has "flipped" the wrong fraction. This error is what leads the student to an incorrect answer.

103. Dayna's teacher asks her to solve the division problem 384 ÷ 3 using an area model. Dayna solves the problem incorrectly, as illustrated below. Select the item that best describes Dayna's error.

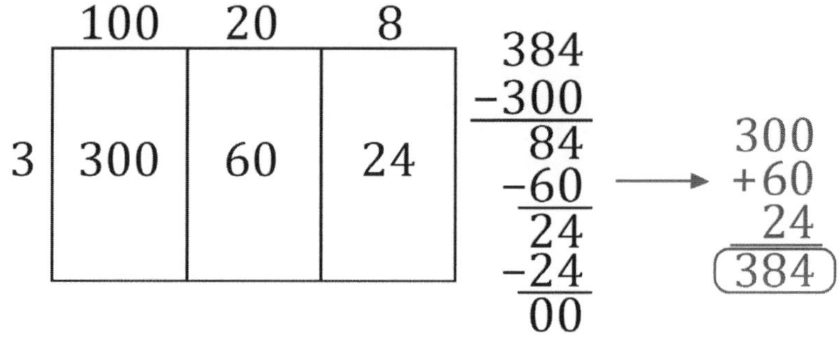

a. Dayna has misunderstood where to locate the answer within the model. The final answer should have been calculated as the product of all three numbers above the model, 100, 20, and 8.
b. Dayna's error was that she needed to set up the area model vertically, not horizontally.
c. On the final step, Dayna needed to subtract the three values, not add them.
d. Dayna has misunderstood which section of the model represents the final answer. When determining the final answer, she has calculated the sum of the numbers on the inside of the model, instead of calculating the sum of the numbers above the model.

104. Amelia made an array of cubes that is 10 cubes by 10 cubes. Ms. Becker asked her to make the array 10 cubes by 15 cubes. Amelia picks up 15 more cubes. Which of the following statements best describes Amelia's error?

a. Amelia does not yet know number facts above 100
b. Amelia does not fully understand how changes to dimension affect measures of area and volume
c. Amelia does not fully understand the commutative property of multiplication
d. Amelia does not yet understand how to interpret mathematical models

105. Which of the following equations may be used to convert $0.\overline{7}$ to a fraction?

a. $9x = 7.\overline{7} - 0.\overline{7}$
b. $99x = 7.\overline{7} - 0.\overline{7}$
c. $9x = 77.\overline{7} - 7.\overline{7}$
d. $90x = 7.\overline{7} - 0.\overline{7}$

106. Andrea must administer $\frac{1}{12}$ of a medicine bottle to a patient. If the bottle contains $3\frac{4}{10}$ fluid ounces of medicine, how much medicine should be administered?

a. $\frac{17}{60}$ fluid ounces
b. $\frac{15}{62}$ fluid ounces
c. $\frac{3}{19}$ fluid ounces
d. $\frac{17}{67}$ fluid ounces

107. Marlon pays $45 for a jacket that has been marked down 25%. What was the original cost of the jacket?

a. $80
b. $75
c. $65
d. $60

108. Which of the following is an irrational number?

a. $3.\overline{13}$
b. $\sqrt{25}$
c. $\frac{\pi}{2}$
d. $\frac{37}{5}$

109. Which property of numbers states that $1 + 3$ is the same as $3 + 1$?

a. Associative property
b. Distributive property
c. Inverse property
d. Commutative property

110. What is the value of the expression $-3 \times 5^2 + 2(4 - 18) + 33$?

a. -130
b. -70
c. -20
d. 74

111. Which of the following correctly represents the expanded form of 0.867?

a. $8 \times \frac{1}{10^0} + 6 \times \frac{1}{10^1} + 7 \times \frac{1}{10^2}$
b. $8 \times \frac{1}{10^2} + 6 \times \frac{1}{10^3} + 7 \times \frac{1}{10^4}$
c. $8 \times \frac{1}{10^3} + 6 \times \frac{1}{10^2} + 7 \times \frac{1}{10^1}$
d. $8 \times \frac{1}{10^1} + 6 \times \frac{1}{10^2} + 7 \times \frac{1}{10^3}$

112. Kendra uses the pie chart below to represent the allocation of her annual income. Her annual income is $40,000.

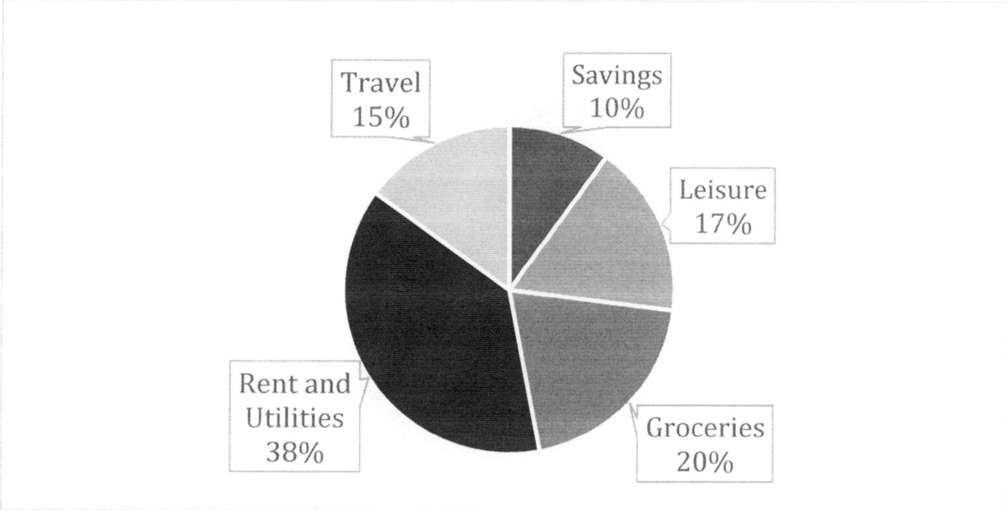

Which of the following statements is true?

a. The amount of money she spends on travel and savings is more than $11,000.
b. The amount of money she spends on rent and utilities is approximately $15,000.
c. The amount of money she spends on groceries and savings is more than $13,000.
d. The amount of money she spends on leisure is less than $5,000.

113. Given the two-way frequency table below, which of the following *best* represents *P*(bowl or chicken soup)?

	Chicken Soup	Vegetable Soup	Total
Cup	329	248	577
Bowl	642	591	1,233
Total	971	839	1,810

a. 70%
b. 75%
c. 80%
d. 85%

114. A teacher recorded the dates that students turned in projects in two different classes to compare trends and noticed that a large number of students were submitting their work late. She plotted charts to see how many students in each class were turning in late work and how late they were.

Which of the following is a true statement for these data?

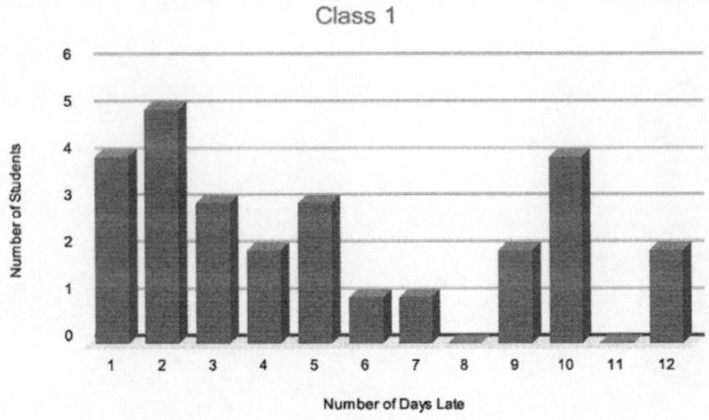

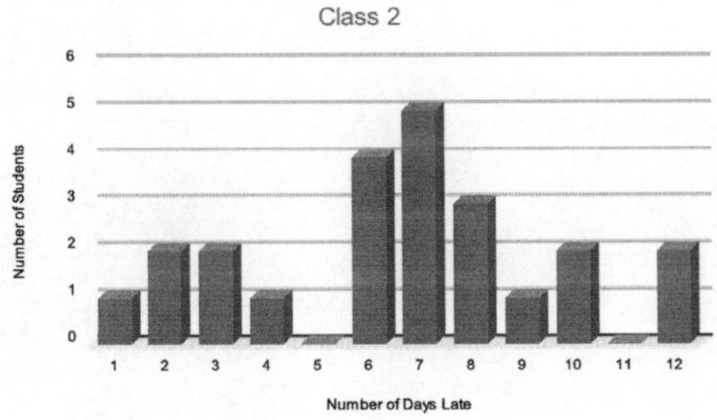

a. The median number of days late in Class 1 is 2 days less than in Class 2.
b. On average, students turned in work 4 days later in Class 2 than in Class 1 (round to nearest whole number).
c. The mode late time is higher for Class 2 than for Class 1.
d. The median late time for Class 1 is greater than the mean for Class 1.

115. Mark's nightstand currently holds 6 books, 12 pencils, and 1 highlighter. If he must place one item from each category into his backpack, how many possible selections are there?

a. 19
b. 72
c. 144
d. 180

116. A random sample of 90 students at an elementary school were asked these three questions:

Do you like carrots?
Do you like broccoli?
Do you like cauliflower?

The results of the survey are shown below. If these data are representative of the population of students at the school, which of these is most probable?

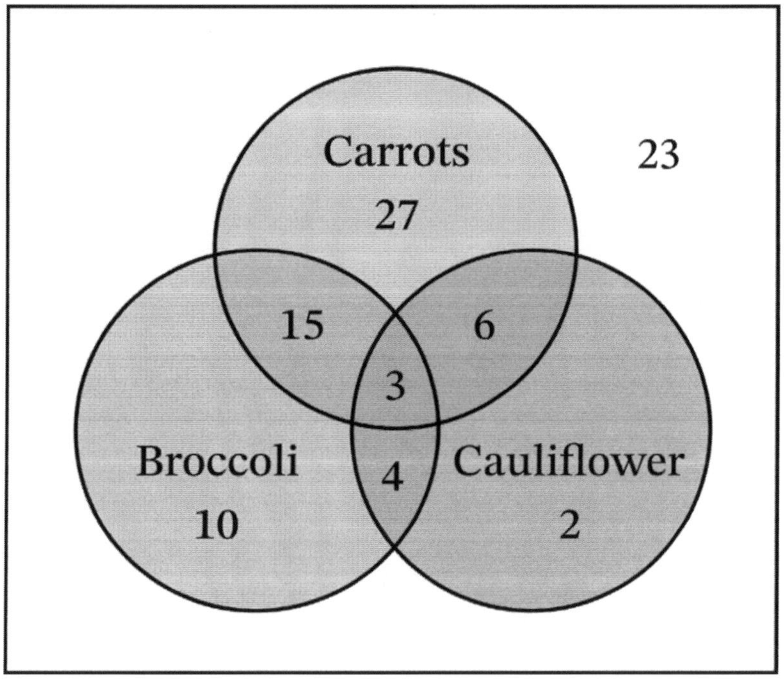

a. A student chosen at random likes broccoli.
b. Given a student chosen at random likes carrots, they will also like at least one other vegetable.
c. Given a student chosen at random likes cauliflower and broccoli, they will also like carrots.
d. A student chosen at random does not like carrots, broccoli, or cauliflower.

117. Eli rolls a six-sided die and tosses a coin. What is the probability that he gets a prime number or tails?

a. $\frac{1}{4}$
b. $\frac{1}{3}$
c. $\frac{1}{2}$
d. $\frac{3}{4}$

118. The x-axis in the scatter plot below represents the number of miles Cyndi drives. The y-axis represents the gallons of gas left in her car's tank. About how many gallons will remain when she has driven 250 miles? Choose the best estimate.

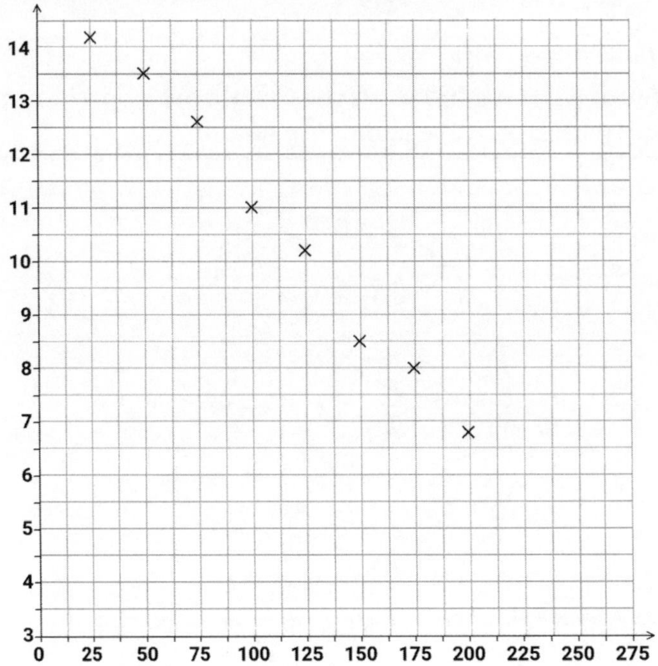

a. 3.5 gallons
b. 4.5 gallons
c. 5.5 gallons
d. 6.5 gallons

119. Given the two-way frequency table below, which of the following best represents P(male or graduate)?

	Undergraduate	Graduate	Total
Male	2,940	2,045	4,985
Female	3,026	2,068	5,094
Total	5,966	4,113	10,079

a. 55%
b. 60%
c. 70%
d. 75%

120. Given the boxplots below, which of the following statements is correct? (Note that the boxes are not drawn to scale with one another.)

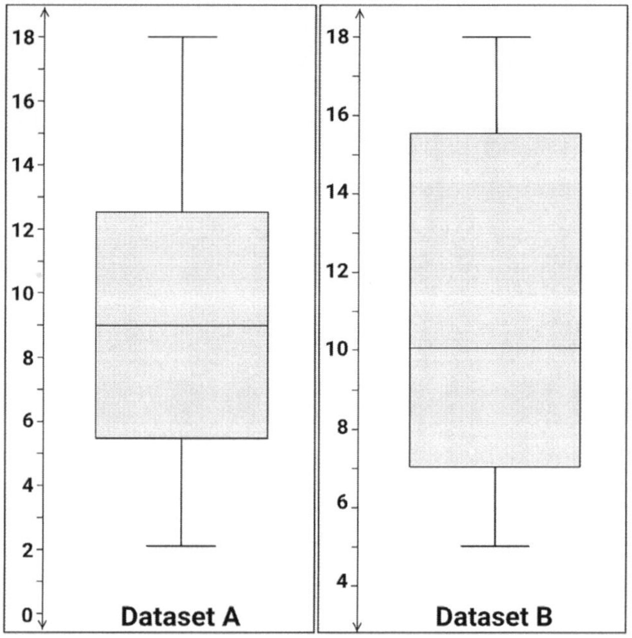

a. Dataset A has a larger range and a larger median.
b. Dataset A has a smaller range and a larger median.
c. Dataset A has a larger range and a smaller median.
d. Dataset A has a smaller range and a smaller median.

Science

121. Which of the following statements regarding the layers of the atmosphere is NOT true?

a. In the troposphere, temperature decreases as altitude increases.
b. In the mesosphere, temperature decreases as altitude increases.
c. In the stratosphere, temperature decreases as altitude increases.
d. In the thermosphere, temperature increases as altitude increases.

122. According to Kepler's laws of planetary motion, which of the following statements is true?

a. The planets orbit the Sun in circular paths.
b. A vector from the Sun to a planet sweeps out equal areas in equal times.
c. Planets located further from the Sun have shorter periods than planets located nearer to the Sun.
d. While orbiting the Sun, the closer the planet is to the Sun, the slower it travels.

123. Which of the following is an example of an absolute age?

a. A fossil is 37 million years old.
b. A rock is less than 100,000 years old.
c. An organic artifact is between 5,000 and 10,000 years old.
d. All of the above

124. In the field of geology, the term "uniformitarianism" refers to the belief that:

a. Catastrophic events like mass extinctions are the main forces that have shaped the Earth.
b. The Earth's crust has not undergone any dramatic changes since its formation.
c. The natural forces that shape the Earth have remained relatively constant over geologic time.
d. The Earth's stratigraphy is more or less uniform at any given geographic location.

125. Which of the following statements correctly describes an effect of the Gulf Stream?

a. It increases humidity along North America's west coast.
b. It makes the climate of South America colder.
c. It makes the climate of Northern Europe warmer.
d. It makes the climate of the Caribbean milder and less humid.

126. The process that causes lithospheric plates to move over the surface of the mantle is called:

a. Conduction
b. Convection
c. Tension
d. Subduction

127. According to the Köppen Climate Classification System, regions with continental climates are most commonly found:

a. In the interior regions of large landmasses
b. Near the equator
c. Near the Earth's poles
d. In places with high temperatures year-round

128. Which of the following is an example of a descriptive study?

a. Comparing the average height of male vs female penguins of a particular species
b. Investigating the growth rate of fungi in various synthetic media
c. Testing the effectiveness of a drug with a double-blind study
d. Split-testing the impact on sales of a new description of menu items.

129. The principal cause of acid precipitation is:

a. Nuclear power production
b. Soil erosion
c. The burning of coal and petroleum products
d. Water pollution

130. When a population reaches its carrying capacity:

a. Other populations will be forced out of the habitat.
b. Density-dependent factors no longer play a role.
c. Density-independent factors no longer play a role.
d. The population growth rate approaches zero.

131. Two companion models, gradualism and punctuated equilibrium, dominate evolutionary theory. Which of the following statements is most consistent with the theory of punctuated equilibrium?

a. Fossils show changes over large periods of time.
b. Fossils showing intermediate characteristics may not necessarily be found.
c. Speciation occurs gradually.
d. Evolution is a slow, steady process.

132. Which of the following demographic changes would lead to a population with an older age composition?

a. Increased birth rate
b. Environmental pollution
c. Increased availability of food
d. Medical advancements that increase life expectancy

133. Which of the following divisions of plants produces seeds for reproduction?

a. Anthophyta
b. Lycophyta
c. Sphenophyta
d. Pterophyta

Refer to the following for question 134:

Diagram of a complete, perfect flower

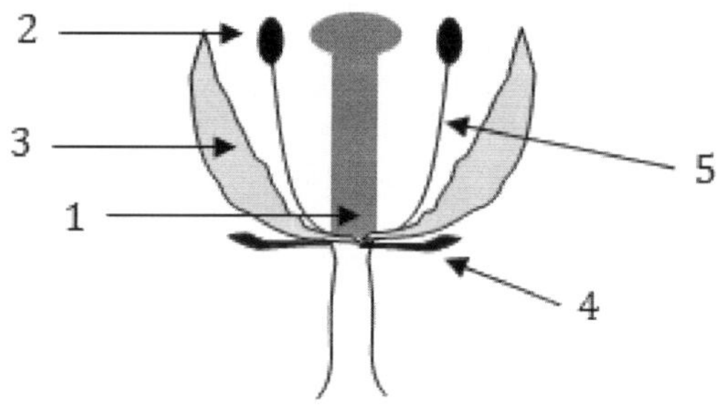

134. Which of the following is NOT considered a reproductive organ of the flower?

a. 1
b. 2
c. 3
d. 4

135. When an animal takes in more energy than it uses over an extended time, the extra chemical energy is stored as:

a. Fat
b. Starch
c. Protein
d. Enzymes

136. Magnesium metal is reacted with hydrobromic acid according to the following equation:

$$Mg + 2HBr \rightarrow MgBr_2 + H_2$$

If 100 g of Mg is reacted with 100 g of HBr, which statement about the reaction is true?

a. Mg is the limiting reagent.
b. HBr is the excess reagent.
c. Mg is the excess reagent.
d. 100 g of $MgBr_2$ will be produced.

137. Which of the following is NOT true regarding exothermic and endothermic processes or reactions?

a. Exothermic reactions release heat energy.
b. The melting of ice is an endothermic process.
c. The burning of butane is an exothermic process.
d. The change in enthalpy is positive for an exothermic reaction.

138. When heat is removed from water during condensation, which of the following are formed.

a. Atoms
b. Covalent bonds
c. Intermolecular bonds
d. Ionic bonds

139. A space station is revolving in a circular orbit around Earth. Consider the following three statements:

I. The center of mass of the space station is necessarily located at its geometric center.
II. The center of mass is moving at a constant velocity.
III. The center of mass of the space station is moving at a constant speed.

Which of the following statements is true?

a. I is true.
b. II is true.
c. III is true.
d. I, II, and III are not true.

140. A substance has a half-life of 2.4×10^4 years. How long does it take for 87.5% of the substance to decay?

a. 2.1×10^4 years
b. 4.5×10^4 years
c. 7.2×10^4 years
d. 9.6×10^4 years

141. According to the kinetic theory of matter, which of the following statements is true?

a. The average kinetic energy is inversely proportional to the square of the average velocity of the particles.
b. The average kinetic energy is inversely proportional to the average velocity of the particles.
c. The average kinetic energy is directly proportional to the square of the average velocity of the particles.
d. The average kinetic energy is directly proportional to the average velocity of the particles.

142. Consider the following statements about Newton's law:

I. A newton is a fundamental unit.
II. Mass and acceleration are inversely related when the force is constant.
III. Newton's first law can be derived from Newton's second law.
IV. Newton's second law can be derived from the universal law of gravity.

Which of the statements are true?

a. I, II, and III.
b. II and III only.
c. III only.
d. None of them

143. Which of the following statements about heat transfer is NOT true?

a. As the energy of a system changes, its thermal energy must change or work must be done.
b. Heat transfer from a warmer object to a cooler object can occur spontaneously.
c. Heat transfer can never occur from a cooler object to a warmer object.
d. If two objects reach the same temperature, energy is no longer available for work.

144. Students experimentally determine that the specific heat of copper is $0.410\ \frac{\text{J}}{\text{g}\cdot°\text{C}}$. If the known value of the specific heat of copper is $0.385\ \frac{\text{J}}{\text{g}\cdot°\text{C}}$, what is the percent error?

a. 6.10%
b. 16.4%
c. 6.49%
d. 15.4%

145. Which of the following is NOT true concerning forming and testing hypotheses?

a. A controlled experiment should have only one independent variable.
b. A controlled experiment may have several constants.
c. A good hypothesis should take all of the available background material on the topic into consideration.
d. A good hypothesis will not be disproved by testing.

146. Why would it be ethical for local and state governments to conduct a risk-benefit analysis in making decisions about city planning and development?

a. Governments must know what the benefits of a new development are for people and the economy in order to persuade opponents and the public who are against it.
b. Knowledge of the environmental risks and benefits to humans is required for gaining building permits.
c. The benefits to people and the economy must outweigh the risks to determine whether their decision to build is fair.
d. The benefits to people and the economy can be used to ignore the risks associated with any new development.

147. What laboratory practice can increase the precision of a measurement?

a. Repeating the measurement several times
b. Calibrating the equipment each time you use it
c. Using metric measuring devices
d. Reading the laboratory instructions before the lab

148. In the scientific method, which of the following steps should come first?

a. Formulating a hypothesis
b. Asking a research question
c. Conducting an experiment
d. Reporting support or refutation

149. In the scientific process, which skill do children employ most when they see patterns and meaning in the results of experiments they make?

a. Measurement
b. Classification
c. Inferences
d. Prediction

150. A teacher tells the class about a new drug that is being tested on 200 volunteer subjects. Half the volunteers are given the new drug while the other half are given a harmless sugar pill. The volunteers who are given the sugar pill serve as the:

a. Control group
b. Experimental group
c. Variable
d. Indicator

Answer Key and Explanations for Test #3

Reading and English Language Arts

1. B: This prompt focuses not only on reading fluency skills, but also on the issue of the young reader's confidence. It is very common for students who feel unsuccessful at reading to avoid the skill altogether. The teacher in this question realizes something important: it is vital to build a student's confidence with reading as he or she builds skill. In choice A there is a faulty assumption that a student could ever memorize enough words to eliminate the need to decode. While some students with processing disorders or different learning styles do rely more heavily on sight words, this practice should not be solely relied upon. In choice C the students will likely feel negatively about being asked to read young children's books; their lack of confidence may be reinforced by this plan. In choice D students may also be frustrated by the extra work they are required to do without any evidence of success with this practice. In choice B, students can build their fluency skills by creating words with various sounds, which is often easier for students than decoding as they are learning to read. As their knowledge of letter-sound relationships grows, they will become better at decoding words they see on the page. Allowing students to encode will also provide them with more chances to feel successful as they learn.

2. A: Phonological awareness refers to an understanding of the sounds a word makes. While phonological awareness leads to fluent reading skills, activities designed to develop an awareness of word sounds are, by definition, oral.

3. C: Decoding, fluency, and comprehension are interrelated. The student is likely spending a lot of mental energy trying to decode unknown words, leaving little energy left to focus on comprehension. Additionally, repeatedly stopping to decode words interrupts fluency. This may cause the reader to struggle to make connections between the disjointed words and sentences. Implicit phonics instruction is not the best intervention option, as research has shown that systematic and explicit phonics instruction is most effective. Additionally, there is not enough information available to determine the cause of the student's decoding difficulties. Therefore, it cannot be assumed that it is related to a lack of phonological awareness skills or a language processing disorder.

4. D: When students take away a sound in a word and say what new word they are left with, they are practicing phoneme deletion. Onset and rime manipulation involve breaking or combining a word between the first sound and the remainder of the word. Segmenting involves breaking a word into its individual sounds. Phoneme isolation involves identifying a specific phoneme within a word.

5. C: Phonic awareness, or phonics (A), is knowing how alphabet letters correspond to speech sounds and vice versa. Awareness of phonetics (B) is knowing specific individual variations in speech sounds within a language. Phonemic (C) awareness is knowing the standard, general, or typical speech sounds used in a language. Alphabetic (D) awareness is knowing the written letter symbols representing speech sounds. (The alphabetic principle is the basis of phonics.)

6. B: When students combine the initial sound in a word with the remainder of the word, they are blending the onset and rime. Syllabification involves breaking a word into syllables. A word may have one or more syllables. Phoneme isolation involves identifying either the beginning, middle, or ending sound in a word. Segmentation involves breaking a word into its individual sounds.

7. B: On a continuum, the simplest level of phonological awareness is represented by being able to recognize and produce rhymes in songs, and show understanding that sentences contain individual words by segmenting them (D). Segmenting words into syllables and blending syllables into words (A) represents a more complex level around the middle of the continuum. A higher level of complexity is segmenting words into onsets and rimes and blending onsets and rimes into words (C). The highest level is phonemic awareness, i.e., understanding that words contain individual phonemes and being able to manipulate (blend, segment, delete, substitute) these (B).

8. B: Automaticity refers to the ability to recognize printed words quickly and effortlessly. Because sight word practice helps increase the number of words students can recognize quickly and effortlessly, it builds automaticity. Sight words can be difficult to decode using typical phonics rules. Phonemic awareness and phonological awareness involve identifying and manipulating sounds rather than reading printed words.

9. D: The word *maple* begins with an open syllable, spelled *ma*. Open syllables end with a vowel and usually have a long vowel sound. Knowing this will help the student decode this word and other words with open syllables. This word does not contain any vowel digraph pairs, r-controlled vowels, or closed syllables. Vowel digraph pairs consist of two vowels that together make one sound. R-controlled vowels consist of a vowel before the letter *r*. Closed syllables end with a consonant and usually have a short vowel sound.

10. C: Of the options, teaching main ideas or strategic integration of ideas refer more to reading comprehension than to phonics and decoding. The best option given is choice B, systematic, explicit, and direct instruction in phonics, as phonics is not as much of an acquired language skill as it is a taught language skill. Explicit instruction in early phonics instruction is most effective. As a child becomes more fluent, increased incidental exposure (choice A) can help to improve fluency in decoding skills. Choice D represents a blended activity, using features of both explicit and implicit instruction and should prove effective in helping students understand phonics and decode words.

11. C: Standardized formal assessments are available for testing alphabetic principle knowledge and skills that equal informal assessments for ease and speed of administration (e.g., the Dynamic Indicators of Basic Early Literacy Skills [DIBELS] for grades K-6, including the Nonsense Word Fluency [NWF] and other measures, all administered in about one minute each). Many formal assessments can be administered to individual students. Teachers can inform their instructional planning using results from both formal and informal assessments. Teachers also use informal assessment to analyze the skills of individual students.

12. B: Ms. Walters' plan does not currently include any specific high-frequency word instruction. High-frequency word knowledge can assist with fluency by enabling readers to quickly and automatically recognize words that appear often and may not always be decodable through normal phonetic structures. Phoneme blending is part of phonological awareness, identification of story elements is part of comprehension, and using the alphabetic principle to spell words is part of phonics.

13. B: Reading responses can take various forms. The most common form of reading response is likely to be targeted student writing. Students may use journals, worksheets, or other formats to construct written responses to something they have read. The purpose of this type of assignment can range from fostering an appreciation of written text to helping a student prepare for an activity in class. Students may also engage in creating an oral reading response in the form of a presentation or debate. Ultimately, reading response increases a student's capacity to understand what is read and to analyze personal responses to the text.

14. B: The term "instructional level" refers to the level at which a child can work on building reading fluency without the text being too easy or too difficult. If the child can read approximately 90% of the words without assistance, the text will be considered "instructional level." If the student needs less help, the teacher should move him to a more challenging piece or consider the text to be "independent level" reading. If the piece is too difficult, the level of difficulty should be lowered or extra help should be provided in the areas of difficulty.

15. C: Oral language development serves as a foundation for building early reading comprehension and writing skills; therefore, it is a significant indicator for achievement both in literacy and across content areas. Children with strong oral language skills begin literacy learning with a more expansive vocabulary, a greater understanding of the basic conventions of standard English, and the ability to express themselves more clearly. Encouraging the use of oral language in the early childhood classroom can be achieved by implementing multiple opportunities for children to speak and listen throughout the school day and across the curriculum. This includes reading aloud to students daily; incorporating rhymes, songs, and chants into instruction; facilitating discussion by asking open-ended questions; and promoting student interaction through purposeful play. Further, teachers can provide families with relevant resources, materials, and suggestions to reinforce oral language skill development at home. Doing so will help young children build a rich vocabulary and the skills necessary for successful reading comprehension and writing fluency development.

16. C: Choice C is correct, since the verbs mentioned in the question all refer to interpreting information in one's own words—which involves the cognitive objective of comprehension. Tasks targeting knowledge recall (A) would ask students to name, label, list, define, repeat, memorize, order, or arrange material. Tasks targeting application (B) would ask students to calculate, solve, practice, operate, sketch, use, prepare, illustrate, or apply material. Tasks targeting evaluation (D) would ask students to judge, appraise, evaluate, conclude, predict, score, or compare material.

17. B: In this paired reading strategy, which improves reading comprehension and helps students identify the main idea in informational text, after silently reading a text selection, the pair of students takes turns following these steps: One student paraphrases what he or she thinks the text's main idea is. The other student agrees or disagrees, explaining why. The pair then develops a consensus as to the text's main idea. Then they take turns finding details in the text that support its main idea.

18. A: One self-monitoring strategy to aid reading comprehension is for students to locate the problem by isolating what part of the text they do not understand, which words were difficult, and specifically what did not make sense to them. Another self-monitoring strategy for students is trying to paraphrase the text they had trouble understanding, which often helps. An additional strategy is to review the text for earlier instances of the same topic or information the student finds unclear to see if those shed light on the current instance. Another self-monitoring strategy is to preview the text to see if explanations, elaboration, illustrations or other graphics later in the text might clarify what students are currently reading. Self-monitoring techniques are important tools for those who struggle with reading, and they can be employed at all difficulty levels.

19. A: In (A), the teacher guides previewing of information to show students how to put themselves in the right frame of mind to listen carefully for meaning. Students are then able to listen in a guided way based upon the previewing. By varying the type of comprehension assessment, the teacher will get a better understanding of what the students learned. (B) is a good exercise but does not provide for direct instruction by the teacher or a particularly skilled student. In (C), students are focusing more on reading comprehension than listening since they must read the story to themselves and then write a report. There is then no way to gauge what they have learned. (D) would be useful but does not include teacher-guided previewing, which is very helpful in building comprehension.

20. B: Writing haikus will promote students' vocabularies. The tightly controlled syllabic requirements will cause students to search for words outside their normal vocabularies that will fit the rigid framework and still express the writer's intended meanings. Often, students will rediscover a word whose meaning they know, but they don't often use.

21. C: Having students retell a story that the teacher read with them is an excellent way to make an informal assessment of their comprehension. In Expanded Book Reading, it *is* advisable for teachers to give students summaries (A) or overviews of a book before reading, and it is also useful to ask students to predict what the book might be about (B). Teachers *can* use this method compatibly with integrating literacy across all curriculum (D) subjects, e.g., by planning art, music, math, and science activities using books they and students have read together.

22. B: Response to Intervention (RTI) is a three-tiered model intended to provide students that struggle in a particular content area with additional support. Each tier consists of increasingly intensive services designed to develop students' skills to a grade-appropriate level. Tier-one RTI services are generally applied to all students to promote universal understanding and achievement. Students that continue to have difficulty are typically referred for tier-two RTI services, in which they receive small-group instruction outside the classroom to develop their skills in the given subject area. Tier-three services are directed toward individual students in need of significant support. In this situation, the student likely has not responded to the tier-one interventions applied to the whole class, and therefore would benefit from receiving tier-two RTI services.

23. D: To deepen young children's comprehension of word meanings, teachers should provide them with multiple definitions and examples for each word rather than only one (A). They should introduce new concepts together with new vocabulary words (B) associated with the concepts. They should provide additional information to give children's comprehension of meanings more depth (C).

24. C: Acquisition and comprehension of academic language is a common challenge among young children. Early language development typically occurs in familiar settings, and reflects children's daily interactions and experiences, whereas academic language is content-specific, often more complex in nature, and therefore harder to understand. However, this skill is necessary for literacy development and success in learning across subject areas. In this situation, the teacher implements before-, during-, and after-reading strategies to promote understanding of the academic language students will encounter in the informational text. The teacher contextualizes new vocabulary by providing definitions and examples before students read the text, creating a framework for increased comprehension. By having students complete guided summary frames as they engage with the text, the teacher encourages close reading that promotes students' ability to summarize, and therefore, demonstrate understanding, of what they have read. Additionally, in instructing students to discuss their summaries with a partner, the teacher encourages students to practice using academic language, thus strengthening their comprehension of its meaning.

25. C: Orthographic processing skills are the ability to recognize and recall written words. These skills are necessary for the development of reading and writing fluency, as they are foundational for decoding both familiar and unfamiliar words, as well as using proper spelling and punctuation conventions. Activities to promote orthographic processing skills should include multiple opportunities for students to use and visualize words in written form, such as by tracing and writing sight words and reciting them aloud from a word wall. Such activities help students internalize the spelling, pronunciation, and meaning of new vocabulary, thus building writing and reading comprehension skills.

26. C: While *some* children's reading lacks fluency due to deficits in their word-decoding abilities, this is not *always* (A) the case: some children simply need more reading practice to develop fluency. Children's motivation to read (B) *is* affected by their reading fluency: when reading is laborious, children do not enjoy it and avoid reading; when reading is easy, children enjoy it and want to read. Fluency has much *greater* impact (D) on the performance of students in higher grades, when the volume of reading required of them in school is exponentially greater.

27. B: Before beginning fluency instruction, typically not before halfway through the first grade at the earliest, teachers should ensure that students have strong word recognition skills to provide the necessary foundation. Student speed and automaticity in decoding individual words are directly related to developing reading fluency (A): rapid, automatic word decoding is the precursor to fluent reading. Reading fluency not only indicates faster information processing, it also has a direct impact on comprehension (C) because the faster a student can process information, the better the student can comprehend what she reads. When a student must decode words more slowly and less automatically, both reading fluency and comprehension are decreased (D). Slow, conscious decoding does not increase comprehension by being more careful or thoughtful; instead, laborious student efforts to decode separate words for meaning divert the attention they could devote to overall comprehension if they could decode rapidly, effortlessly, and automatically.

28. D: Self-correction is an important and useful student behavior in reading. Teachers are advised to observe self-corrections during reading fluency screening, but not to mark them as errors. Although self-correction can certainly be incorporated into repeated reading activities, it is not necessarily a repeated reading activity per se. Tape-assisted reading (A) or computer-assisted reading, readers theater (B) activities, and partner reading (C) are all types of repeated reading activities wherein students read the same text repeatedly until they attain fluency.

29. A: Automaticity refers to one's ability to quickly and accurately recognize and comprehend the meaning of written words. This skill is foundational in the development of reading fluency; therefore, it should be practiced and assessed regularly in the early childhood classroom. Doing so is necessary to ensure students are reading at a grade-level appropriate pace, and it allows teachers to identify areas of individual need for additional support. Timing students as they individually read aloud from a grade-level text is an effective method for evaluating automaticity. This strategy allows teachers to determine how many words per minute the student is accurately able to identify and understand, thus providing measurable data specific to this area of reading fluency development.

30. A: The type or pattern of error most damaging to reading proficiency is substituting words with similar appearances or spelling but completely different meanings, because this shows a lack of reading for meaning. Substituting synonyms (B) shows some comprehension of word meaning. Substituting like parts of speech (C) shows some comprehension of grammar and syntax. Substituting correct words or closer approximations for errors based on information from the sentence context (D) shows skills in both reading for meaning and self-correction.

31. D: When students participate in kinesthetic activities, they are physically engaged in the learning process. These activities involve movement, such as hopping along the sight words written in chalk. While the other activities can also be used to practice sight words and may involve tactile experiences, they involve less movement and physical activity than hopping.

32. C: Although the names of the stages vary, readers generally progress through four stages of reading development: emergent reading, early reading, transitional reading, and fluent reading. The name "transitional phase" refers to the transition from having to learn to read to being able to read to learn. The greatest need for students in the transitional phase is to be able to navigate unfamiliar words in passages. To do so, they need to be able to use morphology (C), such as prefixes, suffixes, and parts of speech, to help determine the meaning of newly-encountered words. Students in the transitional stage should already have many sight words memorized (A) and have letter/sound correspondence (D) nearly mastered. Identifying themes in abstract texts (B) is probably beyond the capability of students in the transitional stage.

33. D: Teachers can effectively use conversation with young children to teach them grammar and vocabulary in natural contexts. When a child uses a word incorrectly in conversation, for example, the teacher can recast the word to show its correct usage (e.g. if the child says someone was driven to the hospital "in the siren," the teacher can respond, "They took her to the hospital in an ambulance with the siren sounding?"). When children speak in incomplete sentences, teachers can and should extend them by repeating what the child said in a complete sentence (A). Young children enjoy talking about themselves most (B); about what they are doing; and about familiar people, objects, and events (C) that access their knowledge. Lessons are not better than conversation for teaching grammar and vocabulary, especially for children who are too young to "sit still and listen" and learn better through natural interactions like conversations.

34. C: The demonstration of learning should show whether or not a student met the daily objective. For students working on reading fluency, reading a short passage that is timed will show if they met the daily reading fluency objective. This is designed to be a quick assessment without any assistance from the teacher. Answer A is incorrect because reading a short story and answering questions may not be the best way to assess reading fluency. Answer B is incorrect because listening to a passage does not allow Brady to demonstrate his reading fluency ability. Answer D is incorrect because the demonstration of learning is designed to be an individual activity without assistance.

35. D: In order to measure reading fluency, it is essential to provide a student with a reading passage and record how many words they can read in one minute. This can help to determine how much progress a student has made and what they may still need to work on. Reading fluency is an important skill for a third grader to practice each day by reading passages and developing a clear understanding of words. Answer A is incorrect because identifying letters is a skill that students typically work on before third grade. Answer B is incorrect because although identifying letter sounds can be important, it is not always the best indicator of reading fluency ability. Answer C is incorrect because although reading sight words can help with reading fluency skills, it is not a measure of reading fluency by itself.

36. D: These are all components (d) of reading fluency. When reading aloud, the student has to use appropriate vocal intonations (a), giving expression suitable to the material to meet the definition of fluency. Whether reading aloud or silently, the student's reading should seem effortless (b) to be fluent. Students who read fast but make errors are not fluent readers, as decoding words accurately (c) must accompany speed to be considered fluent reading.

37. B: When teachers assign cooperative writing partnerships, each student in a pair should not always take only one role (A); they must both take turns writing and reviewing their partner's writing (B) to experience both roles in the process. Each student should provide not only positive feedback (C) or only constructive feedback (D) to a partner, but both. For example, if the assignment is using descriptive adjectives, positive feedback would be identifying specific descriptive adjectives the partner used; constructive feedback could be identifying sentences that could use more descriptive adjectives.

38. D: Research studies have shown that setting specific goals for writing promotes student motivation and sense of accomplishment. Developing student writing goals should not be a responsibility confined either to teachers or students: both teachers and students may develop writing goals, such as including more ideas within one paper, or incorporating specific elements of certain genres in compositions. Teachers and students may develop goals individually, in collaboration, or both: students together, teachers together, and students with teachers—including individual students, student groups, individual teachers, and team/co-teachers.

39. B: Studies show that cooperative learning is an effective practice for teaching many things, including writing (A). Experts recommend that when assigning cooperative writing partners or groups, teachers provide students with both a structure (C), and explicit expectations (D) for both partnership/group and individual performance.

40. C: According to experts, research shows that teachers should explicitly teach their students writing strategies, including prewriting planning, composition, revision, and editing, by first modeling the strategies; then guiding students in practicing them; and then, once they have learned the strategies, letting students practice using them independently. They should not skip the guided practice step (A); students need assistance learning to apply demonstrated strategies before practicing on their own. Students learn better with, not without, teacher models (B), which must be presented before, not after, guided practice (D).

41. A: Research into writing instruction has led to specific findings on the effectiveness of certain techniques. Teacher modeling and think-alouds have been found effective, so choice A is correct. Providing students with temporary support (i.e., scaffolding) that can be gradually removed as their skills grow has not been shown to slow learning, so choice B is incorrect. Merely exposing students to writing processes has been found to be insufficient in teaching writing, so choice C is incorrect. Finally, explicit instruction has been found to be more effective than implicit or embedded instruction, so choice D is incorrect.

42. C: This sentence contains the grammatical error of a misplaced modifier. The modifying phrase "a great animal lover" does NOT modify "his pets" but *him* (e.g., "A great animal lover, *he had* pets including...."). Choice A contains a spelling error: *friend* is misspelled. A common student error is to transpose vowel combinations like this. Choice B has a punctuation error: these two independent clauses should be separated by a semicolon, not a comma. (In this example, a colon would also be acceptable, but not a comma, which creates a run-on sentence.) Choice D has a capitalization error: *South* and *West* are only capitalized when used as names, e.g., "the wild West" or "the sunny South," but when used as directions, they are lowercase.

43. C: It is most appropriate for students to write using more casual language on their own age level when writing for classmates. This applies whether they are writing narrative, argumentation, exposition, or speculation. When students want to share a particular experience with their readers (A), they should write using descriptive form, rather than persuasive or explanatory form, for example. Age/reading level will be determined by the audience. When students want permission for a desired activity (B), they should write using persuasive form, with mature, serious diction and more sophisticated vocabulary to appeal to parents. To write a story that younger children can read (D), they should write in narrative form, using simpler vocabulary and sentence structure; shorter sentences; more vivid, entertaining word choices; a lighter tone; and humor when appropriate.

44. D: Choice D is correct because quotes that are integrated into the text of a paper should read in a way that flows with the other writing in that sentence or paragraph. The other choices are incorrect because they refer to practices that should be avoided when writing research papers. The important points of a research paper should be the writer's original ideas. Therefore, they should be made in the writer's own words (A). Long quotations tend to include information that is not relevant, in which case it would be better to paraphrase (B). Discussion of sources should not inhibit or replace discussion of the original ideas in the research paper. Sources are only necessary insofar as they prove the writer's point; they themselves cannot be the writer's point (C).

45. C: Helping young children understand that communication can occur in different ways, including both verbally and nonverbally, is an important component of developing their speaking and listening skills. Verbal communication refers to spoken language, volume, and intonation, whereas nonverbal communication includes such elements as eye contact, gestures, physical distance, and body language. Incorporating both forms of communication into the classroom for different purposes helps students learn to listen and respond appropriately in a variety of contexts. Further, this strategy supports students' oral language development, as accompanying verbal communication with nonverbal cues strengthens their understanding of its meaning.

46. C: The passage discusses how the Industrial Revolution brought significant changes to society that reshaped the world in profound ways. Artists and writers responded to these changes by capturing the human experience during this period. *Upheaval* accurately reflects the tumultuous and transformative nature of the Industrial Revolution. It implies a state of disruption, change, and instability, which aligns with the context described in the passage.

47. C: In choices "a" and "b," students are primarily using written language in order to present to the class. They are required to use what they have composed as the text for their oral presentations. In Choice "c", students have the chance to learn how to prioritize information they have read and written, and also learn to modify the written word to create an oral presentation based upon specific parameters. This exercise highlights the differences between the written and spoken word. Choice "d" does not necessarily involve all of the students and less directly increases the students' oral skills in a relevant way.

48. B: Folk tales are stories that have been passed down orally through generations and typically contain a kind of moral or lesson. Folk tales are most appropriate in this case because they are so influenced and bear a strong relationship to oral traditions across all cultures that could be present in the classroom. This genre provides many opportunities not only to read aloud but also to discuss the importance of oral language in learning lessons about culture and behavior.

History and Social Science

49. C: A caste system is a system wherein individuals' social, economic, and political destinies are determined by group membership within the caste. Systems fitting this description have been in place throughout the world and directly impact each individual's economic destiny by circumscribing upward economic and social mobility regardless of ability. Class and caste are distinct in the sense that class is assigned based upon an individual's life path, while caste membership is assigned at birth and is essentially immutable. Also, caste systems have well-defined functions for each group, whereas class distinctions are based solely on wealth (as opposed to social function).

50. D: Proponents of legislating greater societal income equity support imposing a progressive income tax, which taxes the wealthy at a higher rate; an inheritance tax, which prevents the wealthy from passing all their wealth on to the next generation; and a gift tax, which prevents the wealthy from simply giving their wealth away.

51. D: When the FOMC sells bonds, they raise interest rates. This draws money out of the American economy, and attracts foreign investors. This causes the value of the American dollar to rise overseas, which makes American goods more expensive to overseas buyers and causes American exports to drop.

52. A: As people have more and more of something, they value it less and less. This is the law of diminishing marginal utility, and it is what causes the downward slope of the demand curve.

53. B: In order to prosper, a nation should not try to increase its imports. Mercantilism is an economic theory including the idea that prosperity comes from a positive balance of international trade. For any one nation to prosper, that nation should increase its exports but decrease its imports. Exporting more to other countries while importing less from them will give a country a positive trade balance. This theory assumes that money and wealth are identical assets of a nation. In addition, this theory also assumes that the volume of global trade is an unchangeable quantity. Mercantilism dictates that a nation's government should apply a policy of economic protectionism by stimulating more exports and suppressing imports. Some ways to accomplish this task have included granting subsidies for exports and imposing tariffs on imports. Mercantilism can be regarded as essentially the opposite of the free trade policies that have been encouraged in more recent years.

54. C: One geographical concept is distance. For example, product prices are affected by the cost of transportation, which in turn is affected by how far away raw materials are from the factories that process them, and prices for land closer to highways are higher than for land farther away from them. Location is another geography concept. Absolute location is determined by a place's latitude and longitude, not land prices (A). Relative location is determined by a region's changing characteristics, which surrounding areas can influence; one example is that land costs more in urban than rural areas. Relative location is not determined by latitude and longitude (B). Achievability is related to the accessibility of a geographical area; for example, villages with surrounding forests or swamps are less accessible than those on beaches. The dependency of an area, and hence its achievability, *does* change (D) as its technology, transportation, and economy change.

55. C: Brazil is the 10th largest producer of oil in the world and the largest in South America. Venezuela is the second largest producer of oil in South America and has the world's largest oil reserves. Bolivia and Guatemala produce oil but are not major producers in Latin America. Uruguay has no significant petroleum production.

56. D: A flow-line map describes the movement of people, trends, or materials across a physical area. The movements depicted on a flow-line map are typically represented by arrows. In more advanced flow-line maps, the width of the arrow corresponds to the quantity of the motion. Flow-line maps usually declare the span of time that is being represented. A political map depicts the man-made aspects of geography, such as borders and cities. A cartogram adjusts the size of the areas represented according to some variable. For instance, a cartogram of wheat production would depict Iowa as being much larger than Alaska. A qualitative map uses lines, dots, and other symbols to illustrate a particular point. For example, a qualitative map might be used to demonstrate the greatest expansion of the Persian Empire.

57. C: Physical geography focuses on processes and patterns in the natural environment. What people eat in any given geographic region is largely dependent on such environmental factors as climate and the availability of arable land. Religion, family, and language may all be affected by geographical factors, but they are not as immediately affected as dietary preferences.

58. D: All of the available answer choices are geographically parts of Southeast Asia. The countries of Myanmar (Burma), Laos, Cambodia, and Thailand are considered Mainland Southeast Asia, as are Vietnam and the Malay Peninsula. Brunei, East Malaysia, Indonesia, and the Philippines are considered Maritime Southeast Asia, as are Singapore and Timor-Leste. The Seven Sister States of India are also considered to be part of Southeast Asia, geographically and culturally. (The Seven Sister States of India are Arunachal Pradesh, Assam, Nagaland, Meghalaya, Manipur, Tripura, and Mizoram, which all have contiguous borders in northeastern India.)

59. D: The Bill of Rights was drafted by Congress to limit the authority of the government and protect the rights of individual citizens from abuse by the federal government. It was the first document to detail the rights of private citizens.

60. C: George Washington served 2 four-year terms as president. This interval of time was not specified in the Constitution, but future presidents followed suit (until FDR).

61. D: According to Article III of the Constitution, Justices of the Supreme Court, judges of the courts of appeals and district courts, and judges of the Court of International Trade are appointed by the president with the confirmation of the Senate. The judicial branch of the government is the only one not elected by the people.

62. B: Congress has the authority to shape the judicial branch. The Supreme Court once operated with only six members. Nine has been the standard number since 1869.

63. A: Anyone may write a bill, but only a member of Congress can introduce a bill. The President often suggests bills. Bills can change drastically throughout the review process.

64. D: The vice president also serves as the president of the Senate. If a tie occurs in the Senate, the vice president casts his vote to break the tie.

65. D: Teachers can use not only history books (A); they can also assign students to read well-constructed and well-written biographies (B) of famous figures in history and works of historical literature (C), which set even fictionalized stories within real historical periods and events. Historical narratives written in "storytelling" style are also good for engaging student attention while establishing chronological sequences in history.

66. C: The cycle of demographic transition is best illustrated by a line graph. Demographic transition is a phenomenon in which a region's growth rate increases rapidly, peaks, and then decreases slowly over a long time. In the early phase of a region's development, both the birth and death rates are high, which can cause the population to fluctuate. As the people of the region become settled, the growth rate calms down, and the region enters a period of rapid increase. Political maps are better at depicting borders and the locations of cities, while pie charts are better at representing proportions. Flow-line maps are good for illustrating the movement of people, goods, or trends across a physical area.

67. C: The graph shows a shift in demand, with a corresponding increase in the price of SuperCell Batteries. The shift is illustrated by the two demand curves, with Demand 2 curve illustrating an increase in price. Because the price has increased, not decreased, this eliminates option A. The equilibrium point is the point at which the quantity demanded equals the quantity supplied. The graph shows two equilibrium points, the first where Demand 1 meets the supply curve, and the second where Demand 2 meets the supply curve. Because equilibrium has shifted, option B can be eliminated. Regarding option D, a double coincidence of wants occurs when two people each have a good or service the other wants, giving rise to the possibility of trade (without money). The graph does not illustrate anything regarding a double coincidence of wants, so option D can be rejected on that basis.

68. D: Indentured servants agreed to work for a set period of time in exchange for transportation to the New World and such basic necessities as food and shelter. They did not receive wages and were generally not highly-educated people. Employers often viewed indentured servants with scorn and treated them as harshly as they treated slaves.

69. D: Because the Puritans took on a Reformed theology, they were in this sense Calvinists. However, many Puritans endorsed radical views that criticized such Calvinists as John (Jean) Calvin and Huldrych (Ulrich) Zwingli in Switzerland. Not only were Puritans critical of Calvinists despite their mutual Reformed approaches, reciprocally many Calvinists were opposed to the Puritans as well. The Puritan movement changed less in American colonies than in England during the 1660s. Following the Restoration (1660) and the Uniformity Act (1662) in England, nearly all of the Puritan clergy objected and left the Church of England, thereby creating a dramatic change in the movement in that country. Nevertheless, in America, the Puritans who had emigrated from England continued their original Puritan traditions for a longer time, as they had neither the same Anglican Church as in England nor the legislation restoring earlier church status against which the English Puritans had reacted.

70. B: Growth of industry was concentrated in urban areas, which cyclically drew laborers into cities, growing the population of cities and increasing efficiency and quality in industry.

71. B: The Trail of Tears was the forcible removal of Native American tribes from their homes in the Southeastern US to Oklahoma. The name came due to the high number of Native Americans who died on the journey.

72. A: James Madison, John Jay, and Alexander Hamilton published *The Federalist* in the *Independent Journal* and other publications in New York. It was a response to the Anti-Federalists in New York, who were slow to ratify the Constitution because they feared it gave the central government too much authority.

73. A: Fascism was not opposed to nationalism and patriotism. Fascism was a radical political movement that was nationalistic in character. In fact, Fascism opposed Marxism (B) because Fascists saw Marxism as anti-nationalist and anti-patriotic. Fascism was both collectivist and saw itself as patriotic. Fascists were also against the bourgeoisie (B) for their individualism, which was the opposite of collectivism. Fascism did purport to be an alternative to Bolshevism (C). Nonetheless, despite this, the Fascist movement did have several things in common with Bolshevism (D). For example, both political movements believed in a single-party state, in appealing to the proletariat, and in the ruling over the masses by an elite group.

74. D: Increases in population growth supplied additional labor forces, helping to enable the Industrial Revolution. These increases were due to the prosperity brought through Europe's Commercial Revolution, which preceded the Industrial Revolution. The rediscovery of concrete, new advances in iron making, and the invention of the steam engine are all examples of developments that occurred during the Industrial Revolution.

75. A: In the 1780s, the French national debt was very high. The French nobility adamantly resisted attempts by King Louis XVI to reform tax laws, which led to a high tax burden on the French peasantry. The French government spent almost 50% of its national expenditures on debt-related payments during the 1780s; thus, it could not and did not spend almost 70% to finance luxuries for the French nobility. This eliminates choice B. King Louis XVI temporarily banned the guild system to bolster, rather than stifle, free trade. Because this system gave skilled craftsmen economic advantages, journeymen opposed ending the system. This eliminates choice D. Regardless of the status of guilds before the French Revolution, French society did not offer many opportunities for upward social mobility. Few peasants were able to advance. This eliminates choice C.

76. B: As production shifted to factories, a large number of unskilled workers were needed to operate the machinery that was beginning to put many skilled craftsmen out of work. As farms grew larger and increasingly mechanized, the number of people who owned their own farm began to decrease. The rural population declined as people flocked to the cities in search of employment.

77. A: The Industrial Revolution did create a new working class composed of professionals like doctors and lawyers, industrialists, and businessmen. Formerly, Europe was dominated by royalty and landed gentry over the poor working class. Industrialization allowed many ordinary people to start and run businesses. It did NOT, however, improve working conditions in the 18th and early 19th centuries, but the opposite occurred: Big factories with machines made conditions more dangerous, and child labor caused many deaths, injuries, illnesses, and so on. Women and children were only banned from working in mines in the mid-19th century; housing and work conditions only improved in the late 19th century. Urbanization was the result of industrialization and not vice versa: Mechanization allowed factory construction, and people moved to cities for jobs. Labor unions developed out of the Industrial Revolution, not vice versa, to establish and defend factory workers' rights.

78. C: The Ottoman Empire joined with the Central Powers in 1914 during World War I. The original Triple Alliance was formed by Austria-Hungary, Germany, and Italy in 1882 and renewed in 1902. The Ottoman Empire signed the Turco-German Alliance in August 1914, joining with the Central Powers. In October 1914, with the bombing of Russian ports on the Black Sea, Turkey formally entered World War I. The Allied Powers of the Triple Entente (Great Britain, France, and Russia) declared war on the Ottoman Empire in November 1914.

Mathematics

79. C: Aaron ran four miles from home and then back again, so he ran a total of eight miles. Therefore, statement III is false. Statements I and II, however, are both true. Since Aaron ran eight miles in eighty minutes, he ran an average of 1 mile every 10 minutes, or 6 miles every 60 minutes, which is 6 mph. He ran two miles from point (A) to (B) in 20 minutes, which is a rate of 1 mile per 10 minutes, and four miles from (D) to (E) in 40 minutes, which is also a rate of 1 mile per 10 minutes, so his running speed between both sets of points was the same.

80. C: His monthly salary may be modeled as $\frac{1}{8}x = 320$. Multiplying both sides of the equation by 8 gives $x = 2{,}560$.

81. B: The equation $y = -4x - 6$ is in slope-intercept form, $y = mx + b$, where m is the slope and b is the y-intercept. All four graphs show the correct y-intercept, −6, but only one shows the correct slope, −4. The slope of a line can be found by picking any two points (x_1, y_1) and (x_2, y_2) on the line and calculating $m = \frac{y_2 - y_1}{x_2 - x_1}$. For choice B, we can choose points $(0, -6)$ and $(-2,2)$, which gives us $m = \frac{2-(-6)}{-2-0} = -4$. None of the other graphs have a slope of –4.

82. B: The equation $y + 3 = 7$ is solved by subtracting 3 from both sides to yield $y = 4$. Substituting $y = 4$ into $x - 1 = y$ yields $x - 1 = 4$. Adding 1 to both sides of this equation yields $x = 5$.

83. D: All four answer choices are linear equations in slope-intercept form, $y = mx + b$, where m is the jogger's rate (slope) and b is the jogger's distance from his front door at the beginning of his run (y-intercept). To find the rate, choose any two times (e.g., $x = 0$ and $x = 3$) and divide the change in distance by the change in time: $m = \frac{25.0-5.2}{3-0} = \frac{19.8}{3} = 6.6$. Therefore, the rate is 6.6 meters per second. The starting distance from the door is the distance at $x = 0$, which is $b = 5.2$ meters. The linear equation that represents this situation is $y = 6.6x + 5.2$.

84. B: Rate in miles per hour can be expressed as, mph $= \frac{\text{distance in miles}}{\text{time in hours}}$. So, Zeke's driving speed on the way to Atlanta and home from Atlanta in mph can be expressed as $\frac{d}{3}$ and $\frac{d}{2}$, respectively, where d is the distance between Zeke's house and his destination. Since Zeke drove 20 mph faster on his way home, (speed home) − (speed to store) = 20. Substitute Zeke's speeds and solve for d.

$$\frac{d}{2} - \frac{d}{3} = 20$$

$$\begin{aligned} 6\left(\frac{d}{2} - \frac{d}{3} = 20\right) \\ 3d - 2d = 120 \\ d = 120 \end{aligned}$$

Since the distance between Zeke's house and the store in Atlanta is 120 miles, Zeke drove a total distance of 240 miles in five hours. Therefore, his average speed was $\frac{240 \text{ miles}}{5 \text{ hours}} = 48$ mph.

85. B: The vertex form of a quadratic equation is $y = a(x - h)^2 + k$, where $x = h$ is the parabola's axis of symmetry and (h, k) is the parabola's vertex. The vertex of the graph is $(1,2)$, so the equation can be written as $y = a(x - 1)^2 + 2$. The parabola passes through the point $(0,1)$, so $1 = a(0 - 1)^2 + 2$. Solve for a:

$$\begin{aligned} 1 &= a(0 - 1)^2 + 2 \\ 1 &= a + 2 \\ -1 &= a \end{aligned}$$

So, the vertex form of the parabola is $y = -(x-1)^2 + 2$. Write the equation in standard form: $y = ax^2 + bx + c$.

$$y = -(x-1)^2 + 2$$
$$y = -(x-1)(x-1) + 2$$
$$y = -(x^2 - 2x + 1) + 2$$
$$y = -x^2 + 2x - 1 + 2$$
$$y = -x^2 + 2x + 1$$

86. A: The situation may be modeled by the inequality $3x + 2y \geq 20$. Isolating the y-term gives $2y \geq -3x + 20$. Solving for y gives $y \geq -\frac{3}{2}x + 10$. Thus, the y-intercept will be 10, the line will be solid, the slope will be $-\frac{3}{2}$, and the shading should occur above the line because y is greater than or equal to the expression on the other side of the inequality.

87. C: Substitute 2 for each x and simplify.

$$f(2) = \frac{(2)^3 - 2(2) + 1}{3(2)} = \frac{8 - 4 + 1}{6} = \frac{5}{6}$$

88. B: All regular polygons have rotational symmetry. The angle of rotation is the smallest angle by which the polygon can be rotated such that it maps onto itself; any multiple of this angle will also map the polygon onto itself. The angle of rotation for a regular polygon is the angle formed between two lines drawn from consecutive vertices to the center of the polygon. Since the vertices of a regular polygon lie on a circle, for a regular polygon with n sides, the angle of rotation measures $\frac{360°}{n}$. Therefore, a square has rotational symmetry about the angle 90° and its multiples. A regular hexagon has rotational symmetry about the angle 60° and its multiples. A regular octagon has rotational symmetry about 45° and its multiples. And a regular decagon has rotational symmetry about 36° and its multiples. Since 120° is a multiple of 60°, the correct answer is a regular hexagon.

89. A: A hexagon has six sides. A hexagonal prism has 8 faces consisting of two hexagonal bases and six rectangular lateral faces. This results in 18 edges and 12 vertices. Therefore, the correct choice is A.

90. C: The center of the sphere is shared by the center of the cube, and each of the corners of the cube touches the surface of the sphere. Therefore, the diameter of the sphere is the line that passes through the center of the cube and connects one corner of the cube to the opposite corner. In the illustration below, notice that the diameter d of the sphere can be represented as the hypotenuse of a right triangle with a short leg measuring 4 units. (Since the volume of the cube is 64 cubic units, each of its sides measures $\sqrt[3]{64} = 4$ units.) The long leg of the triangle is the diagonal of the base of the cube.

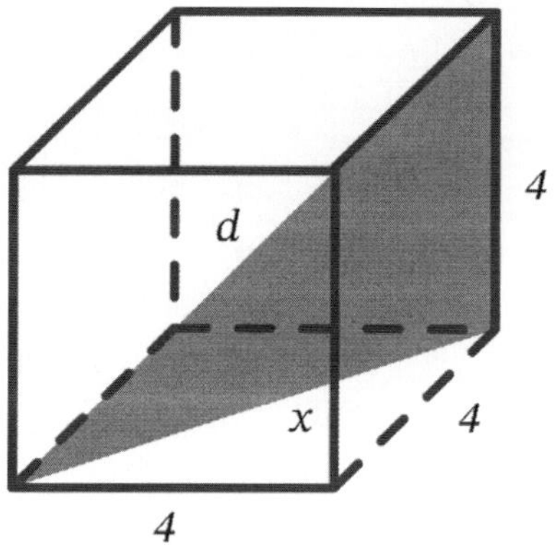

The length of the long leg can be found using the Pythagorean theorem:

$$x^2 = 4^2 + 4^2 = 32$$
$$x = \sqrt{32} = 4\sqrt{2}$$

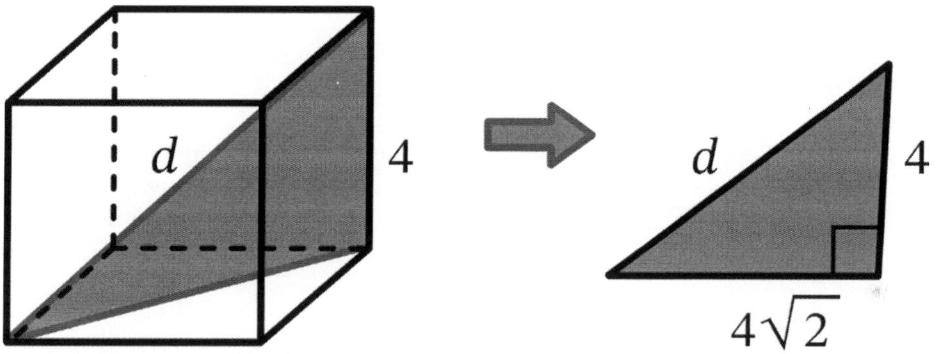

Use the Pythagorean theorem again to find d, the diameter of the sphere:

$$d^2 = \left(4\sqrt{2}\right)^2 + 4^2 = 32 + 16 = 48$$
$$d = \sqrt{48} = 4\sqrt{3}$$

To find the volume of the sphere, use the formula $V = \frac{4}{3}\pi r^3$. Since the radius r of the sphere is half the diameter, $r = 2\sqrt{3}$, and $V = \frac{4}{3}\pi(2\sqrt{3})^3 = \frac{4}{3}\pi\left(24\sqrt{3}\right) = 32\pi\sqrt{3}$ cubic units.

91. C: The volume of a cylinder may be calculated using the formula $V = \pi r^2 h$, where r represents the radius of the circular base and h represents the height of the cylinder. Substituting 3.14 for π, 1.5 for r, and 3 for h gives $V = (3.14)(1.5)^2(3) = 21.195$, which rounds to 21.2. Therefore, the volume of the can is approximately 21.2 in^3.

92. C: The surface area of a sphere may be calculated using the formula $SA = 4\pi r^2$. Substituting 9 for r and 3.14 for π gives $SA = 4(3.14)(9)^2$, which simplifies to $SA = 1{,}017.36$. So, the surface area of the ball is approximately 1,017.36 square inches. There are twelve inches in a foot, so there are $12^2 = 144$ square inches in a square foot. In order to convert this measurement to square feet, the following proportion may be written and solved for x: $\frac{1}{144} = \frac{x}{1{,}017.36}$. So $x = 7.07$. He needs approximately 7.07 square feet of wrapping paper.

93. B: Since the figures are similar, the following proportion may be written and solved for x.

$$\frac{6}{4} = \frac{8}{x}$$
$$6x = 4 \times 8$$
$$6x = 32$$
$$x = \frac{32}{6} = 5\frac{2}{6} = 5\frac{1}{3}$$

Therefore, the measure of x is $5\frac{1}{3}$ in.

94. A: This may be solved in a few different ways, each of which involves calculating the area of two rectangular sections whose areas can be calculated directly. The area of the "L" can be split into two pieces: a 300 ft by 50 ft section and a 50 ft by 50 ft section, or, secondarily, a 250 ft by 50 ft section and a 100 ft by 50 ft section. In either case, the areas can be calculated directly and then summed. The alternative is to view the "L" as a larger rectangle that has had a smaller rectangle removed from it. In this method, the large rectangle is a 300 ft by 100 ft section, and the smaller rectangle is a 250 ft by 50 ft section. These areas can be calculated and the smaller subtracted from the larger. In both methods, the area comes out to 17,500 square feet.

95. C: A reflection across the x-axis will result in a triangle with vertices at $(2, -3)$, $(4, -7)$, and $(6, -3)$. A rotation of 270 degrees counterclockwise is denoted by the following: $(x, y) \rightarrow (y, -x)$. Thus, a rotation of the reflected triangle by 270 degrees will result in a figure with vertices at $(-3, -2)$, $(-7, -4)$, and $(-3, -6)$. The transformed triangle indeed has these coordinates as its vertices.

96. B: Two of the angles, and one side not included between the angles, are congruent to the corresponding angles and side of the other triangle. Thus, the AAS (angle-angle-side) theorem may be used to prove the congruence of the triangles.

97. B: Deductive reasoning moves from one or more general statements to a specific, while inductive reasoning makes a general conclusion based on a series of specific instances or observations. Whenever the premises used in deductive reasoning are true, the conclusion drawn is necessarily true. In inductive reasoning, it is possible for the premises to be true and the conclusion to be false since there may exist an exception to the general conclusion drawn from the observations made.

98. D: This sequence lists the sum of the squares of natural numbers and 1. For example, $1^2 + 1$ is 2, and $2^2 + 1$ is 5. The next number in the sequence can be determined squaring 5 and adding 1, $5^2 + 1$, which is 26. Note also that the differences between consecutive numbers in the sequence are consecutive odd integers starting at 3. For example, $2 + 3$ is 5, $5 + 5$ is 10, and $10 + 7$ is 17, so the next number in the sequence is $17 + 9$, or 26.

99. B: When adults ask children questions, give them time to think, and then attend to their answers, they help children learn to reason. Rather than analyzing and explaining children's own thought processes to them (A), adults do better allowing children to analyze their own thinking and then explain it. Children have this ability; encouraging them to use it gives them practice, developing their reasoning skills. They need these to understand and apply early math and science concepts, and to negotiate everyday life. Rather than tell children why something is a certain way and discussing it with them (C), adults should ask children why without expecting particular answers. This allows children to think for themselves; adults should listen to their ideas. Adults should encourage children to use logic to classify things rather than doing it for them (D). While occasional examples can help get struggling children started, it is generally better if adults invite children to use their existing logical abilities.

100. B: Frances correctly implements the long division strategy to solve the problem. However, she does not include the remainder in her answer, which results in an incomplete answer. The remainder of 2 needs to be included in the final answer. This was Frances' only error. Based on the work provided, she is very close to mastery.

101. D: The model that Julie constructed consists of 2 groups of 1,000, 4 groups of 100, and 6 groups of 10. This combines to 2,460, which is not equivalent to 246. Julie needs to adjust her model so that it includes 2 groups of 100, 4 groups of 10, and 6 groups of one.

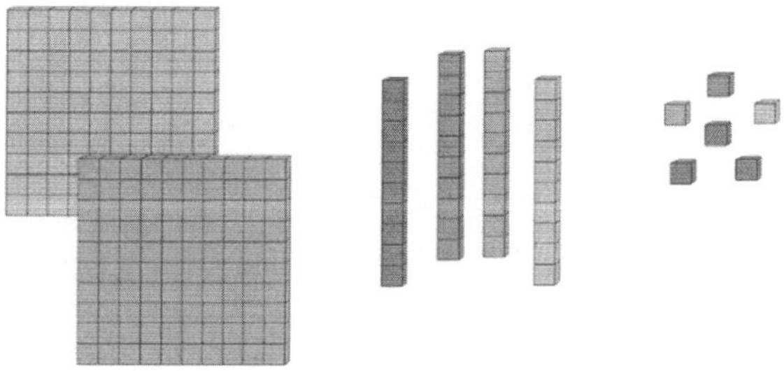

102. D: The strategy of "Keep, Change, Flip" is commonly used for division of fractions. The process involves keeping the first fraction in its original form, changing the division symbol to a multiplication symbol, and flipping the second fraction to its reciprocal. The student has "flipped" the first fraction instead of the second fraction, which is the error that derails the process.

103. D: Dayna has set up the model correctly, and most of the work is correct. However, an error occurs regarding a misunderstanding of how to interpret the answer within the model. Dayna assumes that the numbers inside the model represent the final answer. However, the answer is located above the model. Dayna knows to calculate the sum of three numbers, but the wrong three numbers were used. Choice D best describes this error.

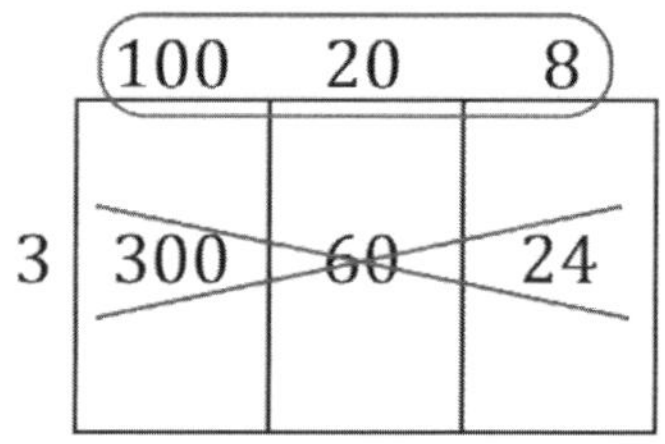

104. B: Amelia underestimated how many more cubes she would need to fill an area when provided with a change in dimension. Choice C would also be correct if it referred to the distributive property rather than the commutative property of multiplication Amelia could have chosen the correct number of cubes if she understood that $10(15) = 10(10) + 10(5)$.

105. A: The repeating decimal may be converted to a fraction by writing:

$$\begin{array}{r} 10x = 7.\overline{7} \\ - \quad x = 0.\overline{7} \\ \hline \end{array}$$

which simplifies as $10x - x = 7.\overline{7} - 0.\overline{7}$, or $9x = 7.\overline{7} - 0.\overline{7}$.

106. A: The amount to be administered may be written as $\frac{1}{12} \times \frac{34}{10}$, which equals $\frac{17}{60}$. Thus, she should administer $\frac{17}{60}$ fluid ounces of medicine.

107. D: The original cost may be represented by the equation $45 = x - 0.25x$ or $45 = 0.75x$. Dividing both sides of the equation by 0.75 gives $x = 60$.

108. C: The decimal expansion of an irrational number does not terminate or repeat. The number π is considered irrational because it does not terminate or repeat.

109. D: The commutative property states that the order in which numbers are added does not change the answer.

110. B: Use the order of operations to find the value for this expression. The order of operations is: parentheses, exponents, multiplication and division, addition and subtraction.

$$\begin{aligned} &-3 \times 5^2 + 2(4 - 18) + 33 \\ &= -3 \times 5^2 + 2(-14) + 33 \\ &= -3 \times 25 + 2(-14) + 33 \\ &= -75 + (-28) + 33 \\ &= -70 \end{aligned}$$

The value of the expression is –70.

111. D: The 8 is in the tenths place, the 6 in the hundredths place, and the 7 in the thousandths place. Thus, 0.867 is equal to the sum of the product of 8 and $\frac{1}{10}$, the product of 6 and $\frac{1}{100}$, and the product of 7 and $\frac{1}{1{,}000}$.

112. B: The amount she spends on rent and utilities is equal to 0.38($40,000), or $15,200, which is approximately $15,000.

113. D: Let $P(B)$ represent the probability of choosing a bowl, and let $P(CS)$ represent the probability of choosing chicken soup. Then $P(B \text{ or } CS) = P(B) + P(CS) - P(B \text{ and } CS)$. Substituting values from the table, we find: $P(B \text{ or } CS) = \frac{1{,}233}{1{,}810} + \frac{971}{1{,}810} - \frac{642}{1{,}810} = \frac{1{,}562}{1{,}810} = 0.8629834254 \ldots \approx 85\%$.

114. C: In Class 1, 27 students submitted late work, so the median is between the 13th and 14th piece of homework. Both the 13th and 14th fall on Day 4, so the median for Class 1 is 4. In Class 2, 23 students submitted late work, so the median is at the 12th piece of homework. This falls on Day 7.

So, because $7 - 4 = 3$, the median number of days late in Class 1 is 3 less than the median number of days late in Class 2.

To find the mean late time for each class, find the sum of the late times and divide by the number of students turning in late work in each class. If the frequency of a one-day late time is 4, the number 1 is added four times (1×4), if frequency of a two-day late time is 5, the number 2 is added five times (2×5), and so on. So, to find the average turn-in time, divide the sum of the products of each late time and its corresponding frequency by the number of late turn-ins in each class. For Class 1, the mean late time is 5.22 days, which rounds to approximately 5 days.

$$\text{Mean} = \frac{4(1) + 5(2) + 3(3) + 2(4) + 3(5) + 1(6) + 1(7) + 2(9) + 4(10) + 2(12)}{4 + 5 + 3 + 2 + 3 + 1 + 1 + 2 + 4 + 2} = \frac{141}{27} \approx 5.22$$

For Class 2, the mean late time is 6.57, which rounds to approximately 7 days.

$$\text{Mean} = \frac{1(1) + 2(2) + 2(3) + 1(4) + 4(6) + 5(7) + 3(8) + 1(9) + 2(10) + 2(12)}{1 + 2 + 2 + 1 + 4 + 5 + 3 + 1 + 2 + 2} = \frac{151}{23} \approx 6.57$$

So, because $7 - 5 = 2$, the students in Class 2 turned in work 2 days later than in Class 1.

The mode late time is the date for which the frequency is the highest. For Class 1, the mode late time is 2 days, and for Class 2, the mode late time is 7 days.

The median late time for Class 1 is 4 and the mean is 4.96, so the median late time is less than the mean.

115. B: This is a counting problem. The number of possible selections equals the product of the possibilities for each category: $6 \times 12 \times 1 = 72$. There are 72 ways for Mark to fill his backpack.

116. B: Determine the probability of each choice.

For choice A, this is the total number of students in the broccoli circle of the Venn diagram divided by the total number of students surveyed:

$$\frac{10 + 4 + 3 + 15}{90} = \frac{32}{90} \approx 35.6\%$$

For choice B, this is the total number of students in the carrots circle and also in at least one other circle divided by the total number in the carrots circle:

$$\frac{15 + 3 + 6}{15 + 3 + 6 + 27} = \frac{24}{51} \approx 47.1\%$$

For choice C, this is the number of students in the intersection of all three circles divided by the total number in the overlap of the broccoli and cauliflower circles:

$$\frac{3}{3 + 4} = \frac{3}{7} \approx 42.9\%$$

For choice D, this is the number of students outside of all the circles divided by the total number of students surveyed:

$$\frac{23}{90} \approx 25.6\%$$

Since choice B has the highest percentage, it is the choice that is most probable.

117. D: Let $P(T)$ represent the probability of getting tails on the coin toss. We can see that $P(T) = \frac{1}{2}$. Let $P(P)$ be the chance of getting a prime number on the die. Of the possible outcomes (1 through 6), three are prime (2, 3, and 5), so $P(P) = \frac{3}{6} = \frac{1}{2}$.

Since $P(P)$ and $P(T)$ are not mutually exclusive, $P(P \text{ or } T) = P(P) + P(T) - P(P \text{ and } T)$. Because the events are independent, $P(P \text{ and } T) = P(P) \times P(T)$. Substituting the probability of each event gives $P(P \text{ or } T) = \frac{1}{2} + \frac{1}{2} - \left(\frac{1}{2} \times \frac{1}{2}\right) = \frac{1}{2} + \frac{1}{2} - \frac{1}{4} = \frac{3}{4}$.

118. B: The points may be entered into a graphing calculator to find the least-squares regression line. This line is approximately $y = -0.044x + 15.59$. Substituting 250 for x gives $y = -0.044(250) + 15.59 = 4.59$. Thus, 4.5 gallons is a good estimate for the amount of gas that will be left after 250 miles.

Alternatively, if you visually predict a line of best fit using any two points, for example, the points (25,14.2) and (100,11), the slope between those points is approximately –0.043, and the line passes through the y-axis around $y = 15$. Using slope-intercept form ($y = mx + b$, where m is the slope and b is the y-intercept), we get the equation $y = -0.043x + 15$. At $x = 250$ we get $y = -0.043(250) + 15 = 4.25$. Thus, another good estimate would be 4.25 gallons, which is also close to 4.5.

119. C: The probability may be written as $P(M \text{ or } G) = P(M) + P(G) - P(M \text{ and } G)$. Substituting the probabilities yields $P(M \text{ or } G) = \frac{4{,}985}{10{,}079} + \frac{4{,}113}{10{,}079} - \frac{2{,}045}{10{,}079}$, which simplifies to $P(M \text{ or } G) = \frac{7{,}053}{10{,}079}$, or approximately 70%.

120. C: The ends of Dataset A are farther apart (from 2 to 18 instead of 5 to 18), indicating a larger range. The horizontal line in the middle of a boxplot represents the median, so Dataset A has a smaller median (9 instead of 10).

Science

121. C: In the stratosphere, temperature increases as altitude increases. The stratosphere contains the ozone layer, which absorbs ultraviolet radiation and then reemits this energy as heat.

122. B: According to the first law of planetary motion, planets move in elliptical orbits, not circular. According to the second law of planetary motion, a radius vector connecting a planet to the sun sweeps out equal areas in equal amounts of time. According to the third law of planetary motion, the square of the period of a planet is directly proportional to the cube of the mean distance.

123. A: When a fossil is determined to be 37 million years old, this is an example of an absolute age. Absolute dating, which can be accomplished through the use of radiometric techniques, establishes precise ages for materials, while stratigraphic techniques only produce relative dates. Relative dating can establish approximate ages for rocks and fossils based on clues in the surrounding rock, but it cannot be used to determine absolute age.

124. C: In the field of geology, the term "uniformitarianism" refers to the belief that the natural forces, laws, and processes that shape the Earth have remained relatively constant over geologic time. This belief contradicts catastrophism, which maintains that dramatic events have been the primary forces involved in shaping the Earth.

125. C: The Gulf Stream, which is a surface current that originates in the Gulf of Mexico and travels across the Atlantic Ocean, makes the climate of Northern Europe warmer. After traveling up the eastern coast of the US, the Gulf Stream splits into two forks. The North Atlantic Drift travels across the ocean to warm Europe, while the southern fork travels toward West Africa.

126. B: The process that causes lithospheric plates to move over the surface of the mantle is called convection. The mantle rock in the lower portion of the mantle is heated by the Earth's core and slowly rises to the surface, pushing aside cooler rock that is already there. This hotter rock eventually cools and is pushed aside by hotter rock that rises from below. This cycle, called convection, creates constant movement in the mantle that contributes to the motion of the tectonic plates.

127. A: According to the Köppen Climate Classification System, regions with continental climates are most commonly found in the interior regions of large landmasses. Continental climates are characterized by large seasonal temperature variations, with warm or hot summers and cold winters. Precipitation is often moderate and can occur throughout the year.

128. A: Descriptive studies look at and analyze the characteristics of a population or compare aspects across multiple populations. These studies seek information about the state of a population as it is rather than experimentally investigating cause-and-effect relationships by manipulating variables and observing outcomes. Comparing the heights of male and female penguins is an example of a descriptive study. The subject is strictly an observable measure (height) of established populations (male and female). For the other studies, the focus is on the cause-and-effect relationship between a manipulated variable (different media, drug vs. placebo, and old vs. new descriptions) and a result of interest (growth rate, drug efficacy, sales).

129. C: Acid rain results from the release of nitrogen and sulfur oxides into the atmosphere. The generation of electricity, especially by coal power plants and gasoline-powered motor vehicles, are the main sources of these destructive pollutants. Although the production of nuclear power may carry other risks, it does not contribute to the problem of acid precipitation.

130. D: Within a habitat, there is a maximum number of individuals that can continue to thrive, known as the habitat's carrying capacity. When the population size approaches this number, population growth will stop.

131. B: Gradualism states that evolution occurs slowly, with organisms exhibiting small changes over long periods of time. According to gradualism, the fossil record should show gradual changes over time. Punctuated equilibrium states that evolution occurs in spurts of sudden change. According to punctuated equilibrium, the fossil record should have large gaps.

132. D: Prolonging the life of individuals in a current population will lead to an older age composition. An increased birth rate will cause population growth, but a greater proportion will be younger, not older.

133. A: Anthophyta is a division of plants that produces seeds as part of reproduction. Spermatopyta is the broader group that includes all plants that produce seeds for reproduction, which includes gymnosperms and angiosperms (the same group as anthophyta). Anthophyta are also known as the group that contains flowering plants. It is the largest and most diverse grouping of plants and includes many food, clothing, and medicinal uses for humans. Grains, beans, nuts, fruits, vegetables, spices, tea, coffee, chocolate, cotton, linen, and aspirin are all derived from plants from anthophyta. Lycophyta is a small group of plants including club mosses and scale trees. Sphenophyta contains about thirty species including horsetails, foxtails, or scouring rushes.

Pterophyta contains non-seed plants like ferns. Lycophyta, sphenophyta, and pterophyta all use spores to reproduce sexually.

134. D: In the image, the parts of the flower are as follows:

1. Ovary – the pollen-receiving portion of the flower that resides at the base of the pistil.
2. Anther – the pollen-bearing tip of the stamen.
3. Petal – The soft, colorful parts of the flower that attract pollinators and protect the inner parts.
4. Sepal – The outermost part of a flower that protect the developing bud before blooming.
5. Filament – The stalk that supports the anther.

Of the available choices, only choice D, the sepal, is not considered a reproductive organ of the flower.

135. A: Long-term energy storage in animals takes the form of fat. Animals also store energy as glycogen, and plants store energy as starch, but these substances are for shorter-term use. Fats are a good storage form for chemical energy because fatty acids bond to glycerol in a condensation reaction to form fats (triglycerides). This reaction, which releases water, allows for the compacting of high-energy fatty acids in a concentrated form.

136. C: 100 g of HBr equals 1.23 moles, and 100 g of Mg equals 4.11 moles. From the coefficients of the balanced equation, the ratio of HBr to Mg is 2 : 1. This means that to react 1.23 moles of HBr, 2.46 moles of Mg would be required. Since 4.11 moles of Mg are present, Mg is in excess.

137. D: Exothermic reactions release heat energy, while endothermic reactions absorb heat energy. Since the burning of butane releases heat energy, the reaction is exothermic. Since the melting of ice absorbs heat energy, the process is endothermic. Since an exothermic reaction releases heat energy, the change in enthalpy is negative.

138. C: A physical change occurs when water condenses. The only thing formed during condensation is new intermolecular bonds. Therefore, no new covalent bonds form (B). The only time new atoms form is during a nuclear reaction (A). The water molecule is not ionizing, so no new ionic bonds form (D).

139. C: In a uniform gravitational field, such as occurs near Earth's surface, an object will move like a point mass located at the center of mass. However, this does not necessarily mean that the geometrical center of an object is the same as its center of mass, depending on its shape, design and mass distribution. The center of mass of a sphere or cube is at its geometric center because you can imagine the sphere as consisting of a large number of point masses located at certain points in space. Multiplying the point masses by their location and dividing by the total mass gives the center of mass. Statement I is not true because the space station may not be completely symmetrical. Statement III is true because the space station is undergoing uniform circular motion around Earth. If the orbit had been elliptical, this would not be true because the speed would have changed depending on the station's position. However, even though the speed is constant in a circular orbit, the velocity is not. Since velocity has a direction associated with it, and the space station is moving in a circular path, its velocity is constantly changing.

140. C: In 2.4×10^4 years, 50% of the substance will have decayed. In another half-life, half of this will be gone, or 75%. 87.5% represents 3 half-lives, or a total of $3 \times 2.4 \times 10^4$ years = 7.2×10^4 years.

141. C: According to the kinetic theory of matter, the kinetic energy of a particle is found by $KE = \frac{1}{2}mv^2$ in which KE is the kinetic energy in Joules, m is the mass of the particle in kilograms, and v is the velocity of the particle in meters per second. This formula shows that the average kinetic energy is directly proportional to the square of the average velocity of the particles.

142. B: The newton can be defined in terms of the fundamental units of meters, kilograms, and seconds as $\text{N} = \text{kg} \times \text{m/s}^2$, so it is not a fundamental unit. Statement II is a result of $F = ma$, Newton's second law, which is true. If $F = 0\text{ N}$, then the acceleration is $0\ \text{m/s}^2$. If the acceleration is $0\ \text{m/s}^2$, then the speed is $0\ \text{m/s}$ or a nonzero constant. This is a nonverbal statement of Newton's first law, meaning Newton's first law can be derived from his second law. Newton's second law cannot be derived from the universal law of gravity.

143. C: Heat transfer can never occur from a cooler object to a warmer object. While the second law of thermodynamics implies that heat never spontaneously transfers from a cooler object to a warmer object, it is possible for heat to be transferred to a warmer object, given the proper input of work to the system. This is the principle by which a refrigerator operates. Work is done to the system to transfer heat from the objects inside the refrigerator to the air surrounding the refrigerator. All other answer choices are true.

144. C: Percent error is calculated by the following equation.

$$\text{Percent error} = \frac{\text{Experimental value} - \text{Theoretical value}}{\text{Theoretical value}} \times 100\%$$

$$\text{Percent error} = \frac{0.410 - 0.385}{0.385} \times 100\% = 6.49\%$$

The percent error for the students' specific heat of copper is 6.49%.

145. D: A good hypothesis must be testable. This means it may be proved or disproved by testing using a controlled experiment. A controlled experiment may have several constants but only one independent variable.

146. C: Weighing the benefits to people and the economy against the risks is why governments would conduct a risk-benefit analysis before making decisions about city planning and development. Answer A, which states that governments must know what the benefits of a new development are for people and the economy in order to persuade opponents and the public who are against it, would be incorrect because the intention would be to build regardless of risk. Answer D, which suggests that the benefits to people and the economy can be used to ignore the risks associated with any new development, would also be incorrect as it would be unethical to ignore the risks.

147. A: Repeating a measurement several times can increase the precision of the measurement. Calibrating the equipment should only be done once for a whole set of measurements. Calibrating for each use will add a source of error and prevent measurements from being able to be compared. None of the other choices are useful strategies to increase the precision of a measurement.

148. B: The first step in the scientific method is to ask a research question to which we want to find an answer. The second step is to formulate a hypothesis (A), which is an educated guess about the answer to the research question. The third step is to conduct an experiment (C) to test the hypothesis. The final steps are to decide whether the results of the experiment support or fail to support the hypothesis and then to report this to others (D).

149. C: When children conduct simple experiments and are able to see patterns and meanings in the results, they are using the scientific process skill of inference. They use the skill of measurement (A) when they quantify the various physical properties of objects, like length, width, height, weight, etc. They use the skill of classification (B) when they group objects, events, conditions, or situations according to the properties they share in common. They use the skill of prediction (D) when they apply their experiences from experimenting to form new hypotheses to test.

150. A: The control in an experiment is not subject to the variable being tested—in this case, the new drug. The volunteers who are given the drug comprise the experimental group.